IS JAPAN REALLY
CHANGING ITS WAYS?

IS JAPAN REALLY CHANGING ITS WAYS?

Regulatory Reform and the

Japanese Economy

LONNY E. CARLILE

MARK C. TILTON

Editors

BROOKINGS INSTITUTION PRESS

Washington, D.C.

ABOUT BROOKINGS

The Brookings Institution is a private nonprofit organization devoted to research, education, and publication on important issues of domestic and foreign policy. Its principal purpose is to bring knowledge to bear on current and emerging policy problems. The Institution maintains a position of neutrality on issues of public policy. Interpretations or conclusions in publications of the Brookings Institution Press should be understood to be solely those of the authors.

Copyright © 1998 by
THE BROOKINGS INSTITUTION
1775 Massachusetts Avenue, N.W., Washington, D.C. 20036

Library of Congress Cataloging-in-Publication data:

Is Japan really changing its ways? : regulatory reform and the Japanese economy /
Lonny E. Carlile and Mark C. Tilton, editors.
p.   cm.
Includes bibliographical references and index.
ISBN 0-8157-1292-8 (cloth : acid-free paper)
ISBN 0-8157-1291-x (pbk. : acid-free paper)
1. Trade regulation—Japan.   2. Deregulation—Japan.   3. Industrial policy—
Japan.   4. Japan—Economic conditions—1989–   5. Japan—Economic
   policy—1989–   I. Carlile, Lonny E.   II. Tilton, Mark C., 1956–
HD3616.J33 I8   1998
338.952—ddc21   98-25374
                                                              CIP

9 8 7 6 5 4 3 2 1

The paper used in this publication meets the minimum requirements of the American National Standard for Information Sciences—Permanence of Paper for Printed Library Materials, ANSI Z39.48-1984.

Typeset in Times Roman

Composition by Princeton Editorial Associates
Scottsdale, Arizona, and Roosevelt, New Jersey

Printed by R. R. Donnelley & Sons
Harrisonburg, Virginia

Preface

The economic crisis in East Asia has given new urgency to the issue of Japanese regulatory reform. Can Japan dismantle its developmentalist regulations so as to open its markets meaningfully to imports and provide the market opportunities desperately needed by its Asian neighbors? Although plagued with slow growth for the last several years, the Japanese economy is still larger than all the other economies of Asia combined, and it could potentially play a major role in helping the region recover. But the weakened yen is currently increasing Japan's trade surpluses at a time when other nations are calling on Japan to help lead Asia out of its economic crisis by absorbing more of the region's exports.

In order to restart their own economy and provide regional economic stimulus by bringing in more imports, Japanese leaders must reform the financial system, expand domestic consumption, and do away with import-blocking regulations. Top Japanese business leaders have long complained that regulations not only block imports but also stifle efficiency and economic growth at home. Japanese citizens are increasingly frustrated with the inability of politicians to carry out the kind of serious economic reform needed to overcome Japan's long period of economic stagnation. Yet when the Japanese political system produces reforms, they are compromised in ways that limit their market-freeing impact.

This book is the culmination of a research project on Japanese deregulation, sponsored by the Japan-U.S. Friendship Commission (JUSFC) and aimed at dispelling some of the confusion surrounding regulatory reform. To most outside observers, regulatory reform in Japan is an incomprehensible blur of grandiose proposals and Byzantine political maneuvering. The difficulty of comprehending what is going on leads to the understandable but unfortunate tendency to alternatively ignore or exaggerate developments that are of tremendous significance to the world at large. The JUSFC project sought to bring together a multinational group of scholars with expertise in various aspects of Japanese regulation who could carry out in-depth studies and dig beneath official claims about regulatory reform. This book attempts to explain the politics behind the reforms, the nature of the reforms, and their effect on both the domestic economy and Japan's international trade.

The support of the JUSFC and its staff made possible a workshop in Honolulu in April 1996 at which chapter drafts were first presented. This meeting provided a chance to learn from one another, discuss the concepts of regulation and reform in Japan, and think about how the various parts of the project could be brought together to create an integrated analysis of Japanese regulatory reform. Earlier versions of chapters in this volume were also presented on panels before the 1996 Association for Asian Studies meeting in Honolulu, the University of Hawaii Center for Japanese Studies seminar series, and a special workshop on deregulation in Washington, D.C., sponsored jointly by the JUSFC and the Japan Information Access Project.

We thank the JUSFC and its staff for their generous financial support for the Honolulu workshop and for the research embodied in this volume. We also thank Sharon Minichiello, Gay Satsuma, and Angela Carbonaro of the Center for Japanese Studies at the University of Hawaii at Manoa for the help they provided, both in organizing the workshop and in preparing the manuscript that became this book. Tanya Dresp of Purdue University also provided important assistance with the manuscript. We acknowledge the tremendous help and support provided by Mindy Kotler and the staff of the Japan Information Access Project. Anonymous reviewers for the Brookings Institution Press provided valuable suggestions for improving the volume. Princeton Editorial Associates provided editorial and composition services and prepared the index. We are most grateful to Nancy Davidson and Janet Walker of the Brookings Institution Press for their instrumental support, guidance, and assistance in the publication process.

Mark Tilton also thanks the Abe Fellowship Program of the Social Science Research Council, Kudō Akira at the Social Science Institute of the University of Tokyo, Sung-jo Park at the Ostasiatisches Seminar of the Free University of Berlin, and David Soskice's research group and Andreas Moerke at the Wissenschaftszentrum Berlin for their support and assistance during his work on the book. He thanks his wife, Pat Boling, and his children, Clio, Ellen, and Andy, for their patience and encouragement. Lonny Carlile thanks his wife, Laura Noda, and his children, Jonathan and Melanie, for their patience and support.

The views expressed are those of the authors alone and should not be attributed to those acknowledged or to the trustees, officers, or other staff members of the Brookings Institution.

Contents

Tables

Figures

CHAPTER ONE

Regulatory Reform and the Developmental State

Lonny E. Carlile and Mark C. Tilton

O ver the past two decades all the advanced industrialized countries have seen efforts to systematically alter the regulatory arrangements that govern the role of the state in their respective economies.[1] The forces and circumstances that have induced these efforts are numerous and varied; a list put forward in a recent Organization for Economic Cooperation and Development (OECD) survey identifies the most common general factors: long-term changes in OECD economies (specifically, the end during the 1970s of the "golden era" of sustained postwar growth); technological changes in key sectors such as communications, information processing, transportation, and energy; globalization (especially in finance); a rethinking among professional economists of their assessments of regulation's costs and benefits; and increased diversity of social values and social groups that has created a need for more choice and flexibility in the provision of goods and services. The thrust of these regulatory reform efforts has in theory been *deregulatory* in nature—that is, they have sought to modify regulatory frameworks in ways that would create new markets, stimulate competition, and increase the weight of market forces in determining economic outcomes. As the same OECD report notes, however, the process of regulatory reform has not been smooth, and these efforts have run into obstacles in the form of entrenched proregulatory habits and resistance on the part of interests and groups that benefit from existing regulation.[2]

Japan has not been an exception in its response to deregulation, and indeed during the same period there has been both widespread and often heated public discussion of regulatory reform, as well as instances of major regulatory reform initiatives being pursued. Given that Japan is the world's second largest national market and also a premier supplier of goods, capital, and technology to the world, the issue of Japanese regulatory reform has naturally been of keen interest to foreign observers, as is evidenced by the recent spate of coverage of Japan's deregulation process in major Western business journals.[3] The stakes involved in Japanese regulatory reform are indeed substantial for the future evolution of the world economy. One recent estimate, for instance, notes that "a thorough deregulation" of the Japanese energy, finance, telecommunications, transport, and distribution sectors would push Japanese GDP up by six percentage points, pump 39 trillion yen ($339 billion at $1 = 115 yen) into the Japanese economy, and increase consumer spending by 370,000 yen ($3,217) per household over the half decade beginning in 1995.[4] It is hardly surprising that government officials and businesses in the United States and elsewhere have taken a keen interest in Japanese regulatory reform.[5]

As for the prospects for Japan's actually implementing such a "thorough deregulation," opinion among observers is divided. At one end of the spectrum are those who—in an assessment that is more commonly found in journalistic treatments than in academic work—see Japan's current regulatory reform effort as positive proof that Japan must and will bow to the universal, inevitable, and irreversible logic of market capitalism (or, alternatively, economic or political development) and in the process become like, or "converge" toward, other advanced industrialized countries.[6] Another school of thought, located at the other end of the spectrum, finds such optimism not only misplaced but naive and uninformed. Such analysts tend to see in the Japanese political economy a fundamentally different form of capitalism in which the state effectively guides the economy through extensive intervention. Or, alternatively, Japan's system is seen as one in which the initiative in economic management has been captured by a panoply of politically powerful special interests who, with the cooperation and mediation of the bureaucracy, have ensconced themselves in protectionist regulatory arrangements that permeate the Japanese economy. Deregulation, in this view, cannot occur, because it goes against the solidly entrenched interests of either or both the all-powerful state bureaucracy or these politically influential and protected interest groups.[7]

Regulatory reform is everywhere a complex and controversial sociopolitical process. In order to effectively comprehend this process in any national context, it is necessary to factor into the analysis the major forces and structures that shape regulatory reforms. Doing this is a difficult task in the case of any country, but the challenge involved in properly analyzing Japanese regulatory reform can be particularly daunting for those whose primary frame of reference is the regulatory environment found in countries of the Anglo-American legal tradition. The semantics of the basic terminology alone reveal this. Whereas in the English context deregulation tends to be commonly understood as a rolling back of state authority in favor of the market, the Japanese equivalent, *kisei kanwa,* literally means and is generally understood to be a relaxation or loosening rather than a removal of regulation. Yet the reasons for the difficulties go beyond the cultural and linguistic hurdles that need to be overcome in order to gain access to relevant information. The very historical trajectory of modern Japan has given rise to a system of regulation that diverges in critical ways from that of a country such as the United States. The development of Japan's regulatory regime, in turn, has created a political context that, despite being carried out in the formal institutional context of a Westminster-style parliamentary system, raises issues and is shaped by a set of dynamics that diverge radically from the Anglo-American experience and to a lesser extent from those of continental Western European nations. These divergences make it essential that the differences in both the regulatory system and consequently in the substance and dynamics of reform be well understood and accounted for if one is to meaningfully assess the prospects and likely direction of Japanese regulatory reform in the future.

The chapters in this volume were prepared in this spirit. Each analyzes an aspect of the Japanese regulatory reform process with an eye toward highlighting the broader institutional contexts and situational imperatives that shape regulatory reform across a range of sectors. Collectively, they represent an attempt to delineate the structure and dynamics of Japanese regulatory reform in a nonnormative, empirically grounded way, explaining why regulatory reform in Japan has unfolded as it has and providing a base for predictions about where it might go in the future. Of the two poles of opinion on the nature of Japanese regulatory reform, the perspective of this volume leans toward the latter approach, that of viewing Japan's as a system with distinctive structures and dynamics that needs to be understood on its own terms rather than examining it with straightforward applications of a universal logic. However, the contributors to this volume also hold the view that it is important not to characterize the system in overly monolithic terms. The issue of whether current Japanese regulatory reform efforts are "genuine" cannot be answered in the abstract or in a priori fashion, but is instead a matter that can only be addressed effectively after careful analysis of existing regulatory reform efforts in light of a nuanced understanding of the context and the institutional setting that characterize Japanese regulatory reform today.[8]

The Distinctive Context of Japanese Regulatory Reform

The chapters that follow provide detailed discussions of the institutional structures of direct concern to the particular aspect of regulatory reform being covered. However, before entering into these more narrowly focused analyses, it is useful to paint in broad strokes a picture of certain key features of the terrain. In addition to providing basic background information, this exercise serves to highlight, in first cut fashion, why analysis grounded in a firm understanding of the distinctive historical, institutional, and political setting of Japanese regulatory reform is essential. Three ways in which the Japanese system differs from the American one are discussed.

First, economic regulation—that is, rules and regulations that govern entry, exit, investment, pricing, and other functions basic to the operation of a capitalist market economy—occurs for a variety of reasons. The dominant tendency in Anglo-American scholarship has been to conceive of economic regulation as involving the provision of the basic framework of rules needed to keep markets operating smoothly and as a response to problems of market failure. This conception is certainly consistent with the emphasis in the Anglo-American "free enterprise" ideology and, as the importance attached to competition and antitrust policy indicates, something emphasized to a considerable extent in practice. This remains generally true even in the extreme case in which the state effectively replaces the market, as in public utilities, for the rationale typically put forward is that such market displacement is needed in order to address "market failure." And although safety, health, and welfare concerns have been recognized as a valid reason for engaging in "social" regulation, such regulation has generally been treated as qualitatively different in character and in a realm separate from that of economic regulation.

In contrast to the discrete compartmentalization of economic and social regulation characteristic of the Anglo-American tradition, in Japan mechanisms of economic regulation have been systematically used to pursue goals that go well beyond the market maintenance functions of the archetypal Anglo-American state.[9] Japan's system of economic regulation has deep roots in the developmentalist ideology and economic system formed during the war mobilization of 1931 to 1945.[10] Developmentalism makes the expansion of domestic production in the context of international competition its principal goal and makes the "developmental state" the means for achieving it. Guided by developmentalist ideology, the developmental state has used economic regulation to actively foster the technological development, capacity growth, and competitiveness of targeted industries considered essential to the future viability of the Japanese economy. The industrial policies of the Ministry of International Trade and Industry (MITI) are by far the best documented but the policies pursued by other ministries and agencies—including the Ministry of Posts and Telecommunications (MPT), Ministry of Transportation (MOT), and Ministry of Health and Welfare (MHW)—also are oriented toward boosting industrial development. Security concerns have also weighed heavily in the developmentalist state agenda. Before Japan's defeat in World War II, security policy focused rather straightforwardly on building up a strong and effective military. With Japan's demilitarization following the war, however, the national security dimension of Japanese economic regulation has taken more subtle but nonetheless real forms, including the fostering of the development of dual use (military and civilian) technology, embedding military production in the commercial economy, and the nurturance of domestic industries.[11]

In contrast to Anglo-American liberalism's faith in free market competition and its limited reliance on regulation for exceptional instances of market failures, Japanese developmentalism has been deeply suspicious of market competition. Private ownership is preferred over ownership by the state, but whereas Anglo-American liberalism views intense competition as a beneficial process that allows more efficient producers to replace less efficient ones, Japanese developmentalism holds that markets are prone to "excessive competition," in which investment is wasted as firms overinvest and underutilize capacity as they drive each other out of business. In light of this, developmentalist policies have sought to economize on national investment resources by using public, private, or mixed regulation to limit competition.

Japanese economic regulation also diverges from the Anglo-American market failure model in the way it has been used to attain social policy goals.[12] Economic regulation has been used to sustain the viability of small producers in retail and distribution, agriculture, leather goods, and other industries. Part of the reason is that these industries have provided a critical base of electoral support for the postwar conservative regime. More fundamentally and in contrast to the American stress on equality of opportunity, in addition to emphasizing the expansion of national production, Japanese developmentalist regulation has emphasized equity in economic outcomes. In an extension of the approach used to promote production, Japan has attempted to achieve such equity by protecting uncompetitive enterprises from competition. The corollary of the widespread use of economic regulation for income redistribution purposes has been that Japan has not developed the extensive income redistribution mechanisms built around direct payments to individuals and families that are associated with the welfare state in Europe.[13] It is arguable that instead even labor markets have been shaped by a kind of social-policy-oriented developmentalist economic regulation.[14]

The extensive use of economic regulation on behalf of goals that go beyond those market maintenance, health, and safety concerns that are the primary drivers of regulation in the "referee" or "regulatory state" model has a number of implications.[15] To the extent that such nonmarket maintenance goals can sustain social and political legitimacy, they will increase the number of vested interests involved and the number of considerations to be taken into account in engineering a given regulatory reform initiative, thereby "corrupting" the regulatory reform process and pushing outcomes in directions that cannot be foreseen if one works exclusively within a strict consumer-producer model of regulatory reform politics.

A second way the Japanese system diverges significantly from the legalistic American model specifically and more generally from the Anglo-American tradition can be found in the extensive overlapping of the public and the private, the stipulated and the discretionary, and the formal and informal, in Japanese administrative practice. What is meant here can be illustrated by the government's own accounting of its "licensing" (*kyoninka*) powers. As shown in table 1-1, licensing in the Japanese context, which (as is argued later in this volume) represents the core of the Japanese regulatory system, covers a wide range of forms and gradations of state intervention that extend far beyond the meaning generally associated with the English term. As the definitions of the groupings in the table suggest, from a technical standpoint licensing in the Japanese context includes exercises of authority based on a blanket imposition of prior restraint from which the state grants exceptions (that is, group A and group B) and ex post facto surveillance mechanisms (group C) in which the clients are merely required to report on activities undertaken. However, this seemingly clear-cut distinction can be meaningless in the event of the commonly noted practice of bureaucratic agencies discouraging submissions or refusing outright to accept *todokede* and other such legally stipulated reports.

Table 1-1. Licensing Categories Used by the Japanese State Bureaucracy, 1985 and 1995

Term	Rough English translation	Number in 1985	Number in 1995	Change in number
Group A: Lifting a general prohibition under specified conditions; establishing specific rights				
Kyoka	Permit	1,345	1,149	−196
Ninka	Authorization	1,441	1,624	183
Menkyo	License	102	100	−2
Shōnin	Approval	988	1,113	124
Shitei	Designation	197	254	57
Shōdaku and others	Consent and others	19	25	6
Subtotal		4,092	4,265	173
Group B: Determining ahead of time whether a particular fact or action meets preestablished criteria and then making this information public				
Nintei	Recognition	297	474	177
Kakunin	Confirmation	94	125	31
Shōmei	Verification	59	126	67
Ninshō	Validation	18	17	−1
Shiken	Examination	102	113	11
Kensa	Inspection	254	247	−7
Kentei	Certification	39	33	−6
Tōroku	Registration	162	181	19
Shinsa and others	Investigation	18	20	2
Subtotal		1,043	1,336	293
Group C: Informing a ministry or an agency of a specified fact; in principle the state agency will merely accept an application upon confirming all items of information have been provided				
Todokede	Notification	3,326	3,435	−109
Teishutsu	Filing	390	555	165
Hōkoku	Report	613	572	−41
Kōfu	Submission	98	89	−9
Shinkoku and others	Statement and others	75	79	4
Subtotal		4,502	4,730	228
Other terms		417	429	12
Total		10,054	10,760	706

Source: Sōmuchō (Management and Coordination Agency), *Kisei kanwa suishin no genkyō* (The current state of progress in regulatory reform) (Tokyo, 1996), pp. 40–41. Translations are from Steven K. Vogel, *Freer Markets, More Rules: Regulatory Reform in Advanced Industrial Countries* (Cornell University Press, 1996), p. 205.

Table 1-2. Items of Licensing Authority by Ministry and Agency, 1985 and 1995

Ministry or agency	Items in 1985 survey	Items in 1995 survey	Change
Defense Agency	26	31	5
Economic Planning Agency (EPA)	26	31	5
Environmental Agency	149	199	50
Fair Trade Commission (FTC)	26	26	0
Hokkaido Development Agency	26	31	5
Management and Coordination Agency (MAC)	29	35	6
Ministry of Agriculture, Forestry, and Fisheries (MAFF)	1,263	1,400	137
Ministry of Construction (MOC)	742	841	99
Ministry of Education (MOE)	310	327	17
Ministry of Finance (MOF)	1,116	1,374	258
Ministry of Foreign Affairs (MOFA)	37	50	13
Ministry of Health and Welfare (MHW)	936	1,221	285
Ministry of International Trade and Industry (MITI)	1,870	1,780	−90
Ministry of Justice (MOJ)	146	168	22
Ministry of Labor (MOL)	532	633	101
Ministry of Local Autonomy (MLA)	104	125	21
Ministry of Posts and Telecommunications (MPT)	265	292	27
Ministry of Transportation (MOT)	2,017	1,607	−410
National Land Agency	81	87	6
National Public Safety Commission	81	141	60
Okinawa Development Agency	27	32	5
Prime Minister's Office (PMO)	27	32	5
Science and Technology Agency (STA)	218	297	79
Total	10,054	10,760	709

Source: Sōmuchō, *Kisei kanwa no genkyō*, p. 39.

As table 1-2 illustrates, the concentration of licensing authority is also heaviest in ministries whose work most directly affects economic activity. The Economic Planning Agency—whose primary function is to collect, report, and analyze macroeconomic statistics rather than administration—represents the one exception.

At the same time, Japan is notably lacking in procedural constraints that bind administrative decisionmakers, and this contributes to a lack of transparency, high levels of discretion, and a high degree of informality in administrative activities.[16] State regulation of private sector activities extends well beyond that which is stipulated in laws and formally legitimated regulations.[17] Administrative guidance, or *gyōsei shidō*—the term used to describe such forays— can be as informal as a quick telephone request by a government bureaucrat to a "regulated" firm on a subject of concern to the state agency over which the agency has the vaguest of grounds for legally exercising authority. Such informal governance creates extremely hazy boundaries between the spheres of state regulation and private sector discretion.

Another mode of informal governance can be seen in the extensive "self-regulatory" activities of private associations such as Japan's many trade associations that constitute a pervasive form of de facto regulation in the Japanese economy. Unlike in the American tradition in which competition policy since the Progressive Era has been devoted almost single-mindedly to rooting out monopolistic and oligopolistic practices, Japanese officials have actively pursued industrial policies that encourage concentration and oligopolistic practices. Such tasks have been hampered, to be sure, by the American-imposed Antimonopoly Law of 1947, but this law has, if anything, encouraged more extensive use of informal regulations by the state and forms of private self-regulation.[18] A further reason for the pervasiveness of informal regulation is that the Japanese system operated within an international system of trade and finance based on liberal principles and norms. The resultant "embedded mercantilism" required Japan to adhere formally to the letter of GATT and IMF stipulations even as it frequently undercut them in spirit with informal policies.[19]

The pervasiveness of informal regulatory mechanisms has a number of implications for analyzing the Japanese regulatory reform process. It means that meaningful treatment of regulatory reform in Japan requires that the scope of analysis move beyond looking simply at the formal regulatory mechanisms and scrutinize the often hidden world of informal administration and private sector regulation. Without this expanded purview, it is impossible to fully grasp the sources of reform initiatives and the roots of resistance to them. Furthermore, it implies that removing statutory and codified rules alone will frequently be insufficient to ensure that the private sector will be given free rein or to guarantee that a competitive market will necessarily follow.

Finally, a third way in which the Japanese regulatory system diverges from the Anglo-American model rests in the distinctive structuring of the policy-making process in Japan that in turn sets the parameters for both regulation and regulatory reform. In addressing this point, it is helpful to bear in mind that the American institutional structure is rather unique in the way that its judicial system, by allowing class action law suits and because of the strength of its judicial review mechanism, has given unusual strength to consumer interests in the regulatory and regulatory reform processes. Other things being equal, producer interests everywhere have greater influence in the regulatory process than consumer interests, which tend to be weakly organized. The position of producer groups in the Japanese system is strengthened further by a fusion of the interests of groups within the governing party, interest groups, and individual regulatory agencies that has grown up over the course of thirty-eight years of single-party majority rule by the Liberal Democratic party (LDP). Although such "subgovernments" are certainly not unknown elsewhere, there is a general consensus among analysts that these tend to be particularly pervasive and self-contained in Japan's "patterned pluralism." Exclusive "iron triangles" consisting of regulators, the regulated firms, and "tribe" (zoku) politicians—as those politicians who broker deals within such subgovernments are known— tend to monopolize policymaking in a given policy sector. As a consequence of their close, insular working relationships, these parties encourage the kind of regulatory informality already described above. And in the absence of countervailing forces, they constitute a major obstacle to deregulatory reforms and impose a conspicuous rigidity on the Japanese system.[20]

Taken together, these divergences of the Japanese regulatory reform context from the Anglo-American model suggest that not only will Japanese regulatory reform be shaped by a distinctive political dynamic, but more fundamentally the issues that animate regulatory reform will often be quite different from those that are characteristic of the Anglo-American, and even continental European, context. Effectively capturing and comprehending the process of regulatory reform in Japan thus requires that the analyst pay careful attention to the characteristics of the institutional setting and its impact, along with the associated constellations of interests and the political dynamics among them.

The Book

The remainder of the book is organized as follows. Chapters 2 through 4 discuss the general historical and institutional context that gave rise to Japan's current regulatory reform drive while they relate this historical context to current issues associated with Japanese regulatory reform. Yul Sohn opens chapter 2 with a discussion of the historical roots of the contemporary Japanese system of regulation. He focuses in particular on the development of licensing, which constitutes the linchpin of the system. Sohn discusses how licensing practices grew out of the circumstances of Japan's modernization. With conventional tariff-based infant industry policies unavailable as an option, due to the "unequal treaties" imposed on Japan in the mid-nineteenth century, the country's leaders were encouraged to engineer a system of finely tuned controls over entry, exit, resources, and production in strategic sectors. This initial impetus was strengthened further by Japan's distinctive position in the global economic system during the interwar period and later by the strategic military concerns in the years leading to and during World War II. The practices and ideology of this system subsequently infused Japan's contemporary regulatory system.

In chapter 3 Hideaki Miyajima explains how regulatory mechanisms and state policies played a critical role in the development of one of the most fundamental Japanese institutions: the large Japanese corporation, or J-Type firm. Beginning with the immediate post–World War II period, he delineates the complex way domestic preferences and imposed institutions interacted to create a system of financing that supported corporate governance by main banks. He then discusses how, during the 1960s, the resulting institutional arrangements were enhanced and used to resist the perceived threat of foreign takeovers of Japanese corporations. His analysis of the role of regulation in the evolution of the Japanese corporate system is then used as a base for discussing the effects of the liberalization of Japanese financial regulations from the late 1970s onward, and he considers how future regulatory reform in this area is likely to affect Japanese corporate performance. According to Miyajima, although the basic long-term planning orientation that characterizes the J-Type firm is still intact, the trend in recent years has been in a direction that encourages short-sighted corporate irresponsibility, such as the speculative overinvestment during the late 1980s. He discusses how the relegalization of holding companies has been put forward as a policy to help resolve this problem despite a lack of agreement among experts as to precisely what the implications of such a move might be.

In chapter 4 Lonny Carlile focuses on the politics of the administrative reform movement, Japan's effort to "reinvent government," and in particular the emergence of deregulation as a topical issue of public debate. His chapter delineates how coalitions of groups and subgroups within the bureaucracy, labor, the business community, and the political parties have interacted in

complex and changing ways to shape and reshape both the discourse of regulatory reform and the concrete policy proposals advanced in its name. He shows
that despite the relatively slow pace of implemented reform, the political and
institutional environment of Japanese regulatory reform has evolved rather
dramatically over time and that as a result, it presents at least the possibility
that a watershed of regulatory reform might be reached, although such an
outcome is by no means guaranteed.

The three substantive chapters in the latter half of the book look systematically at specific aspects of recent Japanese regulatory reform. In chapter 5
Elizabeth Norville reviews the process of financial deregulation from a perspective that highlights the international political economic context of financial
liberalization and the significance of state developmental concerns in shaping
the process of regulatory reform, going so far as to argue that financial liberalization was infused with a concrete developmental purpose. To say that liberalization was intended to serve such puposes, however, is not the same thing as
saying that those goals have been or will invariably be attained, and one of the
things Norville does in the chapter is to assess the mixed bag of accomplishments and nonaccomplishments involved. In the postbubble years, Norville argues, the Ministry of Finance (MOF) has been forced to shift gears
drastically, although the fundamental "illiberal" orientation remains.

In a more narrowly focused but nonetheless broadly insightful contribution,
Kōsuke Ōyama analyzes the political process associated with deregulation in
the Japanese oil industry. After a discussion of the nature of regulation in the
industry before the reform process, he outlines how the regulatory reform was
shaped by a balance of pro- and antireform forces. Initially, reform in the
industry led to modifications of the rules that clearly favored the opponents of
liberalization. Subsequently, the balance shifted in favor of the latter. Critical
to this shift and to the success of the reform effort, according to Ōyama, was the
political change in 1993 that saw the LDP lose control of the government and
be replaced by a reformist coalition under Hosokawa Morihiro. Ōyama cau-
tions that despite this success, industry's structure remains relatively unchanged, and the impact of this reform on the market has been relatively small.
Nor has it necessarily contributed to the realization of a sensible and effective
energy policy for the country, which he argues is beyond the scope of any kind
of deregulation.

Mark Tilton in chapter 7 delineates how the basic features of Japanese
modes of regulation, broadly defined, affect international trade. By using concrete examples, he shows that informal governance and private cartels play a

key role in Japanese economic regulation and explains why, for this reason, changes in the law alone will not be sufficient to predict the actual impact of a given deregulatory innovation in the Japanese context. Tilton also explores the ideological context of Japanese deregulation, in the process demonstrating how two strands of thought, liberalism and developmentalism, have interacted in an asymmetrical way to shape the discourse of Japanese regulation and regulatory reform.

One of the key themes that emerges out of these chapters is how in contrast to conventional images that tend to picture deregulation as the state's "letting go" of a sector, deregulation in the Japanese case continues to be heavily informed by state-centric visions of the desired future course of the economy in light of changing international economic circumstances. The chapters also suggest that the impact has so far been a delimited one and not the landslide of deregulation some observers have hoped for.

Finally, in a concluding chapter, Carlile and Tilton revisit and contextualize key themes presented throughout the book, highlighting once again the point that deregulation in Japan needs to be understood as a highly political process that is unfolding in a distinctive historically generated sociopolitical and institutional context. A key issue of contention is on whose terms—those of business, the bureaucracy, or political parties—will deregulation in Japan evolve. The specific way the contention is settled, the outcome of which is highly uncertain at this point in time, will in turn have a profound and differential impact on what Japan's current era of deregulation will mean to interested parties both inside and outside Japan.

Notes

1. See, for instance, Organization of Economic Cooperation and Development (OECD), *Governance in Transition: Public Management Reforms in OECD Countries* (Paris, 1995); Kenneth Button and Dennis Swann, eds., *The Age of Regulatory Reform* (Oxford: Clarendon Press, 1989); and OECD, *Regulatory Reform, Privatisation, and Competition Policy* (Paris, 1992).

2. OECD Public Management Service (PUMA), *Control and Management of Government Regulation:* World Wide Web URL http://www.oecd.org/puma/regref/pubs/con95/index.htm, accessed January 1998.

3. For instance, "Two Japans," *Business Week,* January 27, 1997, pp. 24–29; "Changing Japan," *The Economist,* January 11, 1997, pp. 19–21; R. Taggart Murphy,

"Don't Be Fooled by Japan's Big Bang: Many Westerners Are Convinced These Financial Reforms Herald the Dawn of U.S. Style Capitalism in Japan. They're Wrong," *Fortune,* December 29, 1997, p. 214; and "Situation Normal: Japan's Government Is Again Backpedaling on Financial Deregulation," editorial, *The Economist,* March 7, 1998, p. 20.

4. *Nikkei Weekly,* May 26, 1997, p. 2.

5. See, for instance, Commission of the European Communities, "List of EU Deregulation Proposals for Japan," November 17, 1997, World Wide Web URL http://europa.eu.int/en/comm/dg01/0227dere.html; "Submission by the Government of the United States to the Government of Japan Regarding Deregulation, Administrative Reform and Competition Policy in Japan," November 15, 1996, as reproduced in Japan Information Access Project, *Japanese Deregulation: What You Should Know, Proceedings* (Washington: Japan Information Access Project and Japan-U.S. Friendship Commission, 1997), pp. 27–48; OECD, *Japan 1995–1996,* OECD Economic Surveys (Paris, 1997); and Dick K. Nanto, "Deregulation as Market Opening in Japan," CRS Report for Congress (Washington, D.C., February 1, 1995).

6. An example of this sort of argument can be found in Jagdish Bhagwati, "Samurais No More," *Foreign Affairs,* vol. 73 (May/June 1994), pp. 7–12. For a recent essay that discusses convergence theory, see Suzanne Berger, "Introduction," in Suzanne Berger and Ronald Dore, eds., *National Diversity and Global Capitalism* (Cornell University Press, 1996), pp. 1–25.

7. Among the most widely read are Chalmers Johnson, *Japan: Who Governs? The Rise of the Developmental State* (New York and London: Norton, 1995); and Karel van Wolferen, *The Enigma of Japanese Power* (London: Macmillan, 1989).

8. Kozo Yamamura has recently argued on behalf of a similar line of approach in "The Japanese Political Economy after the 'Bubble': Plus Ça Change?" *Journal of Japanese Studies,* vol. 23, no. 2 (1997), pp. 291–331.

9. Chalmers Johnson, *MITI and the Japanese Miracle: The Growth of Industrial Policy, 1925–1975* (Stanford University Press, 1982), pp. 17–23.

10. The term *developmentalism* and the discussion of it here draw on Bai Gao, *Economic Ideology and Japanese Industrial Policy* (Cambridge University Press, 1997).

11. Richard Samuels, *Rich Nation, Strong Army: National Security and the Technological Transformation of Japan* (Cornell University Press, 1994), pp. 33–56.

12. Kent Calder, *Crisis and Compensation: Public Policy and Political Stability in Japan, 1949–1986* (Princeton University Press, 1988).

13. T. J. Pempel, "Japan and Sweden: Polarities in Responsible Capitalism," in Dankwart A. Rostow and Kenneth Paul Erikson, eds., *Comparative Political Dynamics* (HarperCollins, 1991), pp. 408–38; Sheldon Garon and Mike Mochizuki, "Negotiating Social Contracts," in Andrew Gordon, ed., *Postwar Japan as History* (University of California Press, 1993), pp. 145–66.

14. Ikuo Kume, "Institutionalizing the Active Labor Market Policy in Japan: A Comparative View" in Hyung-Ki Kim, Michio Muramatsu, and T. J. Pempel, eds., *The Japanese Civil Service and Economic Development* (Oxford University Press, 1995), pp. 311–36.

15. On the concept of the regulatory state, see Johnson, *MITI and the Japanese Miracle*, pp. 17–23.

16. John Haley, "The Context and Content of Regulatory Change in Japan," in Button and Swann, eds., *The Age of Regulatory Reform*, pp. 124–38.

17. For discussion, see Mark Tilton, *Restrained Trade: Cartels in Japan's Basic Materials Industries* (Cornell University Press, 1996), pp. 1–21; and John Haley, "Administrative Guidance versus Formal Regulation: Resolving the Paradox of Industrial Policy," in Gary Saxonhouse and Kozo Yamamura, eds., *Law and Trade Issues of the Japanese Economy* (University of Washington Press, 1986), pp. 107–28.

18. Tilton, *Restrained Trade;* Frank Upham, *Law and Social Change in Postwar Japan* (Harvard University Press, 1987), pp. 167–204.

19. T. J. Pempel, "Regime Shift: Japanese Politics in a Changing World Economy," *Journal of Japanese Studies,* vol. 23, no. 2 (1997), pp. 333–61.

20. John C. Campbell, "Bureaucratic Primacy: Japanese Policy Communities in an American Perspective," *Governance,* vol. 2 (January 1989), pp. 5–22; Michio Muramatsu and Ellis S. Krauss, "The Conservative Policy Line and the Development of Patterned Pluralism," in Kozo Yamamura and Yasukichi Yasuba, eds., *The Political Economy of Japan,* vol. 1: *The Domestic Transformation* (Stanford University Press, 1987), pp. 516–54; Brian Woodall, *Japan under Construction: Corruption, Politics, and Public Works* (University of California Press, 1996); Chalmers Johnson, "Tanaka Kakuei and the Advent of Machine Politics in Japan," *Journal of Japanese Studies,* vol. 12 (Winter 1986), pp. 1–28.

CHAPTER TWO

The Rise and Development of the Japanese Licensing System

Yul Sohn

In recent years, critics have pointed to governmental licensing (*kyoninka*) as the primary source of burdensome and obstructive regulation in Japan. Domestic businesspersons argue that licensing undercuts the competitiveness of the private sector, and foreign exporters and governments cite it as the major source of informal trade barriers. By governmental licensing I mean special exemption from a general ban on an activity. For example, firms are generally prohibited from starting up operations in an industry unless they get a license from the government. In Japan, licensing is used to control not just market entry but also importation, factory expansion, and other major investment decisions. Licensing has been used in (1) sectors relating to public health (for example, prostitution and pharmaceuticals), (2) sectors relating to public safety (for example, explosives, arms, oil pipelines, and high-pressure gas), (3) infrastructural sectors (for example, telecommunications and electricity), and (4) infant industries that are strategically important to national security and economic well-being. Many of Japan's 10,760 licenses are used for industrial policy purposes, as is suggested by the fact that more than 30 percent were granted by the Ministry of International Trade and Industry (MITI) and the Ministry of Finance (MOF).[1] Although it is well known that the Japanese state strategically alters resource allocation toward targeted industries by granting subsidies, preferential lending, and tax breaks, what is often overlooked is that these measures are combined with licensing to create entry barriers in order to

16

organize industries for strategic purposes. The state normally channels various forms of financial assistance and information sharing to preferentially licensed firms.[2] By serving as the gatekeeper to entry into industry, the licensing system gives the state leverage over firms and constitutes the core of Japan's regulatory framework.

The creation of Japan's licensing system was part of Japan's strategy of developing strong domestic industry while minimizing investment by foreign firms. The initial adoption of this mercantilist industrial development goal by Japan in the late nineteenth century was a response to the threat to its national sovereignty posed by Western imperialism. Mercantilist, developmentalist goals are common among late industrializing nations, but Japan's policies were unusual in the extent to which they relied on *non*-tariff measures. This unique twist on developmentalist policies was the consequence of a specific adaptation to the prohibition on tariffs placed on Japan by the unequal treaties with the West. These created a context in which Japan was induced to rely on industrial policies based on the promotion of cartels and mergers, along with governmental subsidies. Later, in the 1930s, an already mercantilist Japan created the licensing system in order to control and limit a wave of imports and direct investment from overseas.

The Rise of Meiji Mercantilism

For late industrializers, the central concern was how to promote national economic development. The path that countries such as the United States, Germany, and later Japan took was to protect strategic infant industries from foreign competition and nurture them to the point of international competitiveness. The oligarchs of the Meiji period (1868–1912) were keenly aware of their new regime's weakness in the face of both domestic political rivalries and Western imperialist threats, and they believed the state needed to control and nurture private industry in order to bolster its own power.[3] This goal was expressed through the slogan "rich nation, strong army." The Meiji leaders were strongly influenced by the mercantilist ideas of Friedrich List, who held that the state should protect and promote domestic industry for developmental purposes.

The foremost early Meiji proponent of mercantilism, Ōkubo Toshimichi, argued strongly for government intervention in industrial development: "In general, a nation's power depends on the prosperity of its people. The prosperity of the people in turn depends on their productive power. The amount of production is determined largely by the industriousness of the people, but more fundamentally it is dependent upon the guidance and encouragement of government officials."[4] Ōkubo considered free trade a metaphor for Western hegemony and a device to perpetuate the Western powers' domination over newly industrializing countries. What he witnessed was gunboat diplomacy and domestic industries too weak to compete with Western economic powers under laissez-faire policies. In order to develop domestic industry, he believed, it was necessary to cut back on Japan's large volume of foreign imports. Ōkubo's goal, however, was not economic autarky but rather to follow the example of England, the prototypical trading state. Ōkubo argued along classical mercantilist lines that as a nation gains political power it increases its trade surplus. The critical variable was how the state chose to manage international trade. Ōkubo argued for protection by citing the example of England: its rise to world power was attributable to seventeenth-century mercantilist policies such as the Navigation Acts, which built up the merchant marine to world dominance by preventing unlimited importation of foreign goods. Only after achieving a dominant global position did England turn to free trade.[5]

Protective tariffs were the preferred mercantilist policy instrument of the time. Itō Hirobumi argued that Japan should imitate the United States in using tariffs to stimulate domestic production before following the free-trade policies espoused by Britain.[6] But Japan lost the right to set its own tariffs when it signed the "unequal treaties" with the West between 1857 and 1868. These treaties limited Japan's tariffs to 5 percent until 1899 and only permitted selected increases after that.[7] Immediately after 1868 a flood of imports, unchecked by tariffs, created economic havoc. The price of both rice and gold soared, and Japan faced a balance-of-payments crisis because it desperately needed imports of raw materials and capital goods to industrialize.

In the early Meiji period Japanese leaders tried repeatedly to increase tariffs, but the Western powers, led by Britain, refused. Not until the end of the Meiji era did Japan recover full control over its tariffs. Japanese leaders thus faced the problem of how to protect and nurture manufacturing without tariffs. As a first step Ōkubo created the Industrial Promotion Bureau within the Home Ministry. The bureau invested directly in sectors where risks were too great for private firms or where private investment was not forthcoming, such as railways and telegraph, and it undertook long-term development programs for improving the quality of exportable handicraft goods, raw silk, and tea.[8] Ōkubo also set up model factories with imported advanced foreign equipment to mechanize silk reeling and cotton spinning, encouraged direct exports by Japanese merchants, and helped to establish a direct export firm.

Along with engaging in heavy-handed government promotion of exports, bureaucratic leaders created forms of regulation that we now call industrial policy to protect infant industry from foreign competition. Ōkubo and his political ally Ōkuma Shigenobu subsidized infant industries and imposed a heavy sales tax on imported goods that escaped tariffs.

Even more important, Japanese leaders began to use industrial restructuring consciously as an industrial policy instrument to enhance the international competitiveness of domestic industry. The goal was to create a market structure that would help Japan to export more and import less. As James Vestal aptly points out, in contrast to the neoclassical economic assumption that industrial structure is a consequence of competition, Japanese bureaucrats saw industrial structure as something to be managed purposefully and saw competition as a tool of industrial policy.[9] One of the earliest attempts at state-led industrial restructuring was Ōkubo's promotion of mergers in the shipping industry in order to enhance its competitiveness.[10] Cartelization was another restructuring strategy. Maeda Masana, in charge of industrial development under Ōkubo and Ōkuma, lamented that Japanese people "vied with one another in commerce in isolation with no thoughts to banding together cooperatively."[11] He argued that in order to achieve international competitiveness, Japanese producers needed to establish cooperatives such as local producer associations to control the quality of export goods. Following this idea, the Ministry of Agriculture and Commerce (MAC, later MITI) helped to form trade associations such as the Japan Spinners Association, which was established under the leadership of Okada Reiko, a bureaucrat who directed a government-owned mill. It aimed at making industry competitive by sharing information and promoting cooperation.[12] In 1884, the MAC put forward a Standing Rule on Trade Associations (Dōgyō kumiai junsoku) to organize producers and traders and encouraged the formation of trade associations in order to control "excess production" and inspect the quality of export goods. In 1900, the MAC supported the establishment of Key Goods Trade Associations (Jūyō bussan dōgyō kumiai) in order to regulate product quality and curb dumping. The Japan Trade Council was founded by major importers and exporters who wanted to encourage foreign trade by exchanging information and conducting research on foreign markets.

In sum, the Meiji leadership's epistemology of trade and commerce reflected Listian mercantilism, which aimed at protecting domestic industry for devel-

opmental purposes. However, without the right of tariff autonomy development policy had to rely on domestic-level measures such as public lending,
preferential taxation, and industrial restructuring through the promotion of
mergers and cartels. Japan's ideas and practices regarding industrial policy
were the result not so much of any application of systematic theories as of a
series of ad hoc adjustments in response to domestic political challenges and
the unequal-treaty system imposed by the West. Because Japanese mercantilism was not based on tariff control but on enforced free trade, it took the form
of export-led industrialization. Yet, lack of tariffs did not imply a liberal economic system. To the contrary, the state used strong market regulations to
compensate for its lack of tariffs.

Arrival of Foreign Investment

Japan was fortunate to have been of little economic interest to the Western
powers when its ports were forced open in the 1850s and 1860s. Japan was not
incorporated into the world economic system to the same degree as China,
even after the unequal treaties were concluded. The United States treated
nineteenth-century Japan largely as a way station to China rather than as an
important market in its own right.[13] Although Western economic interests
imposed unequal treaties on Japan, the lack of significant Western economic
interests there gave Japan a "breathing space" of two or three decades. On its
part, the Meiji state actively discouraged foreign investment and was wary of
taking on foreign loans because of the unhappy experiences of Egypt and
Turkey, which had mismanaged their foreign loans and suffered foreign military intervention as a result.[14] Even as Japan resisted investment and loans
from overseas, its trade with the West flourished.

World War I boosted Japanese industrialization.[15] An unprecedented American economic boom fueled by massive exports of war-related products to
Europe also expanded imports into the United States. Japan benefited from
increased exports of textiles and other products to the rapidly growing U.S.
market, and it made substantial gains in the Asian market because of the
economic vacuum created by the European powers' involvement in the war.
Owing to strong exports, Japan ran a large trade surplus, increased credit to
foreign countries, and expanded its specie reserves. More important, it was
able to finance import-substituting industrialization in heavy industry, a move
that was promoted by state policy but that also resulted from the sudden

scarcity of heavy and chemical goods from war-torn Europe.[16] The economic boom of the World War I years, in turn, made Japan a more attractive place for foreign investors. Domestic income levels rose as the war boom and strong exports continued, while at the same time an active labor movement contributed to the rise of workers' incomes. Urbanization, high consumer prices, the expansion of the domestic market, and the corresponding increase of Japanese purchasing power all created opportunities for imports and investments from overseas, which then adversely affected domestic firms, particularly in the nascent heavy industries.[17]

Despite the long-awaited recovery of tariff autonomy in 1912, for several reasons Japan did not immediately use protective tariffs as its major policy tool for industrial growth. First, high tariffs would make it hard to attract the advanced foreign technology and investment Japan needed to make the transition from light to heavy industrialization. Second, Japanese leaders did not want to squander the international prestige gained from its victories in the Sino-Japanese War of 1895 and the Russo-Japanese War of 1905 by adopting tariff policies hostile to the West. Third, the use of industrial policy as a substitute for trade policy appears to have developed institutional inertia and become entrenched in the national decisionmaking structure and process. And fourth, only two years after Japan's recovery of tariff autonomy the outbreak of the First World War diverted European and American manufactured goods to war uses, making it difficult for Japan to import and obviating the need for tariffs.

Following World War I, the Japanese received an influx of foreign investment. This was facilitated by the Washington Conference System, an East Asian regional treaty regime that encouraged multilateral consultation and cooperation, particularly on economic issues.[18] For some forms of industry, such as electrical machinery and automobiles, the Japanese state actively invited foreign direct investment.[19] As of 1932, fifty major firms were either owned exclusively or partially by foreigners, many of them giant multinationals, such as Standard Oil, Royal Dutch-Shell, Armstrong-Vickers, Dunlop, General Electric, B. F. Goodrich, Siemens-Schukertwerke, Westinghouse Electric, Ford, General Motors, Chrysler, Victor Talking Machine, Associated Oil, Otis Elevator, and International Standard Electric.

Multinationals had begun to invest in Japan at the turn of the century, but many came to Japan after the outbreak of World War I and vastly increased their investment during the 1920s. Although the scale of their investment was not large, its impact on the Japanese economy was substantial.[20] It was concentrated in the heavy and chemical industries that the Japanese state was eager to promote, especially in such sectors as automobiles, machine tools, specialty steels, chemicals, petroleum, heavy electric machinery, and tires.

Toward a Licensing System

Before World War I, the Japanese government never seriously considered using tariffs as a primary means of protecting domestic markets. The Hara cabinet began to use tariffs in the early 1920s to fund expansionary fiscal policy, not to protect domestic industry. Due to fears of inflation and the 1923 Great Kanto Earthquake, further tariff revision was postponed until 1926, when tariffs were at last increased, selectively, in order to protect specific domestic industries.[21] Certain heavy industries received high tariffs, but rates were still lower than those in most advanced industrialized nations. The Kenseikai government of Katō Takaaki and Wakatsuki Reijirō (1924–27) restrained tariffs and tried to promote international trade and cooperation, an approach known as Shidehara diplomacy, after Foreign Minister Shidehara Kijūrō who promoted it.[22] Thus, even though protectionist trends were prevalent worldwide in the 1920s, tariff policy was only a supplementary measure in Japan and was not used to correct overall balance-of-payments deficits.

Beginning in the mid-1920s, under this liberal trade regime private cartels proliferated, initiated by private firms but often with state support. Cartels, aided by government subsidies and protective tariffs, helped to nurture domestic industries in sectors with low levels of foreign investment. One example is the Pig Iron Cartel, which, helped by governmental subsidies and tariff protection, kept prices up and regulated pig iron imports. Government subsidies also supported the domestic soda cartel's successful effort to compete with the international soda cartel led by International Chemical Industries (ICI).[23] Steel products, cement, superphosphate, and electric machineries also successfully followed this pattern. However, the combination of cartelization, tariffs, and subsidies was not enough to shore up domestic firms in sectors with strong foreign investment. When powerful foreign players were included, cartels invariably failed. Domestic firms often allied themselves with powerful foreign firms and opportunistically refused to join cartels. Although instances did exist when domestic and foreign firms joined in setting up cartels to divide market shares, limit production, and stabilize prices, all such agreements were

short lived. Because of the thorough integration of domestic and global markets, fluctuating world market conditions undermined the stability of domestic
collusive arrangements.

In the petroleum industry about half of Japanese prewar market share was
consistently occupied by two of the world's largest multinationals: Standard
Oil and Royal Dutch Shell. As early as 1901, Ōkuma Shigenobu, together with
Shibusawa Eiichi, told domestic oilmen that Japan needed a "grand merger" to
"multiply [Japanese] power and compete with [Standard Oil]."[24] Initially, the
merger movement was stimulated by Standard Oil of New York's setting up of
an oil-drilling and -refining firm on Japanese soil, and it was a recurring subject
through the prewar period. The first attempt at collusion by domestic oil firms
was in 1904. Two leading firms, Nippon Oil and Hoden Oil, believed that
excess competition among domestic firms suppressed oil prices and weakened
domestic competitiveness vis-à-vis the multinationals. They organized the National Oil Sales Union to improve product quality and build up the distribution
system. Despite this initial success, subsequent collusive attempts failed because domestic firms were unable to effectively organize themselves without
including the dominant foreign players. In 1909, the Japanese oil industry
formed the first foreign-domestic cartels to divide up market shares, limit
production, and stabilize prices. These private agreements lasted less than a
year, and later collective agreements were also short lived because domestic oil
firms could not control their distribution networks well enough to implement
the agreements and because international market conditions were extremely
unstable.

The state often responded to industry pleas to help strengthen cartels or even
set them up. Yoshino Shinji, a prominent MAC official who is considered by
many to be the architect of Japanese industrial policy, was the most instrumental in this regard.[25] After the Great Depression hit in 1929, Yoshino initiated
the industrial rationalization movement to restore order in the domestic market
both through better firm-level management techniques and through state support for cartels. Yoshino argued that cartels were not intended to provide
monopolistic rents for big business but were for public purposes. The state, he
asserted, must intervene to restore an industrial order that corresponds with the
national economic interest rather than, as was then perceived to be the case,
individual private interests.[26] State guidance of cartels was intended to "rationalize" the national economy by regulating firms' activities with an eye toward
facilitating the smooth supply of commodities, fair pricing, and fair profits.[27]

This was the idea behind the Important Industry Control Law (1931), which sought to protect and promote key industries without interfering blatantly in international trade by using tariffs.

The law had some success but was hindered by the difficulty of regulating major foreign players both in and outside the cartels. An extreme case was the automobile industry. Ford and GM established assembly plants in Japan and held more than 90 percent of the market share while a handful of domestic firms struggled to survive. The power of the two U.S. firms was so overwhelming that collusive pacts were largely meaningless. Without drastic state measures to restrict both domestic manufacturing and imports, building up a Japanese-owned industry seemed impossible. The state needed to curtail Ford and GM's operations in order to protect its favorites: Nissan and Toyota.

"Restoring industrial order" and "rationalizing the national economy" in the face of foreign competition thus required strict state controls. Yoshino intimated that what was needed in establishing such controls was licensing.[28] Under the licensing system, a firm would need a license to operate and the state would adopt licensing criteria that would limit market players to a few selected firms upon which it would then focus its development efforts.

This idea did not originate within the Japanese economic bureaucracy but in the French petroleum industry licensing system of the mid-1920s, created to give France autonomy from Anglo-American oil companies' hegemony.[29] The French licensing system aimed at protecting domestic industry and securing an adequate supply of oil for emergencies. Licensing had previously been used in Japan to regulate areas clearly related to public safety and health. For example, prostitution has been a licensed business from the late Tokugawa period. Licenses were needed to produce pharmaceuticals beginning in the early Meiji years. Also, licensing was applied in the electricity sector in 1929; firms were allowed to operate only when they met specific government safety requirements. However, using regulation for developmental purposes was a new, borrowed idea. As in France, the goal was to establish national autonomy in strategic industries.

The Japanese military, especially the navy, was instrumental in introducing the idea into Japan. World War I sparked a new discourse about the need for economic autonomy in a world of modern, total war. Advocates claimed that national integrity and economic prosperity depend on autonomous political power and economic self-sufficiency. A number of international events, including World War I, international naval conferences, and the emergence of a mechanized Soviet military on the Asian continent, portended a confrontation with the West that some thought would be a war of attrition, drawing not just on guns and soldiers but on the nation's entire stock of economic resources. The efficient generation and mobilization of industrial power would be crucial to future wars.

These ideas stemmed from World War I when a group of Japanese military officers and civilian bureaucrats studied German war mobilization.[30] Army colonel Koiso Kuniaki concluded that victory in future wars would go to those with strong industrial power and efficient mobilization plans. He recommended that Japan "establish a self-sufficient economy [and] limit the freedom of profit-seeking from the international division of labor" and that because of its limited reservoir of strategic resources, Japan develop productive facilities in Manchuria and Mongolia and bring in raw materials from China.[31] Koiso's views were shared by other young military officers, such as Nagata Tetsuzan and Ishiwara Kanji, as well as by the so-called reform bureaucrats who populated the Cabinet Investigative Bureau (later, the Cabinet Planning Board) in the mid-1930s, and became influential when their political guardian, Konoe Fumimarō, became prime minister in 1937.[32]

Kita Ikki's radical proposal, *An Outline Plan for the Reorganization of Japan,* provided a theoretical grounding for these ideas.[33] The first line of the plan states that "at present, the Japanese empire faces an unparalleled national crisis both at home and abroad."[34] The problems he cites are associated not so much with the Western imperialist threat as with the threats to the crumbling Japanese empire of the spreading impact of the Russian Revolution, the intensification of domestic class struggle, and the rise of national liberation movements within Japan's imperial sphere (the March 1 Movement in Korea and the May 4 Movement in China). In response to these problems, Kita argued for a national socialist program of strict state controls in order to bring about sweeping changes in all sectors of Japanese society. He proposed seven new ministries to carry out coherent economic planning to enhance productive efficiency. These institutions would confiscate large firms because of their excessive concentration of private wealth, manage them, and encourage the formation of trusts and cartels in order to rationalize production.

The military combined the belief in the inevitability of total war and the need for an autarkic empire with Kita's radical ideas for domestic reorganization. The culmination of the autarkic idea came in 1934 from two army ministry proposals, which criticized the organization of the economy for giving too much freedom to individuals who only sought unlimited personal profit and caused class conflict.[35] They advocated "holistic and moral economic concepts" emphasizing national rather than individual profit, on which Japan should establish a "national defense state."[36]

The national defense state required a powerful political economic system that in times of war could regulate industry closely and mobilize resources efficiently. Moreover, because war would interrupt international trade, the state needed a self-sufficient economic empire with enough industrial capacity and natural resources to withstand a trade embargo.[37] Autarky especially required self-sufficiency in militarily strategic industries such as automobiles, petroleum, aircraft, steel, machine tools, and some chemicals. These industries were all dominated by multinationals, and the military was hostile to foreign investment because it believed it to undermine national autonomy.

By the mid-1930s, these beliefs about Japan's strategic needs, combined with a desperate need to stabilize the fluctuating domestic market, led to the implementation of the radical new idea of establishing a licensing system. Economic bureaucrats and the military bureaucrats came to a consensus over the need to regulate foreign economic influence and to do so through licensing. The navy played a significant role in introducing a licensing system into the petroleum industry, borrowing the basic ideas from France. The army was instrumental in establishing the same system in the automobile industry, with close attention paid to Hitler's *Motorisierung* policy. The economic bureaucracy, centered on the Ministry of Commerce and Industry (MCI), helped draft and implement the new policies. Licensing was applied to the petroleum, automobile, aluminum, steel, machine tools, synthetic fuels, and aircraft industries, all of which were of strategic importance and deeply penetrated by foreign multinationals.

The 1930s saw a series of licensing laws: the Aluminum Industry Law (1933), the Petroleum Industry Law (1934), the Automobile Industry Law (1936), the Synthetic Fuels Law (1937), the Steel Industry Law (1937), the Machine Tool Industry Law (1938), and the Aircraft Industry Law (1938). Government licenses were required if firms wanted to either enter these industries or expand operations in them and were granted only if the firms met specific criteria. For example, in the case of petroleum, licenses were given in principle to Japanese-owned firms that could mass-produce refined products. To be qualified and protected, refineries were required to have the capacity to process 50,000 kiloliters of crude oil annually and be equipped with more than one cracking distiller. Licenses were given to Japanese automobile producers who could manufacture more than 3,000 vehicles a year with engines of more than 750 cubic centimeters. This licensing did not, it should be noted, force out of business existing firms that did not meet the criteria—for example, small-scale domestic firms, foreign multinationals, and domestic firms under foreign control. Insofar as they did not try to expand their operations, Ford, Chevrolet, Standard-Vacuum, and others were allowed to operate. But because the licensing system was typically applied to rapidly expanding infant industries, licenses were indispensable for survival and the state used them as leverage to get firms to do its bidding. For example, firms were pushed into truck manufacturing and petroleum refining. Licensing also proved to be an effective means of harassing disfavored firms into exiting an industry. When Ford Japan applied for a license to build a new assembly plant in Yokohama, for instance, the MCI asked innumerable questions and insisted on changes in the plans, only to ultimately turn the application down. Even applications for renovating existing plants typically took nine months to review.

In order to advance the goal of self-sufficiency, the state not only constrained foreign business operations with discriminatory licensing; it provided financial incentives for domestic industry through preferential quotas, tax exemptions, tariff protection, and subsidies. How did the private sector cope with state intervention? Some domestic firms such as Nissan and Toyota expanded their manufacturing facilites in order to qualify for licenses and financial assistance. Jidōsha Industries, later Isuzu, the product of a two-firm merger (Ishikawajima and DAT Motors) in 1933, made another effort to expand its scale through a merger with Tokyo Gas and Electric in 1937 to be designated as the third licensee following Nissan and Toyota. Under state direction, it specialized in manufacturing diesel vehicles. The other way the state attempted to support domestic firms was by helping them establish cartels. The top three domestic oil firms, Nippon Oil, Ogura Oil, and Mitsubishi Oil, were all established in response to the enactment of the Petroleum Industry Law, which set up the Domestic Gasoline Union as a price and sales cartel. This was later supplanted by the Petroleum Union. The Kerosene Union and the Heavy Oil Committee also established cartels. In return for meeting the state-set requirements, however, private firms and their associations were given relatively free rein to administer their cartels through such measures as setting tariff levels.

Conclusion

The licensing system is Japan's core regulatory system, and it was created as a response to market internationalization, bringing about protection of domestic industry from foreign competition without using protective tariffs. Use of the licensing system was not restricted to the interwar period but is ubiquitous in contemporary Japan as well. There are interesting parallels between the pre- and postwar periods. Japan's first market internationalization was brought about by the unequal treaties that forced Japan to open up to imports. Unable to use tariffs, the Japanese government protected key domestic industries with nontariff measures in the form of mergers and cartels, which were combined with subsidies and tax breaks. The state's response to increased inflows of foreign capital in the 1920s was the licensing system, a powerful industrial restructuring policy tool for promoting mergers and cartels, discouraging unwanted foreign investment.

The first wave of internationalization in the pre–World War II period led to the institutionalization of the licensing system. A second, postwar wave of internationalization led to the spread of the system into broader areas. Following Japan's period of postwar recovery, the United States pressured Japan to carry out trade and capital liberalization during the 1960s. Capital liberalization in particular was so feared that it was called "the second coming of the black ships," a reference to the fleet of U.S. admiral Matthew Perry, which arrived in 1853 to force Japan to open its ports. Liberalization itself eliminated two major tools of protective policy for the postwar state. First, the government's ability to protect domestic industry was reduced by the dramatic relaxation of the Foreign Exchange and Foreign Trade Control Law (1949), which had given the state power to concentrate all foreign exchange earned from exports and thereby exert control over domestic industry through the allocation of foreign exchange from a foreign exchange budget. Second, Japan had to drop its Foreign Capital Law (1950), which had required that foreigners wanting to invest in Japan obtain government approval. Tariff rates also had to be lowered.

As in the prewar period, market liberalization again led to proposals for industrial restructuring. Like Yoshino Shinji, postwar policymakers characterized domestic firms as small and unproductive and prone to excess competition that left them too weak to compete with foreign firms.[38] As in the 1930s, the state and the private sector broadly agreed on the need to enhance Japan's international competitiveness.[39] Based on this consensus, for example, the Petrochemical Cooperation Roundtable (Sekiyukagaku Kyōchō Kondankai), composed of representatives of the government and industry, was established to set promotion standards for the licensing of business that would compete with larger foreign firms. Licenses were granted to firms that could achieve economies of scale, that is, firms retaining an annual manufacturing capacity of 300,000 tons of ethylene. Licenses were also tied to scale requirements in the petroleum industry. Under liberalization, the low level of capitalization of domestic oil firms made them easy targets for foreign buyout. Nationalistic concerns that the Japanese oil industry would be at risk and that national security would be compromised led MITI and the Energy Roundtable (Enerugi Kondankai) to search for a way to prevent foreign investment and "excess competition" among domestic firms. These licensing and regulatory powers given to the state in 1962 were the same ones granted in 1934 and repealed in 1945. In the case of the shipbuilding industry, governmental licensing was used to regulate new entry into the industry when the tariff rate dropped from 15 percent in 1964 to zero in ten years.[40] Armed with the powers of licensing, the state promoted industrial restructuring in sectors subject to market instability, to perceived excessive domestic competition, and to competitive pressure from foreign firms, as well as in sectors considered vital to the nation's economic security. The absence of tariff controls was used to justify the use of invasive and extensive regulation based on licensing powers.

Because Japanese regulation has aimed at protecting key industries from foreign competition, it is frequently protectionist in character, and therefore naturally leads to international trade disputes. An important question is whether the relaxation or destruction of the licensing system in and of itself can create open, fair, and free markets. Most likely the answer is no. The purpose of formal regulation through licensing has been to establish informally regulated markets based on monopolistic, cartel-like practices, so in order to create truly open markets the state most likely needs to work more actively to undo the legacy of its licensing policies than simply withdraw from formal regulation.

Notes

1. Sōmuchō (Management and Coordination Agency), *Kisei kanwa suishin no gen-kyō* (The current state of progress in regulatory reform) (Tokyo, 1996).

2. The premier source on Japanese industrial policy is Chalmers Johnson, *MITI and the Japanese Miracle: The Growth of Industrial Policy, 1925–1975* (Stanford University Press, 1982).

3. *Ōkubo toshimichi monjo* (Ōkubo Toshimichi documents), vol. 5 (Tokyo: Tokyo daigaku shuppankai, 1968), p. 55.

4. Ibid., p. 561.

5. Ibid. Ōkubo's ideas were later expanded on by Fukuzawa Yukichi. See Fuku-zawa's theory of "nation building through exports" in Sugihara Shirō and others, eds., *Nihon no keizai shisō yonhyakunen* (Four hundred years of Japanese economic thought) (Tokyo: Nihon keizai hyōronsha, 1990), p. 245.

6. Itō Hirobumi's memorial (*kengisho*) of 1871, in *Shōkō seisakushi V: Bōeki (1)* (History of commercial and industrial policy) (Tokyo: Shōkō seisaku shi kankō kai), p. 201.

7. William Lockwood, *Economic Development of Japan* (Princeton University Press, 1954), p. 326.

8. See Sidney Brown, "Okubo Toshimichi: His Political and Economic Policies in Early Meiji Japan," *Journal of Asian Studies*, vol. 21 (February 1962), pp. 194–96.

9. James Vestal, *Planning for Change: Industrial Policy and Japanese Economic Development, 1945–1990* (Oxford University Press, 1993), pp. 9–10.

10. *Ōkubo Toshimichi monjo*, vol. 6, pp. 414–23. For more detail, see "Ōkubo Toshimichi no kaiun hogo ikuseisaku" (Ōkubo Toshimichi's developmental and protec-tionist policies toward the shipping industry), in Nakamura Masanori, Ishii Kanji, and Kasuga Yutaka, eds., *Nihon kindai shisō taikei* (An outline of modern Japanese eco-nomic thought), vol. 8: *Keizai Kōsō* (Economic ideas) (Tokyo: Iwanami shoten, 1988), pp. 34–37.

11. "Kōgyō Iken" (Advice for the Promotion of Industry), ibid., pp. 119–29.

12. The cotton-spinning industry was not just cartelized but also organized as an interest group to help shape industrial policy for the industry. W. Miles Fletcher, "The Japanese Spinners Association: Creating Industrial Policy in Meiji Japan," *Journal of Japanese Studies*, vol. 22, no. 1 (1996), pp. 49–75. See also Fletcher, *The Japanese Business Community and National Trade Policy, 1920–1942* (University of North Carolina Press, 1989).

13. Frances V. Moulder, *Japan, China, and the Modern World Economy: Toward a Reinterpretation of East Asian Development ca. 1600 to ca. 1918* (Cambridge Univer-sity Press, 1977).

14. See, for example, the Orders on Mining of 1873, which prevented foreigners from investing in mines, the text of which can be found in *Nihon kindai shisō taikei,* vol. 8 (1989), pp. 13–16. On Japan's wary observation of other weak nations' experi-ence, see E. H. Norman, *Japan's Emergence as a Modern State* (New York: Institute of Pacific Relations, 1940), p. 116.

15. For an overview of the wartime economic changes in Japan, see Takeda Haru-hito, *Teikokushugi to minponshugi* (Imperialism and democracy) (Tokyo: Shueisha, 1992), pp. 67–96. See also Takafusa Nakamura, *Economic Growth in Prewar Japan* (Yale University Press, 1983), pp. 144–56.

16. Hashimoto Jurō, *Daikyōkōki no nihon shihonshugi* (Japanese capitalism during the Great Depression) (Tokyo: Tokyo daigaku shuppankai, 1984), chapter 1.

17. For examples, see Takeda, *Teikokushugi to minponshugi,* pp. 166–68.

18. For a discussion of Japan and the Washington Conference System, see Akira Iriye, *After Imperialism: The Search for a New Order in the Far East, 1921–1931* (Harvard University Press, 1965).

19. Mark Mason, "With Reservations: Prewar Japan as Host to Western Electric and ITT," in Takeshi Yuzawa and Masaru Udagawa, eds., *Foreign Business in Japan before World War II* (University of Tokyo Press, 1990), p. 176.

20. Masaru Udagawa, "Business Management and Foreign-Affiliated Companies in Japan before World War II," in Yuzawa and Udagawa, *Foreign Business in Japan before World War II*, p. 5.

21. Miwa Ryōichi, "1926-nen kanzei kaisei no rekishiteki igi" (The historical meaning of the 1926 tariff revision), in Sakasai Takahito, ed., *Nihon shihonshugi—Tenkai to ronri* (The development and logic of Japanese capitalism) (Tokyo: Tokyo daigaku shuppankai, 1978), pp. 174, 179–80.

22. The best account of the Shidehara diplomacy remains Iriye, *After Imperialism*.

23. On steel, see Okazaki Tetsuji, *Nihon no kōgyōka to tekkō sangyō* (Japanese industrialization and the steel industry) (Tokyo: Tokyo daigaku shuppankai, 1993), pp. 35–82. On soda, see Miyajima Hideaki, "Senkanki nihon ni okeru kokusai kyōsō to senryakuteki kainyū" (International competition and strategic intervention during interwar Japan), *Waseda shōgaku*, vol. 362 (1995), pp. 609–40.

24. Inoguchi Tōsuke, *Gendai nihon sangyō hattatsushi* (The history of industrial development in contemporary Japan), vol. 2: *Sekiyu* (Petroleum) (Tokyo: Gendai nihon hattasu shi kenkyukai, 1963), p. 110.

25. For Yoshino's industrial policy ideas, see Yoshino Shinji, *Shōkō gyōsei no omoide* (Memories of commercial and industrial administration) (Tokyo: Shōkō seisaku shi kankō kai, 1971). See also Johnson, *MITI*, pp. 83–115.

26. Yoshino, *Shōkō gyōsei no omoide*, pp. 189, 202, 205–06.

27. See Miyajima Hideaki, "Sangyō gōrika to chūyō sangyō tōsei-hō" (Industrial rationalization and the important industry control law), in Kindai Nihon Kenkyūkai, ed., *Seitō naikaku no seiritsu to hōkai* (Rise and fall of the party cabinet) (Tokyo: Yamakawa shuppansha, 1984), pp. 101–42.

28. Yoshino Shinji, *Nihon kōgyō seisaku* (Japanese industrial policy) (Tokyo: Nihon hyōronsha, 1935), p. 318.

29. Licensed firms were granted various financial benefits from the French state in return for fulfilling the oil stockpiling requirement, which was devised for strategic reasons. For an institutional account of the French oil industry before 1945, see Leslie Grayson, *National Oil Companies* (New York: Wiley, 1981); and Gregory Nowell, *Mercantile States and the World Oil Cartel, 1900–1939* (Cornell University Press, 1994).

30. Michael Barnhart, *Japan Prepares for Total War* (Cornell University Press, 1987), p. 22; Johnson, *MITI*, p. 117.

31. Bōeichō (Defense Agency), *Rikugun Gunjudōin* (The army's munitions mobilization), vol. 1 (Bōei Kenshujō, 1967), pp. 40–42.

32. See Robert Spaulding, "Bureaucracy as a Political Power," in James Morley, ed., *Dilemmas of Growth in Prewar Japan* (Princeton University Press, 1971); and Hata Ikuhiko, *Kanryō no kenkyū* (A study of bureaucracy) (Tokyo: Tokyo daigaku shuppankai, 1983), pp. 112–13.

33. The most comprehensive treatment of the influence of Kita's ideas on strategic thinking in military circles is Itō Takashi, *Shōwa shoki seijishi kenkyū* (A study of political history in the early Showa period) (Tokyo: Tokyo daigaku shuppankai, 1969).

34. *Kita Ikki chosakushū* (The collected works of Kita Ikki), vol. 3 (Tokyo: Misuzu shobo, 1972), p. 291.

35. (The essence of modern national defense and economic strategy) *Kindai kokubō no honshitsu to keizai senryaku kita,* and (The true meaning of national defense and a proposal for strengthening it), *Kokubō no hongi to sore kyōka no teishō* (Tokyo: Rikugunsho, 1934), or the so-called Army Pamphlet.

36. *Kokubō no hongi to sore kyōka no teishō,* p. 281.

37. *Kindai kokubō no honshitsu to keizai senryaku kita* p. 30.

38. Johnson, *MITI,* p. 255.

39. Vestal, *Planning for Change,* p. 47.

40. For a brief review of Japan's industrial restructuring policy in the postwar years, see Iwasaki Akira, "Gappei to saihensei" (Mergers and restructuring), in Komiya Ryūtarō, Okuno Masahiro, and Suzumura Kōtarō, eds., *Nihon no sangyō seisaku* (Tokyo: Tokyo daigaku shuppankai, 1984), pp. 431–44.

CHAPTER THREE

The Impact of Deregulation on Corporate Governance and Finance

Hideaki Miyajima

Thanks to an accumulation of research in recent years on the characteristics of the J-Type firm, as the ideal typical model of the Japanese corporation has come to be known, it is widely recognized that the Japanese corporate system has characteristics significantly different from those of the Anglo-American type of firm in such areas as internal structure, transaction relations, corporate finance, and corporate governance. These distinctive characteristics have been sustained by the regulatory framework that emerged out of the period of reforms following the end of World War II and are considered a major factor in making possible the vaunted rapid growth of the Japanese economy during the so-called high-growth era (HGE) of the 1950s and 1960s, Japanese industry's successful adjustment to the radically changed economic context of the 1970s, and the maintenance of the competitive edge of Japan's assembly industries during the 1980s.[1] Recently, however, the financial deregulation that has occurred in Japan since the late 1970s, together with other macroeconomic factors, has begun to have a major impact on the patterns of corporate finance that had earlier undergirded the J-Type firm. These changes have resulted in a metamorphosis of the J-Type firm system during the late 1980s and early 1990s that has, in turn, induced further deregulation.

As the Japanese economy struggles through an exceptionally long period of low growth in the wake of the collapse of its late 1980s "bubble economy," it is frequently claimed that the J-Type firm system is no longer viable. Business leaders and researchers have been engaged in heated debates over how best to establish a vigorous new economic system for the next century that can effectively replace the existing system built around the J-Type firm. Mindful of the ongoing controversy, this chapter describes the evolution of the J-Type firm system in the light of the regulatory framework that sustained it and explores the consequences of deregulation for that system.[2] The focus is on the aspect of corporate finance and governance, and within this context the topic of main bank-client firm relations will be of central importance. Following a brief description of the J-Type firm model in the first section, the second section reviews the process of the J-Type firm's emergence and its mode of operation during the HGE (1955–70). It argues that the J-firm system was a rational response to the regulatory framework established during the period of postwar reform. The third section, focusing mainly on the 1980s, describes the process of financial deregulation and its impact on the J-Type firm. The crucial development during this period was the decline in the monitoring capacities of main banks. The fourth section summarizes the current change in the J-firm system and follows with a discussion of the current debates over whether to rescind the Glass-Steagall–type separation of the Japanese banking and securities industries and over the recent lifting of the ban on the establishment of holding companies. Incorporated into these sections are regression analyses that use data concerning the 150 largest Japanese corporations in the years 1955, 1964, and 1972. Due to the appearance and disappearance of some companies on these lists, the number of companies included in the three years totals 202. In the regression analysis for turnover and corporate performance 100 companies were picked at random from this data set.

The J-Type Firm Defined

The J-Type firm is an ideal typical depiction of the essential features of the type of corporate organization that has predominated in Japan's big business sector since the 1950s. The J-Type firm system is composed of subsystems such as a subsystem of cooperative industrial relations based on "lifetime" employment and a subsystem of interfirm contracting built around long-term relationships linking suppliers and assemblers. The focus in this chapter will be on the corporate finance and corporate governance aspects of the J-firm system, the essence of which can be generalized as follows[3]:

1. The board of directors of a J-Type firm is composed mainly of corporate "insiders"—salaried managers promoted from within the company—and the

membership of this board overlaps with the membership of the top management team. It is quite common, in fact, for large Japanese firms to have boards
that do not contain any "outsiders" whatsoever, and to that extent even representatives of large shareholders are absent. The one exception to this general
rule is that the firm's main bank (see item 3) is represented on the board. This
structure is quite different from both the Anglo-American model, where boards
of directors regularly include outsiders who represent large shareholders and
who closely monitor the activities of the top management team. It is also
different from the German model, in which the top management team is moni-
tored by a supervisory board composed of representatives of shareholders and
employees.[4]

2. Thanks to stable patterns of cross-shareholding among the members of
corporate groups, or *keiretsu,* the top managers of the J-Type firm are freed
from the short-term pressures of the stock market. This relationship between
top managers and the capital market is different from the Anglo-American
model, in which the capital market functions as an effective device for monitoring, controlling, and disciplining firm managements. It is often argued that the
growth-oriented behavior and long-term time horizon of the J-Type firm were
encouraged by this institutional setting.[5]

3. The so-called main bank, which engages in ex ante, interim, and ex post
monitoring of client companies, plays an active role not only in supplying
funds to a firm, but also in disciplining the firm's top management team.[6]
Under this system, a main bank is charged with the task of supplying new
money for the investment projects of client companies—that is, it plays an
initial or first lender role. The basis on which it decides whether to lend is ex
ante monitoring, and it is the main bank that organizes a de facto syndicate to
supply the remainder of the funds. Main banks also rely on passive, stable
shareholders who do not interfere in firm management, to mitigate agency
problems that might occur as a consequence of the dispersed ownership of the
corporation. And main banks do not themselves intervene in the affairs of their
client companies when the latter are doing well. In times of financial distress,
however, main banks carry out rescue operations by dispatching representatives to client companies, at times taking over the boards of these companies,
reorienting client company managements, and taking the initiative in restructuring the company in question. This main bank disciplinary mechanism is a
form of "contingent governance" and differs from the arm's-length Anglo-
American system based on takeovers and bankruptcy procedures. It is somewhat like the German system in which the *grosse Bank* plays a key role in
corporate governance.[7]

Regulation and the J-Type Firm during the High-Growth Era
HGE

The J-Type firm system emerged as a result of postwar reform initiated by the U.S. occupation army (i.e., the Americanization of Japanese economic institutions) and its subsequent modification (i.e., the Japanization of the American system). It evolved during the era of high economic growth and served to encourage that growth.

The Antimonopoly Law and the Problem of Shareholder Stabilization

Shareholding was unregulated in prewar Japan, and holding companies were a prevalent form under this laissez-faire system. There was a broad spectrum of holding companies ranging from those of the big three corporate groups called *zaibatsu* (Mitsui, Mitsubishi, Sumitomo) to the headquarters of relatively small, family-based corporate networks. Following the end of World War II, general headquarters (GHQ) of the Allied powers regarded this concentrated ownership structure as undemocratic and a potential resource that could be exploited by a renewed Japanese militarist regime. Under a plan initiated by GHQ, the *zaibatsu* system was dissolved completely with the intent of replacing it with a more dispersed and "democratic" system via a redistribution of ownership that was expected to produce an equity-based system of corporate finance. The Antimonopoly Law of 1947, adopted as part of the occupation forces' extensive economic reform program, regulated share ownership for the first time. Article 9 prohibited the establishment of holding companies (defined as companies with 25 percent or more of their assets in the securities of other companies).[8] U.S. antitrust law, on which the Antimonopoly Law was modeled, does not require this, and in this sense the Japanese legal stipulations can be considered somewhat distinctive. The main reason behind the provision was to prevent a revival of the concentrated ownership structure of the *zaibatsu* system. The original law also banned manufacturing companies from owning any stock in other companies (Article 10). Under Article 13 of the original version of the law a financial institution was not allowed to own more than 5 percent of a company's total stock issues.[9]

It proved impossible to sustain these highly restrictive provisions in their original form in the wake of the imposition of the draconian 1949 Dodge Line retrenchment policy on Japan's fragile, war-devastated industrial economy. A stock market collapse was precipitated in October of that year by an oversupply of stocks and an increase in real interest rates. The crash affected the economic system that GHQ had established in Japan in two ways. First, it made recapitalization virtually impossible. With share prices dropping to almost below par value, Japanese firms found themselves unable to raise the capital needed to attain the "sound capital composition" that GHQ was demanding as a prerequisite for its capital-market–based system.[10] A second consequence of the stock market crash was that the top managers of Japan's leading firms found themselves faced with the threat of takeover bids by outside interests. This was especially true for ex-*zaibatsu* companies, whose stock issues were being liquidated as part of GHQ's *zaibatsu* dissolution program, and several former *zaibatsu* companies experienced hostile takeover bids. With their autonomy under siege, the top management teams of Japan's largest corporations sought to maintain their firms' stock prices through measures that represented the functional equivalent of leveraged buyouts, the latter being technically prohibited under Japanese commercial law.[11]

Actions of this sort were conspicuous in late 1949 and early 1950 and were assisted by modifications of the corporate law framework. With the Japanese government pressing for measures to sustain equity prices and under orders from Washington to rapidly rehabilitate the Japanese economy, GHQ began to retreat from its original plan to reform the Japanese corporate system along the lines of the market-based system of corporate governance in the United States.[12] As a part of its policy for maintaining stock prices, GHQ authorized a revision of the antimonopoly statutory framework that it had established only a few years earlier. A 1949 amendment of the Antimonopoly Law made it possible for manufacturing companies to own other companies' stocks, subject to the qualification that this did not substantially reduce competition. A further amendment in 1953 included a revision of Article 13 that raised the ceiling on financial institution ownership from the previous 5 percent to 10 percent. The prohibition of holding companies was not touched at that time.[13]

As figure 3-1 suggests, these changes in policy made possible a modest shift from individual- toward institution-centered ownership. Cross-shareholding among ex-*zaibatsu* companies advanced during the early 1950s. Given that holding companies were prohibited and bank shareholding restricted, cross-shareholding represented one of the few avenues of response available to the ex-*zaibatsu* companies facing takeover bids. Despite these developments, ownership of leading Japanese firms was still widely dispersed in the 1950s, and shares in most other firms were held mainly by individuals or investment trust funds (the equivalent of mutual funds in the United States). The prevailing

**Figure 3-1. Distribution of Stockholdings in All Listed Nonfinancial
Companies by Type of Investor, 1945–93**

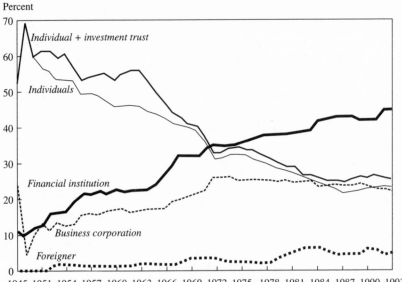

Source: Nomura, Tokyo Stock Exchange, *Annual Securities Statistics* (1996).

corporate governance structure, in other words, remained characterized by the
market model that was envisioned in GHQ's original plans.[14] The percentage of
shares held by individuals had decreased by only 5 percent between 1955 and
1963. If the percentage of shares held by mutual funds is added to individuals'
shares, the aggregated share in 1963 exceeded that of 1955 (see figure 3-1).

A turning point came with the implementation of capital liberalization in the
mid-1960s. The Japanese government (that is, the Ministry of Finance [MOF]
and the Ministry of International Trade and Industry [MITI]) and business
leaders were determined to protect Japanese companies from the takeover bids
of foreign companies that were expected once capital liberalization occurred.
Given Japan's diffuse ownership structure, government officials and top managements of large firms were worried that foreign firms would quickly take
control of Japan's leading companies. Fears of this sort were exacerbated after
1962 by a prolonged bear market. The average listed share price in the first
section of the Tokyo Stock Exchange (TSE) fell by almost 50 percent between

its October 1961 peak and April 1965 trough. The government decided to shore up stock prices in response and used these operations to facilitate the establishment of a retinue of stable shareholders in Japan's leading firms. In the process, the state's previously neutral stance toward the structure of corporate ownership shifted to a decidedly activist one.

How, concretely, did this shift unfold? Initially, the big business community strongly favored the abolition of the ban on holding companies found in Article 9 of the Antimonopoly Law as a way to counteract the threat of foreign takeovers of Japanese firms. Other measures proposed to counter such takeovers included raising the 10 percent ceiling on shareholding by financial institutions and placing provisions in a company's articles of incorporation (*teikan*) that would prohibit foreign investors from owning shares and attaining board member status in a company. A committee of businesspersons in 1967 argued that the introduction of holding companies would make it easier in situations in which mergers would be difficult or impossible to realize for the companies involved to achieve economies of scale through holding-company–organized cooperative efforts.[15] MITI drafted a number of plans that incorporated these ideas, and the Council on Foreign Capital initiated discussions about the authorization of holding companies for the purpose of establishing stable shareholders and encouraging mergers and acquisitions.[16]

The proposed abolition of Article 9, however, never materialized. This failure was not just a result of Fair Trade Commission opposition but was also due to the fact that in the interim significant progress had been made in establishing stable shareholders. A Deliberation Council for Coordinating Capital Increases (Zōshi Chōsei Kondankai) was organized in 1961 and actively attempted to suppress increases in corporate capital during the mid-1960s. This was followed by the creation of new joint public-private institutions known as the Japan Joint Securities Corporation (Nihon Kyōdō Shōken Kabushiki Kaisha) and the Japan Securities Holding Association (Nihon Shōken Hoyū Kumiai). Nominally these two quasi-governmental organizations were charged with the task of maintaining stock prices. Using special loans provided by the Bank of Japan, they ultimately purchased approximately 6 percent of all shares listed in the first section of the TSE from the stock market itself, from investment trusts (mutual funds), and from securities companies.[17] This volume of purchases proved sufficient to attain the desired effect on stock prices. The two quasi-governmental institutions then systematically resold the shares they had purchased to "stable" shareholders—that is, to financial institutions with a common *keiretsu* affiliation and to other companies that were expected not to resell or transfer their shares in the short term. About 80 percent of the shares purchased were resold to corporations during the ensuing five years.[18] In addition, the Commercial Code was revised to make it easier for firms to stabilize their shareholders on their own. One of the most important measures involved was an amendment to Article 280 that made it possible for a firm's board of directors to increase capital through private placements without obtaining the formal approval of a general meeting of current shareholders. By private placement (third-party allocation) we are referring to sales of equity, often at below market prices, to selected persons or firms (typically, directors, employees, suppliers, or distributors). Another amendment made it possible for a company to restrict share ownership to Japanese citizens in a firm's articles of incorporation, although in practice this step was not used much due to the fact that the rules of the TSE were such that a company could not get listed if such a restriction were included in its articles. One well-known instance of the application of this provision can be found at Toyota, where the company's articles of incorporation were revised to limit shareholding to Japanese nationals and legal persons.[19]

The stabilization of corporate shareholding advanced steadily as a consequence of these measures. This trend was particularly conspicuous with regard to cross-shareholding among ex-*zaibatsu* firms, with the cross-shareholding ratio reaching nearly 30 percent in the case of the members of the Mitsubishi and Sumitomo presidents' clubs. Non-ex-*zaibatsu* companies organized presidents' clubs of their own, and cross-shareholding increased among these firms as well. In the automobile and electrical industries, large firms used their vertical supplier networks as a basis for stabilizing their shareholders by asking subsidiaries or related companies to hold their shares. The result was the dramatic change in the nature of the corporate ownership structure that can be seen in figure 3-1. Changes were especially marked in the auto industry, in which the threat of foreign takeover was considered most serious. Eight of the fifteen firms that experienced the largest increase in the percentage of shares held by other firms and financial institutions between 1964 and 1972 were in the auto industry.[20]

The Role of Main Banks in the J-Firm System Prior to Deregulation

Heavy regulation and controls in the financial sector were instituted during the war and immediate postwar years.[21] Convinced that close ties between *zaibatsu* banks and firms in the wartime economy had created an "interrelated solvency" problem that led to their dominance, GHQ took it upon itself to dissolve these financial ties.[22] GHQ attempted to create in place of the debt-financing–based structure of the wartime banking system a market-based financial system in which long-term funds would be raised in the capital market and short-term money would be supplied by commercial banks. A strict division of labor among financial institutions was implemented in line with this vision. The most important of these was the separation of the banking and securities businesses, modeled after the American Glass-Steagall Act, that was mandated by Article 65 of the Securities Transaction Law of 1948. The so-called city banks, as Japan's largest banks are known, which used to be heavily involved in the business of underwriting and brokering bonds, were no longer allowed to participate in these businesses.[23]

The financial system that emerged in 1955 was not the one GHQ had originally envisioned. A key problem was that the capital market did not expand sufficiently to meet investment needs. The proximate cause for this was the stock market crash that followed the implementation of the Dodge Line. The longer-term structural reasons were that household savings levels were too low to allow for substantial popular investment in equities and that there was a lack of credible institutions capable of reducing investment risks for small investors.[24] The banking sector therefore came to serve as the primary source of corporate investment funds. It was this prevalence of financial intermediaries, in turn, that provided the context for the emergence of the so-called main bank system.

Government regulations facilitated and sustained the main bank system. In addition to initiating the segmentation of banking and securities businesses, the regulatory framework established in the financial sector during war and postwar reform periods involved the following[25]:

1. The regulation of international capital inflow and outflow through the Foreign Exchange and Foreign Trade Control Law of 1950, which prevented foreign capital from undercutting the various financial controls imposed on the domestic market. Within this framework, firms were required to get government permission before borrowing money from foreign banks or issuing securities in overseas markets.

2. The restriction of bond issuance to a small number of companies through the imposition of secured issuance (collateral) requirements and detailed accounting criteria relating to the size and financial situation of eligible firms (for example, net assets, dividend and profit per stock, the ratio of net assets to

capital stock, equity ratio, and the rate of return on assets). Furthermore, the Bond Issuance Committee (Kisai Chōsei Iinkai) tightly regulated the amount and the conditions of bond issuance with an eye toward the market situation and interest rates. As a result, it proved virtually impossible for companies, especially relatively new companies without an established reputation and with a high debt-equity ratio, to raise funds by issuing bonds.

3. The strict control of bank deposit rates through the Temporary Interest Rate Adjustment Law of 1947. Based on this law, the MOF pursued an interest rate policy aimed at artificially maintaining interest rates below what the market would have produced and that constituted a de facto subsidy for the banks. Nominal lending rates remained stable during the HGE, but banks could raise effective lending rates by requiring that client companies maintain compensating balances.

As a result of these regulations, patterns of corporate finance were biased strongly in favor of debt financing. In addition to the role played in this trend by the tax advantages of debt financing, the fact that corporate bond issuance was highly regulated meant that manufacturing firms with internal funds insufficient for financing investment projects had little choice but to resort to borrowing as a means of increasing capital. This bias strengthened in the 1950s or, more specifically, after the arrival of the Jimmu Boom in 1956.

For the banking sector, this framework provided strong incentives to develop good clients because the profitability of a city bank was conditioned by the number and size of its client firms as well as by its ability to collect deposits. Main banks were in a position to collect a main bank rent from strong or promising client companies in the form of decreased ex ante monitoring costs, a lowering of the costs involved in attracting client deposits, commissions earned on various client transactions, and the additional business generated from the transactions of client-affiliated companies.[26] The top managers of the city banks recognized that a retinue of good client companies provided them with a huge advantage in the early stages of the HGE. For instance, at a meeting of branch managers in 1954 the president of Fuji Bank stated: "Now that the economy has largely returned to normal, the accumulation of capital has made it possible for well-performing companies to improve their position and strengthen their [vertical] keiretsu relationships. . . . If a bank establishes business with these high-performance, group-affiliated firms, then this bank will strengthen its position and, at the same time, lay the foundation for growth in the future."[27] After having decided to adopt this strategy, Fuji enlarged its screening and research divisions by dividing the former screening division into a first and second division. The first division focused on screening large clients. Parallel moves by other city banks resulted in fierce competition for good clients.

Competition among main banks was accelerated by the rivalry between ex-*zaibatsu* and non-ex-*zaibatsu* banks. Each of the ex-*zaibatsu* banks (Mitsubishi, Mitsui, and Sumitomo) had easy access to a client base of big firms that were former members of the same prewar *zaibatsu*. By contrast, the non-*zaibatsu* Fuji, Sanwa, and Daiichi Banks had few good clients and were in a far weaker position than the ex-*zaibatsu* banks because of the smaller size of their clients and the newness of their business relationships with their clients.[28] The non-*zaibatsu* banks therefore tried, beginning in the early 1950s, to obtain a client base of large firms with the aim of achieving economies of scale in their loan structure and to enhance their competitiveness vis-à-vis the ex-*zaibatsu* banks. Their strategy, in turn, influenced that of the ex-*zaibatsu* banks.

Other arrangements were put into place to support the main bank system and *keiretsu* financing (main bank financing) during the 1950s and early 1960s. First, main banks made it a practice to dispatch representatives of the bank to large client corporations in order to facilitate monitoring of the firm. According to my sample of 100 companies, the number of companies to which bank representatives were dispatched increased from 23 in 1958, to 36 in 1963, and to 53 in 1969. Furthermore, main banks tended to hold equity in client companies up to the limits stipulated by the regulatory framework, a phenomenon that came into its own during the first phase of the HGE. It has been demonstrated that the higher a company's dependence on loans from a bank and the higher a company's debt-equity ratio, the greater the share of the client firm's stock held by a main bank. It was in this manner that the main bank system came to be firmly established by the mid-1960s.[29]

The J-Type Firm in Its Heyday

The change in ownership structure and the emergence of the main bank system had a profound effect on corporate behavior. One way this impact was felt can be found in the way the main bank system facilitated corporate investment by mitigating information problems. A number of companies such as Honda and Sony, which are now considered firmly established, did not have a good reputation in the capital market in the late 1950s. But these new companies' main banks, as first lenders, were willing to provide them with an ample supply of venture capital because of the assurance provided by the

Table 3-1. Dividend Rate (*DR*) and Sensitivity of *DR* to Return on Equity (*ROE*), 1957–94

Estimated equation: $DR = a + a_1 ROE^a$ (N = 204)

Period	Average of DR	a_1	$\bar{R}^2$
1957–64[b]	.122	.643* (11.579)	.259
1965–73	.106	.002** (2.574)	.003
1974–82	.103	.001 (.624)	.000
1983–89	.112	.042* (5.215)	.018
1990–94	.134	.388** (9.244)	.080

Sources: Japan Development Bank, *The JDB Corporate Finance Data Bank,* CD-ROM (Tokyo: Japan Economic Research Institute, 1996).

t-value in parentheses:

* = Significant at the 1 percent level.

** = Significant at the 5 percent level.

a. Each regression includes year dummy and industry dummy.

b. The sensitivity of *DR* (dividend payout ratio) to *ROE* before 1964 is still tentative because of lack of data.

banks' long-term relationships with them and the monitoring arrangements that were part and parcel of the main bank system.[30] Another example of the impact of the regulatory changes can be seen in the way that the success of the shareholder stabilization program freed top management from stock market pressures. An empirical corroboration of this point can be found in the results of a regression of dividend payout ratios (*DR*) on the rates of *ROE* of Japan's largest firms after 1957, tabulated in table 3-1. A positive correlation between the *DR* and *ROE* indicates that shareholders were obtaining increased dividends from a firm's increased profits. A positive correlation of this sort, it might be noted, is in evidence during the prewar period and the early 1950s.[31] *DR* remained sensitive to *ROE* during the first phase of the HGE (1957–64), but the degree of sensitivity declined during the era's later phase (1965–73). The degree of correlation decreased further during the 1970s—indeed, so much so that $\bar{R}^2$ declined to almost zero. This suggests that with the stabilization of shareholders, Japan's largest firms adopted stable payout ratio policies unaffected by fluctuations in the capital market.

Table 3-2. Estimation of Investment Functions, 1957–64 and 1965–72

Model: $I_t/K_{t-1} = a_0 + a_1(L_{t-1}/K_{t-1}) + a_2(CF_{t-1}/K_{t-1}) + a_{3q_{t-1}} + a_4Y_{t-1}$[a] $(N = 204 \times$ years$)$

Variable[a]	1958–64	1965–73	1974–82
L_{t-1}/K_{t-1}	0.007	-0.008	-0.015*
	(0.661)	(-0.966)	(-4.341)
CF_{t-1}/K_{t-1}	1.063*	0.659*	0.282*
	(11.497)	(11.943)	(11.471)
q_{t-1}	0.046**	0.000	0.029***
	(2.354)	(-0.26)	(1.832)
Y_{t-1}/K_{t-1}	0.008***	0.007**	0.001*
	(1.945)	(2.188)	(4.341)
$\overline{R}^2$	.268	.188	.215

Sources: Japan Development Bank, *The JDB Corporate Finance Data Bank;* BOJ, *Economic Statistics Annual,* 1985.

t-value in parentheses:

*Significant at the 1 percent level.

**Significant at the 5 percent level.

***Significant at the 10 percent level.

a. Each regression includes year dummy and industry dummy.

b. Notations of variables are as follows:

I_t = capital investment, the increment of tangible fixed assets during the current fiscal year.

K_{t-1} = stock of capital, the tangible fixed assets outstanding at the end of the previous fiscal year $t - 1$.

L_{t-1} = borrowing, the total of borrowing outstanding at the end of the previous fiscal year $t - 1$.

CF_t = cash flow in the previous year by $Dep_t + Prof_t - D_t$, where Dep_2, $Prof_t$, and D_t denote depreciation, net profit, and dividend, respectively.

q_{t-1} = Tobin's q and is calculated by $(V_{t-1} + Debt_{t-1})/A_{t-1}$, where V_t, $Debt_t$, and A_t denote the total value of firm, debt, and asset, respectively.

Total value of firm is issued stock at the end of the previous fiscal year $t - 1$ valued at stock market price. However, the simple average of highest and lowest price is taken as a market price instead of market price at the end of the previous year.

Y_{t-1} = lagged production: sales plus the change in final goods inventory.

Table 3-2 provides further insight into the characteristics of corporate behavior that emerged with the spread of stable shareholders. It measures the effect on investment of Tobin's q, cash flow, and other variables in accordance with a formula developed by Hoshi, Kashyap, and Scharfstein.[32] Here Tobin's q is understood as a proxy for pressure from the capital market. Although there are several measurement problems and for that reason the results are still tentative, it would appear arguable that although the positive influence of Tobin's q on investment was statistically significant during the first phase of HGE (1957–64), it was no longer apparent in the later phase (1965–

Figure 3-2. Borrowing-Asset Ratios of Large Companies, 1957–93ᵃ

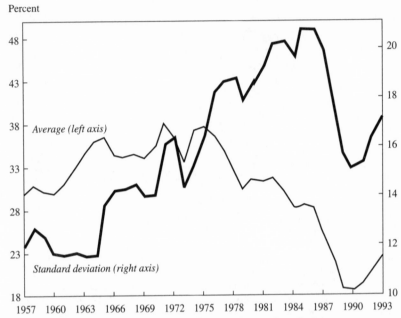

Percent

Source: Japan Development Bank, *The JDB Corporate Finance Data Bank.*
a. Sample consists of the 204 largest companies in the manufacturing sector that made up the top 150 firms based on assets in 1957, 1964, or 1972.

72). This result is consistent with the proposition that the investment decisions of top management in the latter phase of the HGE were shielded from the external pressures of the capital market.

Companies with stable shareholders grew increasingly dependent on debt financing. As shown in figure 3-2, the borrowing-asset ratio of Japan's leading firms increased steadily despite serious misgivings on the part of the MOF about the direction of this trend in corporate capital composition.[33] The coefficient of cash flow decreased by almost half between 1957 and 1964 and between 1965 and 1972, indicating that cash flow constraints on investment were being steadily mitigated. Under normal circumstances, the effect of such increases in borrowing-asset ratios would be to raise the cost of capital and reduce the investment levels of the firms involved because of increased risk and agency costs. The effect in HGE Japan, however,

Table 3-3. Ownership Structure, Leveraging Ratio, and Growth Rate of Firms, 1957–64 and 1965–72

Model:[a] $G = a + a_1 Asset_{t0} + a_2 \Delta SH\text{-}Fin + a_3 SH\text{-}Fin_{t0} + a_4 \Delta Bor + a_5 Bor_{t0} + a_6 Ind\text{-}dum$

Years	$Asset_{t0}$	$\Delta SH\text{-}Fin$	ΔBor	$\bar{R}^2$
1957–64	−0.752**	0.030**	0.748	.226
	(−1.905)	(2.028)	(0.532)	
1965–72	0.130	0.025*	0.938**	.303
	(0.838)	(4.201)	(1.975)	

Sources: Japan Development Bank, *The JDB Corporate Finance Data Bank;* Diamondo, *Kaisha-yōran* (Handbook for listed companies) (1958, 1964, 1965, 1973).

t-value in parentheses:
*Significant at the 1 percent level.
**Significant at the 10 percent level.
a. Notations of variables are as follows:
G = growth rate of asset: asset at the beginning of a period divided by that at the end of the period.
$Asset_{t0}$ = logarithm for asset at the beginning of a period.
$Ind\text{-}dum$ = industry dummy according to a two-digit code.
$\Delta SH\text{-}Fin$ = change of holding share of financial institutions from the beginning of a period to the end of the period.
$SH\text{-}Fin_{t0}$ = holding share of financial institutions at the beginning of a period.
ΔBOR = the change of borrowing-asset ratio from the initial time of period to the end of period.
Bor_{t0} = borrowing-asset ratio in the initial period.

was exactly the reverse. By taking advantage of the opportunities for maintaining high levels of debt financing made possible by the regulated financial system and by alleviating pressures from the external capital market through the shareholder stabilization program, Japanese firms were in a position to realize high, investment-driven growth.

This point can be demonstrated with a simple regression analysis (table 3-3), in which the growth rate of firms (asset based) is regressed on changes in the borrowings-to-assets (leveraging) ratio (ΔBor) and the percentage change in shares held by the financial institutions ($\Delta SH\text{-}Fin$). The goal of this regression is to see whether increased dependence on borrowing and shareholder stabilization resulted in increased firm growth rates. According to table 3-3, the growth rate of assets was positively correlated with ΔBor in the latter phase of the HGE, whereas this was not the case during the HGE's first phase. The growth rate was also positively correlated with $\Delta SH\text{-}Fin$, which was presumably indicative of shareholder stabilization actions during the later phase of the HGE.[34] These results suggest that, in line with our earlier discussion, the more a company depended on debt financing and the more it had stabilized its shareholders, the higher the growth rate of its assets in the later phase of the HGE. They are also consistent with the model of the J-Type firm.

The main bank system played a rather different role during the mid-1970s, when the oil crisis made an impact on J-Type firm behavior. As part of a larger drive to rationalize and reduce costs (popularly referred to as "quantity reduction management," or *genryō keiei*), Japanese firms reacted to high interests rates by attempting to reduce their borrowing. In the process, the positive correlation between firm growth and debt dependence disappeared. A regression using the variables in Table 3-3 other than $\Delta SH\text{-}Fin$ showed that in contrast to the period 1965–72, during the period 1975–80 the coefficient of ΔBor was negative with a 1 percent significance level. This means that the less a company depended on debt, the more rapidly a company grew in terms of assets. The data suggest that, as far as the companies sampled are concerned, the role of the main bank in reducing the agency costs associated with debt financing decreased. The main bank's first lender role that was so conspicuous during the HGE (and in its first phase in particular) was no longer as critical in the period 1975–80 period.

Nevertheless, the main bank still played a significant role in supplying funds to the companies in the sample that could not easily raise money in the capital market due to their poor performance. According to figure 3-2, variance in the borrowing-to-assets ratio rose after the oil crisis. This indicates that there were two types of companies: those that reduced their dependence on borrowing and those that were unable to. The main bank relationship still played a role for the latter type of company in supplying money for restructuring and in rescuing them when they fell into financial distress.[35] After the oil crisis, many companies in such industries as aluminum, petrochemicals, and automobiles fell into financial distress. Main banks took the initiative in rescuing their client companies by reducing required interest payments. The Sumitomo Group's rescue of Mazda represents one prominent example.[36]

In the area of corporate governance, the main bank system played a crucial role in disciplining top management teams when a firm's financial performance declined. A statistical elaboration of this point, provided in the appendix to this chapter, shows a correlation between the turnover of company presidents in Japan's largest firms and poor corporate performance, with this relationship most pronounced during the latter phase of the HGE (1965–69). This finding suggests that if a company had an operational profit rate below the norm (that is, below the industry average, indicating a high probability that the company was in financial distress) or showed excess employment relative to its operational profit rate (that is, it was not using its human resources efficiently), it was likely that the main bank would intervene by replacing the members of the firm's board of directors. In another study I suggest that the poorer the firm's performance, the higher the degree of main bank intervention as measured by the importance of the positions held in the firm by representatives of the main bank.[37] In sum, one can clearly see during the late 1970s a contingent governance structure at work—that is, a systematic shift of control from insiders to outsiders that was contingent on the financial situation of firm.

Financial Deregulation and the Metamorphosis of the Main Bank System

Deregulation since the 1980s drastically changed the nature of bank-firm relationships. As a result of structural changes in the economy and deregulation, Japanese firms as a whole came to depend less on bank borrowing for their external funds and the level of bank monitoring of client companies accordingly decreased. A process of self-selection unfolded in which less-profitable firms continued to depend on bank borrowing (private debt) while more-profitable firms sought funds in the capital markets (public debt).

Deregulation and the Changing Nature of Corporate Finance since the 1970s

The J-Type firm system, whose emergence and functioning were discussed in the preceding section, began to undergo changes from the latter half of the 1970s onward as the pattern of corporate financing in large Japanese firms shifted from one based on debt financing to a more diversified, more internationalized, and more sophisticated pattern. One of the driving forces behind this trend was structural change in the post-oil-crisis Japanese economy. As the anticipated rate of corporate growth decreased, so too did the rate of corporate investment. As this occurred, large Japanese corporations gradually came to rely on internally generated funds and began to actively reduce their level of borrowing and to diversify their modes of raising funds. Companies in cash-rich, export-oriented assembly industries such as automobile, electronics, and other machinery were no longer net-borrowers by the late 1970s, and in the early 1980s they substantially increased their issuance of bonds. Likewise, companies in the basic materials sector (for example, chemicals, metals, and steel) began paying off their loans on a net basis and were also issuing more bonds in the early 1980s. The faster-growing nonmanufacturing sector stepped in to absorb the loans previously absorbed by the manufacturing sector.

This change in the pattern of corporate financing was accelerated in the mid-1980s, when the Japanese economy experienced a huge and steady rise in stock prices following the Plaza Accord of October 1985. Helped by the low interest rates instituted as a countermeasure against the yen's appreciation, prices on the TSE increased by two and a half times between 1985 and 1989. Bond issuance in the domestic market, which was mainly composed of convertible bonds, grew sharply from 1986 on. Japanese corporations also began to raise money in the Euromarket, where bonds with warrants (that is, bonds with an option to buy shares at a specific price during a specified period) were prominent (figure 3-3). It has been reported that the capital costs of equity-related bonds as perceived by corporate managers were extremely low because of the increase in stock prices.[38] In this phase, all industries, even material-related industries, depended on bond issuance for new money.

This change in the pattern of corporate finance was made possible by financial deregulation and the consequent development of an effective capital market. As already indicated, the securities market, or more precisely the secondary market for securities, remained underdeveloped during the HGE. However, it expanded rapidly after the early 1970s, with its size growing from under 50 percent of nominal GNP in 1970 to over 100 percent by 1990.[39] The large-scale flotation of government bonds was the first factor that contributed to the development of the Japanese securities market. The Japanese government, hoping to use its spending power to stimulate the economy, emerged as a major borrower after 1975. As a result, the so-called bond-financing ratio—that is, central government bond flotation as a proportion of total general account expenditures—rose from under 5 percent in the late 1960s to 34.7 percent in 1979 (in 1994, this figure was 20 percent). These developments, in turn, forced the government to deregulate the financial sector by removing restrictions constraining private bond issuance, which were closely linked to government bonds. The Bond Issuance Committee stopped regulating yield rates while continuing to relax bond issuance criteria. The authorization of unsecured straight and convertible bond issues in 1979 was epochal in that it replaced collateral requirements with eligibility criteria. Another important step in

Figure 3-3. Equity Finance, 1976–94

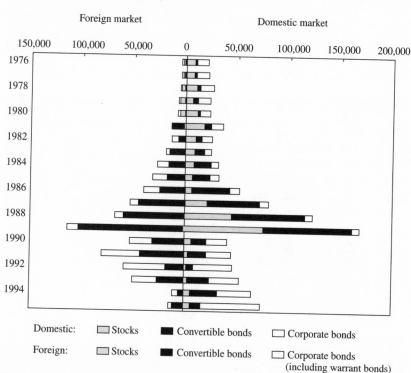

Source: Nomura, Tokyo Stock Exchange, *Annual Securities Statistics* (1996).

the deregulation of bond issuance was the amendment of the Commercial Code in 1981, which made it possible for companies to issue warrant bonds. Thus, in addition to straight bonds, companies were now allowed to issue equity-linked bonds, thereby paving the way for convertible bonds and warrant bonds to become popular corporate-financing instruments in the 1980s (see figure 3-3).

Another factor that encouraged the expansion of the capital market was internationalization initiated in the early 1970s, when private sector firms were first allowed to accumulate foreign claims and foreign banks to enter the Japanese market. In 1980, the Foreign Exchange and Foreign Trade Control Law was revised in order to liberalize cross-border transactions in principle. As a result of this reform, there was a large increase in turnover by nonresidents in the bond market and Japanese firms could now issue bonds in foreign markets without explicit government permission. In 1984, the MOF abolished the so-called real demand principle, and Japanese residents were now free to conclude forward contracts for foreign currencies without having to demonstrate a "real" need (an export or import transaction, a maturing foreign security, and so on). From the 1980s on, Japanese corporations were increasingly in a position to choose an optimal mix of fund-raising mechanisms in both domestic and foreign capital markets.[40]

However, despite these forms of deregulation and internationalization, a company that hoped to issue bonds still faced numerous forms of rigid regulation. For instance, bond issuance regulations required that a company satisfy such accounting criteria as a specified level of net worth, net worth ratio, paid-in capital, dividends per share, and ordinary after-tax profits per share.[41] The strictest criteria were imposed on unsecured convertible bonds. Although the number of companies eligible to issue such bonds rose as a consequence of several deregulatory measures that relaxed the criteria, in 1989 there were still only 500 eligible companies among the 1,800 companies listed on the TSE.[42]

It was this strict regulation that caused the huge increase in the issuance of warrant bonds on the Euromarket after 1983.[43] Given the strict regulation of domestic bond issues, Japanese companies preferred to issue their bonds on the Euromarket, where bond issuance was basically unsecured and the commission charged was much lower than in Japan. It is a well-known fact that the primary purchasers of such warrant bonds were Japanese investors. This situation, referred to as financial hollowing (kin'yū-kūdō ka), in turn, provided the impetus for further relaxation of bond issuance criteria in the late 1980s and early 1990s.

Another noteworthy point is that the increase of bond issuance in the Euromarket after 1983 and the subsequent increase in bond issuances domestically did not imply an abandonment of the main bank system. The warrant bonds issued by firms in the Euromarket were generally backed by bank guarantees. In fact, it is reported that 77 percent of all warrant bonds issued between 1984 and 1987 were guaranteed by banks and that the bank guarantee was normally given by main banks.[44] The rigid criteria applied to unsecured bonds induced a big increase in domestically issued secured straight and convertible bonds in the late 1980s. Under the Secured Bond Trustee Law, the collateral trustee was saddled with major responsibilities in the administration of properties being held as collateral and it was normally a firm's main bank that was the collateral trustee. The corporate bonds issued in the 1980s were thus a form of public debt as well as a private debt supported by the main bank relationship.[45]

Secured bonds and warrant bonds backed by bank guarantees can be understood to be another form of bank borrowing in the sense that the main bank would still be in charge of managing the debt if the company issuing the bonds faced financial distress.

Thus, as statistics indicate clearly, Japanese companies responded to the changed environment by increasing their dependence on the capital market. However, there was nonetheless a substantial degree of continuity with respect to the bank-firm relationship. The key difference is that compared with the bank-firm relationship of the HGE, since the 1970s the main banks have generated less revenue for their services and their level of monitoring of client companies has been reduced.

The Changing Relationship between Banks and Firms

Deregulation in the 1980s undermined the advantageous position occupied by the banking sector as a consequence of the previous system of financial regulation. The elimination of controls on interest rates reduced the margin that city banks used to enjoy. Certificates of deposit offering unregulated interest rates (minimum denomination, a half-billion yen) were introduced in 1979. Two other instruments with unregulated interest rates—large time deposits and money market certificates—were introduced in 1985. The minimum deposit required for these savings methods was lowered step by step thereafter. The removal of interest rate controls was virtually completed by 1992. As minimum balance requirements declined, the share of deposits in accounts whose rate of interest was unregulated grew rapidly. As a result, as demonstrated by recent research, the "rent" accruing to the city banks has been declining since the late 1970s and became almost negligible in 1990.[46] Faced with these circumstances, banks changed from a strategy that emphasized the development of quality clients to one centered on retail banking. With the amount of loans to large Japanese firms decreasing drastically from the mid-1970s onward, city banks attempted to diversify their clientele by shifting their focus from manufacturing to service industries (real estate and construction), pursuing the business of small and medium-sized firms, and expanding their international operations.[47] The share of such clients in the city banks' overall business grew from 36 percent in 1974 to more than 50 percent in 1985. The share of large overseas clients in their overall business grew to 17.3 percent for loans, 30 percent for deposits, and 21 percent for gross profits on average from 1986 to 1990.[48]

The organization of the city banks changed accordingly in the face of these circumstances. First, city banks overhauled their function-based organizational structures. Sumitomo Bank's reorganization in 1979 with the help of the consulting firm McKinsey & Company marks an important milestone in this regard. Sumitomo switched from a structure based on a functional division of labor to a client-oriented, multidivisional format composed of three divisions: a retail division (mainly for small and medium-sized firms and households), a wholesale division (large firms), and an international division. Sumitomo's reorganizational lead was followed by the other city banks in the 1980s.[49] Second, city banks tried to transform their relations with their large-firm clients from their earlier loan-centered relationships to a more diversified relationship that encompassed bond issuance-related services, consulting, and assistance with operations overseas. One example of innovation in this area was Sumitomo Bank's introduction of relation-based management (RM) in 1979. The core idea behind RM was to move from servicing client firms individually to addressing the needs of client firms in groups that included their affiliates and foreign subsidiaries. A team in the bank's wholesale division would serve as a unified window for the various transactions of group members.[50] As banks became more deeply involved in bond-related services and the foreign operations of their clients, the segmentation of banking and securities industries came to be recognized as one of the major obstacles blocking the expansion of their businesses. It is worth noting in this context that this segmentation also applied to their overseas business activities. During the 1980s, when the banks began establishing foreign subsidies to assist their client companies at overseas sites, MOF administrative guidance prohibited them from underwriting the equity-related bond issues of client firms.[51]

Third, the status of the screening divisions within the organizational structure of the city banks changed. Formerly, the screening divisions were autonomous units that operated independently of other divisions. They were divided up and integrated into newly created retail, wholesale, and international divisions. The ability of the new screening to serve as a check on the operating divisions was thus limited. In addition, the total number of employees engaged in screening was reduced. If the history of the city bank screening divisions during the HGE can be understood to be a history of steady expansion, that of the late 1970s onward was just the reverse—steady downsizing. The collateral requirements for loans were stiffened in tandem with this movement. As a number of researchers have pointed out, in contrast with what occurred during the first phase of the HGE, when banks often approved uncollateralized loans on the basis of ex ante monitoring, during the 1980s the common practice was for banks to virtually automatically approve collateralized loans to investment projects that used land as security.[52] Business involving real estate developments consequently became the primary replacement for the business of large manufacturing firms that had earlier been the banks' primary domestic clients, and the banking sector turned into a cash-generating machine for a collective speculative binge that continued to 1992.

Soft Budget Constraints and Firm Self-Selection under the Bubble Economy

The changes in the lending behavior of banks under the bubble economy were accompanied by changes in the behavior of nonfinancial corporations. As a number of researchers have stressed, a "moral hazard" problem was created by the softening of budgetary constraints on nonfinancial firms as a result of deregulation and the bubble.[53] During the HGE, "hard" budget constraints provided a context within which main banks could monitor nonfinancial firms and compel compliance on the part of their top managements. Their capacity to do so declined during the period of the bubble economy. This was due in part to the fact that the corporate sector no longer depended on the banks for their funds and in part because the incentives for city banks to engage in ex ante monitoring of clients weakened as the bubble economy gave rise to expectations of continual increases in the value of the collateral that the banks held. From the standpoint of corporate insiders, this created what Jensen calls "free cash flow"—that is, "cash flow in excess of that required to fund all projects that have positive net present values when discounted at the relevant cost of capital."[54]

Although it is difficult to demonstrate quantitatively the existence of a free cash flow situation, circumstantial evidence suggests that this was indeed what was occurring. From the mid-1980s onward, the internal funds of Japanese firms exceeded their investment levels (figure 3-4A).[55] That is, even though available internal funds were sufficient to finance their levels of investment, companies continued to raise huge amounts of money through equity financing. Anecdotal evidence suggests that firms during the bubble period tended to invest this excess in either land, trust funds, or other financial assets (a practice referred to as *zaiteku*). Another piece of evidence is the low returns on equity after 1986 (figure 3-4B). Whereas return on investment recovered after the yen-appreciation–induced recession of 1986, as is shown in figure 3-4, *ROE*

Figure 3-4A. Indexes of Corporate Finance (All Industries), 1978–93

Percent

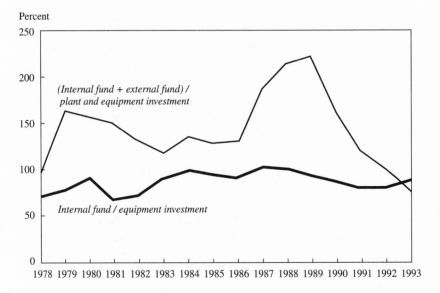

Figure 3-4B. Trend of *ROE* and *ROA* in the Postwar Period, 1956–93[a]

Percent

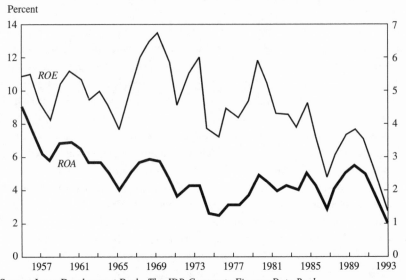

Source: Japan Development Bank, *The JDB Corporate Finance Data Bank.*
a. Sample consists of the 204 largest companies in the manufacturing sector that made up the top 150 firms based on assets in 1957, 1964, or 1972.

levels were far less than in the early 1980s. Using firm-level data, A. Horiuchi insists that the issuance of equity-related bonds was not necessarily profitable for shareholders but instead increased the amount of free cash flow available to managers. He reports that the firms most actively involved in the issuance of corporate equity-related bonds during the latter half of the 1980s tended to suffer more drastic declines in their rate of profit after 1990 than those that issued no bonds at all.[56]

Further evidence supporting the assertion that the main banks lost their monitoring capacity can be found in the appendix. That data shows that the negative correlation between financial performance on the one hand and turn-over in the board of directors and other indicators of main bank intervention on the other no longer applied during this period in the way that it did during earlier ones. One interpretation of this result is that company insiders held freely disposable assets (so-called unrealized assets, or *fukumi-shisan*) due to rises in land and stock prices. Thanks to these unrealized assets, corporate insiders could avoid the intervention of outsiders for short periods even if a company faced financial distress in the sense of low profitability (that is, low OR, operational profit divided by sales) or excess employment (low operational profit per employee, OR/L).

In short, then, during the bubble economy period corporate governance of the J-Type firm was characterized by a conspicuous decline in main bank monitoring. Given that these firms could now easily avail themselves of forms of financing other than borrowing, the influence of the main banks on client companies decreased in tandem. In the absence of a market-based system of control such as that found in the United States, Japan was left without an effective system for monitoring and disciplining the top managements of large Japanese firms.

A second aspect of the changes wrought by the bubble economy is the emergence of a process of self-selection among firms in the area of corporate financing. By the late 1980s, changing circumstances associated with deregulation and a transformed economic structure had dramatically altered the function and significance of the contingent governance structure built around the main bank system. As previously noted, debt mediated through a main bank relationship is in effect debt with a rescue option. As deregulation offered companies a widened range of financing options, those low risk firms with high expected profit levels gravitated toward public bond offerings in the capital market because they no longer required the rescue options offered at a premium by their main banks. High risk companies with lower expected profit levels tended to maintain their main bank relationships by borrowing money from main banks directly or through warrant bonds guaranteed by their main banks, thereby continuing to maintain access to the rescue option offered by their main bank. The risk burden borne by the main banks rose accordingly as their best customers severed earlier ties.[57]

The J-Type Firm and Deregulation: Current Issues

As the Japanese economy has entered a long recession, further deregulation issues have surfaced, which are closely related to the question of whether J-type firms have been converging on a more Western style of capitalism.

Convergence, Stasis, or Diversification?

As outlined in the preceding section, financial deregulation in Japan starting in the late 1970s gave impetus to a change in corporate-financing patterns that, in turn, modified the main bank system. The bubble economy accelerated this trend in the late 1980s. When the Japanese economy entered into a long-term recession in the 1990s in the wake of the bubble economy's collapse, Japanese firms were faced with a new set of challenges. One of them has been to deal with the aftereffects of the bubble economy, some of the most problematic aspects of which include (1) a serious delay in restructuring the manufacturing sector, (2) huge accumulations of bad debt in the financial and nonfinancial sectors, and (3) a credit crunch caused by a turn on the part of the city banks away from aggressive lending to excessive caution (*kashi-shiburi*). The other task is to adjust to the increased economic competition caused by the globalization of economic activities stemming from the rapid expansion of trade in east Asia and the acceleration of capital flows among nations. Under these new conditions, nations now compete with one another to develop appropriately "deregulated" economic institutions. In the face of these circumstances, Japan's remaining financial regulations are being relaxed. The accounting criteria for bond issuance were abolished in 1990, the banks' role as trustee was simplified in 1993, and the bond issuance criteria were finally abolished in 1995.[58] Thus, the regulation of bond issuance has basically been abolished. More drastic financial deregulation is scheduled under the Hashimoto cabinet's plan for economic structural reform, including the so-called financial Big Bang.

Does all of this mean that the J-Type firm, and Japanese capitalism along with it, have been totally transformed? What is the future direction of the evolution of the J-Type firm? Some researchers insist that there has been a convergence of the J-Type-firm system toward the Anglo-American–style market-based system. In support of the convergence argument, observers note that the financial policies of big firms continue to be independent of bank borrowing. These firms basically rely on internal funds to finance their investments, and when external funds are needed, they can take advantage of the deregulated capital market by issuing bonds. There are also signs of convergence in ownership structure. According to recent estimates, the share of corporate stocks held by stable shareholders has decreased over the past few years.[59] This would be consistent with the fact that in the 1990s the DR grew more sensitive to ROE when compared with the 1970s and 1980s. As shown in table 3-1, the coefficient of DR to ROE increased and the $\bar{R}^2$ of this estimate improved, suggesting that the influence of shareholders on the appropriation of net income has been growing. This result suggests that the power of shareholders may have increased in the governance structure.

The various subsystems that constitute the J-Type firm have also been changing. One of the most conspicuous subsystems is the long-term transactional ties (*keiretsu*) that link assemblers and suppliers as well as producers and the distributors (wholesalers and retailers). The *Keizai hakusho* (Economic White Paper) of 1996 reports that such long-term relationships have been relaxed of late for various reasons, including the movement of production facilities to foreign countries and the decreasing price of imported goods under yen appreciation.[60]

At the same time, however, there is considerable evidence to suggest that the essential features of the J-Type firm system are still in place. According to the flow-of-funds account of the national economy, the share of capital supplied by the banking sector was greater than 50 percent, still relatively high compared with other advanced industrialized countries.[61] Perhaps more significant, the nonfinancial companies themselves still regard the main bank relationship as a necessary one and, stressing the importance of the lender-borrower relationships and the main bank's provision of bond-related services, do not betray any signs of an intention to abandon these ties.[62] Nor has the pattern of cross-shareholding among the six major *keiretsu* groups shown any sign of drastic change thus far, despite the aforementioned decline in the overall share of stocks held by stable shareholders.[63] In this context, it is interesting to note that when a 1994 amendment to the Commercial Code required that an outside auditor be added to the membership of the corporate board, the new auditor invariably came from a company in the same main bank group. It is, to be sure, rather ironic that introducing an "outside" auditor would strengthen *keiretsu* relationships.[64] Furthermore, with respect to the result that the power of shareholders in the governance structure may have increased as far as our own sample is concerned, there was no instance of a CEO turnover occurring as a result of a takeover bid and few cases of a company accepting an outside director from a financial institution other than the main bank. Shifting our focus to another subsystem of the J-Type firm, the lifetime employment and seniority wage system that is often regarded as the system's core, it seems that this subsystem has also been sustained despite serious challenges and a modification of the wage profile.[65]

It is probably unrealistic to characterize the current situation as one of either convergence or a straightforward continuation of the J-firm system. Instead, there has been considerable variation in the amount of change in the J-Type bank-firm relationship among different industries.

In engineering-intensive assembly industries such as autos, electronics, and general machines, in which Japanese companies have adjusted to changing external conditions and kept their competitive edge, the old bank-firm ties have disappeared and been replaced by more arm's-length relationships. These firms have been able to raise money on the open market through public debt. Their managers are disciplined by the capital market as well as by globalized product markets.

In the traditional materials industries, such as iron and steel, nonferrous metals, and chemicals, which are now in the process of restructuring, firms still keep their close relationships with their main banks. The companies that issued equity-related bonds in the late 1980s had to redeem these bonds in the 1990s, depending for this refinancing on their main banks. In these sectors, the bank-firm relationship has a significant role in corporate finance as well as corporate governance.

A third sector, perhaps the most crucial, is the nonmanufacturing sector, especially real estate and construction. These two industries increased their borrowing in the 1990s as banks lent additional money to clients suffering from bad debts after the bubble collapsed. This lending can be understood as similar to other rescue operations that have taken place since the oil crisis of the mid-1970s. However, this additional lending unfortunately delayed rather than encouraged the necessary restructuring of these companies. In 1997, some

medium-sized companies with huge amounts of bad debt began to be liquidated as main banks gave up their rescue operations. These incidents suggest a
reduced commitment to borrowing firms on the part of banks.

The New Phase of Deregulation

Given these ambiguous changes in the J-firm system, there is an ongoing
controversy among researchers and business leaders concerning the role of
deregulation in creating a viable economic system for the next century. Along
with the widely discussed need to restructure the financial system in order to
cope with the problem of massive bad debt, Japan's Glass-Steagall–like separation of the banking and securities industries and the ban on holding companies that was institutionalized during the postwar reform period have become subjects of heated debate. For instance, the partial relaxation of the
segmentation of securities and banking industries in 1992 that authorized
banks to establish securities subsidiaries stimulated public discussion over
whether further deregulation was needed. Subsequently, the total abolition of
segmentation has been decided on as a part of the financial Big Bang.[66] The
abolition of the Antimonopoly Law's ban on holding companies became another hot topic and was also realized during 1997. On these issues there is,
interestingly, a consensus of views in favor of deregulation, although the
reasons for supporting such an amendment differs depending on whether a
proponent favors preserving or abandoning the J-Type-firm system.

One side in the debate sees the J-Type–firm system converging toward the
Anglo-American version and argues for deregulation that would facilitate this
trend. Among the advocates in business circles is the Japanese Association of
Corporate Executives (Keizai Dōyūkai). In his New Year's speech of 1996, for
instance, the chairman of the Dōyūkai stated that the present highly regulated
Japanese economic system must be transformed into a more transparent one
governed by a system of rules that is more or less identical to those of the other
advanced industrialized countries.[67] The association's 1996 *Kigyō hakusho*
(white paper on the firm) advocates changing the corporate governance structure of the J-Type firm to a more open, shareholder-based one.[68] There are
many advocates of a complete removal of the Glass-Steagall–like separation in
this camp. They tend to believe that allowing city banks to operate in the
securities market would encourage competition between city banks and securities companies. As for the holding company ban issue, Mabuchi insists that
because the globalization of finance is leading to an international convergence

of financial institutions, the establishment of financial holding companies represents the only way for Japanese financial institutions to improve their competitive edge.[69]

However, other researchers stress that the subsystems making up the J-Type–firm system are highly interdependent and complementary, and for that reason modifying just one subsystem along the lines of the Anglo-American model would be ineffective. Emphasizing that the long-term time horizon of J-Type firms is an essential element in sustaining their competitive edge internationally as well as an important contributor to Japan's comparatively egalitarian income distribution, Teranishi Juro recommends that deregulation of the financial system be planned in a way that would augment the monitoring function of the main banks based on short-term loans and cross-shareholding among the members of a corporate group.[70] Aoki Masahiko, who played a leading role in the development of the J-Type–firm concept, argues for a modification of the main bank system and the contingent governance structure in a way that will ensure their survival while at the same time making them compatible with the newly internationalized, securitized, and deregulated operational environment. From this perspective he and others propose drastic deregulation involving the elimination of the Glass-Steagall–like separation of the banking and securities industries. Specifically, Aoki argues that a legacy of the main bank system is that in Japan human resources skilled in screening investment projects have accumulated not in securities companies but in the city banks. Allowing banks to enter securities-related businesses would harness these resources and through delegated monitoring would allow for an economization of monitoring costs, in addition to a number of other specific advantages.[71] Eliminating the ban on holding companies is justified from a similar standpoint. According to Aoki, holding companies can be expected to use such human resources in a manner that will revive the system's currently moribund monitoring capacity.[72]

My own view is that the current situation is not a complete convergence with the Anglo-American type but a diversification of the former J-firm system and that the argument that elements of the J-Type–firm system should be restructured in a way that would maintain its key features while adapting the system to a radically changed environment is more persuasive. In any event, it is clear, and impressive from a historian's perspective, that the deregulation of the Japanese economy is now entering a new phase. As shown in this chapter, Glass-Steagall–like separation and the ban on holding companies represent the pillars of the basic regulatory framework within which the J-Type firm has emerged and operated. Although financial reform up to now has not substantially undermined the J-Type–firm system, proposals are being discussed that would drastically alter Japan's basic regulatory framework. The precise way in which this process unfolds is likely to have profound, if unpredictable, implications for the future evolution of Japan's economic system.

Appendix

The assertion that main banks played a role in disciplining the top managements of large Japanese corporations has not been systematically tested. Table 3-4 represents an attempt to conduct such a test using a database of 100 leading firms developed by the author.[73] Table 3-4 regresses top manager turnover (*TURN*) on several corporate performance indicators using the logit model.

1. The data were divided into five periods, which correspond to specific phases in the evolution of the postwar Japanese economy. Period 1 (turnover data 1959–63; performance data 1957–62), period 2 (1965–69; 1963–68, respectively), period 3 (1974–78; 1972–77), period 4 (1984–88; 1983–88), and period 5 (1990–94; 1988–93). Period 1 corresponds to the initial phase of the HGE; period 2 to the HGE's second phase, also reflecting the impact of securities depression; period 3 to the post–oil-crisis period; period 4 to the yen-appreciation–induced recession that followed the Plaza Accord and the period of the so-called bubble economy; and period 5 to the postbubble recession years.

2. The dependent variables are as follows: *TURN 1* indicates instances in which the company president was replaced by an insider (someone recruited from the ranks of the company's existing management) but in which no other major change occurred in the membership of the board of directors. *TURN 2* is when the company president was replaced by an insider and there was also a major change in the membership of the board (that is, three or more directors were replaced, and at least one of the new members was dispatched from the main bank). *TURN 3* indicates that the company president was replaced by an outsider. *TURN IN* is an instance of *TURN 1* and *TURN 2* both occurring, whereas *BIG TURN* consists of *TURN 2* and *TURN 3* together, and *ALL TURN* is made up of *TURN 1, TURN 2,* and *TURN 3* occurring together.

Table 3-4. Abstract of Managerial Turnover and Firm Performance, 1959–94, Selected Years

Model:[a] turnover $= a_1 + a_2$ (unique performance) $+ a_3$ (average performance) $+ s_4 LS$

Turnover	1959–63	1965–69	1974–78	1984–88	1990–94
ALL TURN	1 = 43, 0 = 468	1 = 41, 0 = 444	1 = 67, 0 = 435	1 = 72, 0 = 433	1 = 69, 0 = 435
RRS	−	⋯	⋯	⋯	⋯
ER	⋯	⋯	⋯	⋯	−***
OR	−**	−*	⋯	⋯	−***
OR/L	−	−*	⋯	⋯	−**
LS	+**	+	+*	+*	+*
TURN IN	1 = 28, 0 = 468	1 = 33, 0 = 444	1 = 60, 0 = 435	1 = 59, 0 = 433	1 = 60, 0 = 435
RRS	⋯	⋯	⋯	⋯	⋯
ER	⋯	⋯	⋯	⋯	−***
OR	−	−	⋯	⋯	−***
OR/L	+	⋯	⋯	⋯	−**
LS	+*	+	+*	+*	+*
TURN 1	1 = 22, 0 = 448	1 = 22, 0 = 444	1 = 41, 0 = 435	1 = 47, 0 = 433	1 = 51, 0 = 435
RRS	⋯	⋯	⋯	⋯	⋯
ER	⋯	⋯	⋯	⋯	⋯
OR	⋯	⋯	⋯	⋯	⋯
OR/L	⋯	⋯	⋯	⋯	−
LS	+**	+	+*	+*	+*

TURN 2

	1 = 6, 0 = 468	1 = 11, 0 = 444	1 = 19, 0 = 435	1 = 12, 0 = 433	1 = 13, 0 = 435
RRS	–	: :	: :	: :	–**
ER	–*	: :	: :	: :	–***
OR	–**	–**	–**	: :	–*
OR/L	–***	–**	–**	: :	–*
LS	+	: :	: :	+****	+****

TURN 3

	1 = 15, 0 = 468	1 = 8, 0 = 444	1 = 7, 0 = 435	1 = 13, 0 = 433	1 = 9, 0 = 435
RRS	–***	–	: :	: :	: :
ER	–**	–*	–	: :	–
OR	–*	–*	–***	–**	–***
OR/L	–*	–*	–***	–**	–****
LS	+	+	+	+	+

BIG TURN

	1 = 21, 0 = 468	1 = 19, 0 = 444	1 = 26, 0 = 435	1 = 25, 0 = 433	1 = 22, 0 = 435
RRS	–***	: :	: :	: :	: :
ER	–*	–**	–	–	–
OR	–*	–*	–***	–**	–*
OR/L	–*	–*	–**	–**	–*
LS	+**	: :	+	+****	+****

Notes continued on next page

Source: MOF, JDB Database.

Confidence level:

*Significant at the 1 percent level.

**Significant at the 5 percent level.

***Significant at the 10 percent level.

Sign of the coefficient is added when significance level is satisfied at the 15 percent level.

a. Estimation method: probit model, in which dependent variables are 1 if any type of turnover occurs and otherwise 0. Possible observations are 510, or 102 firms times five years. Actual observations are less than 510 because of missing variables.

Dependent variables: *TURN 1* = insider president replaced by insider

TURN 2 = *TURN 1* and change in board membership (see text)

TURN 3 = insider president replaced by outsider

TURN IN = *TURN 1* + *TURN 2*

ALL TURN = *TURN 1* + *TURN 2* + *TURN 3*

BIG TURN = *TURN 2* + *TURN 3*

Independent variables: *PR* = profit rate of equity

RRS = rate of return on stock

OR = operating income/sales

OR/L = OR/number of employees

ER = rate of increase in the number of employees

SR = rate of sales growth

TAR = rate of increase in total assets

LS = length of service as a president in previous year

All variables are two-year averages.

3. The independent variables are as follows: rate of return on stocks (RRS), which is used as a proxy for stockholder interests; operational profit divided by sales (OR) and operational profit per employee (OR/L), which are used as proxies for the bank's interests; and the rate of increase in the number of employees (ER), which is a proxy for insiders' interests. All regressions included the previous company president's length of service (LS) to control for routine turnover based on seniority rules.

4. As shown in table 3-4, turnover is regressed on unique Pi and average Pi. Both are measured as a two-year average and unique Pi is standardized by calculating its divergence from the industry average (average Pi). Only the signs of the coefficients of unique Pi are reported.

The following points can be drawn from the regression results in table 3-4:

1. Although the direct replacement of presidents by bank representatives ($TURN\ 3$) decreased from period 1 to period 3, $TURN\ 3$ was negatively correlated with OR in period 1 and period 2. $TURN\ 3$ was also negatively correlated with RRS in period 1, which seems to be consistent with the fact that the market for corporate control still survived and coexisted with the main bank system in the first phase of the HGE.

2. However, $TURN\ 2$, which represents cases in which the bank influenced client company personnel decisions, increased in frequency from period 1 to period 3. The correlation between $TURN\ 2$ and OR and OR/L is clear in periods 2 and 3.

3. As a result, $BIG\ TURN$—that is, when turnover of the president and in the board was influenced by the main bank—was negatively correlated with OR and OR/L in periods 1 through 3. $ALL\ TURN$ was negatively correlated with OR in periods 2 and 3.

4. It is safe to say that by period 3, OR and OR/L became the most important factors in the replacement of company presidents. This indicates that if a company could not realize the average profit rate (that is, there was a high probability that the company was in financial distress) or showed excess employment, it was likely that the main bank would intervene by replacing the firm's board.

5. There is some indication that control over the governance of large companies shifted from outsiders to insiders during period 3. In other words, there was a negative correlation between turnover by an insider ($TURN\ 1,\ TURN\ IN$) and ER. This indicates that, unless the performance of a company was particularly poor, the insiders could appoint a president from among themselves based on seniority rules.

6. It is noteworthy that with the exception of *TURN 3,* the correlation between turnover and company performance disappeared in period 4. The only variable that can explain turnover is the length of service of the previous president. The coefficient of *LS* in period 4 is three times larger than in period 3, although this is not shown in table 3-4.

7. Recently, it seems that the correlation between turnover and company performance has returned. In particular, it is worth noting that the proxy of insider interest *(ER)* shows a negative correlation with turnover by insiders, while outsider turnover is again negatively correlated with *OR.* These findings suggest that the governance structure of Japanese firms has diversified into two types: low-debt companies in which insiders now play a significant disciplinary role in presidential turnover, and high-debt companies in which the main bank still plays an important role in disciplining the top management team. However, the data cover only the year 1994 for turnover and 1993 for company performance. It will take a few more years before any solid conclusions can be drawn.

Notes

1. Aoki Masahiko, *Information, Incentives, and Bargaining in the Japanese Economy* (Cambridge University Press, 1988); Aoki Masahiko and Ronald Dore, *The Japanese Firm: The Sources of Competitive Strength* (New York: Oxford University Press, 1994); Aoki Masahiko and Hugh Patrick, eds., *The Japanese Main Bank System: Its Relevance for Developing and Transforming Economies* (New York: Oxford University Press, 1994). Recent work in Japanese includes the following: Hashimoto Jūrō, *Sengo nihon keizai* (Postwar Japanese economy) (Tokyo: Iwanami shoten, 1995); Yoshida Kazuo, *Kaimei nihon gata keiei-shisutemu* (Investigation of the Japanese-type management system) (Tokyo: Tōyō keizai shinpōsha, 1996); Itō Hideshi, ed., *Nihon no kigyō shisutemu* (Japanese firm system) (Tokyo University Press, 1996). On the emergence of the J-Type–firm system, see Okazaki Tetsuji and Okuno Masahiro, eds., *Nihon-gata keizai shisutemu no rekishi-teki genryū* (Historical origin of the Japanese-type economic system) (Tokyo: Nihon keizai shinbunsha, 1993); and Hashimoto Jūrō, ed., *Nihon kigyō shisutemu no sengoshi* (The postwar history of the Japanese firm system) (Tokyo: Tōkyō daigaku shuppankai, 1996).

2. This chapter owes much to recent work on the J-Type firm by Aoki Masahiko and attempts to expand on his work by looking at the aspect of ownership structure through an analysis of a data set developed by the author. See Aoki Masahiko, "Monitoring Characteristics of the Main Bank System: An Analytical and Historical View," in Aoki and Patrick, *The Japanese Main Bank System;* and "Contingent Governance of the

Team: An Analysis of Institution Complementarity," *International Economic Review,* vol. 35 (1994), pp. 654–76.

3. James C. Abegglen and George Stalk Jr., *Kaisha: The Japanese Corporation* (New York: Basic Books, 1985); Aoki, "Monitoring Characteristics of the Main Bank System"; Hashimoto Jūrō, "Nihongata kigyō shisutemu no keisei" (The emergence of the Japanese-type firm system), in Yui Tsunehiko and Hashimoto Jūrō, eds., *Kakushin no keieishi* (History of innovation in business) (Tokyo: Yūhikaku, 1995); Horiuchi Akiyoshi, "Nihon ni okeru kōpōrate gavanansu no mekanizumu to yūkōsei," *Kin'yū kenkyū,* vol. 13 (June 1994), pp. 121–54; Hashimoto Jūrō, *Gendai no nihon keizai* (The contemporary Japanese economy) (Tokyo: Iwanami shoten, 1995).

4. Regarding the German case, see J. Edwards and K. Fisher, *Banks, Finance and Investment in Germany* (Cambridge: Cambridge University Press, 1993); and W. Corlin, "West German Growth and Institutions, 1945–90," CEPR Discussion Papers Series 896 (London: Center for Economic Policy Research, 1993).

5. However, this is a point that has so far not been subjected to systematic empirical testing. For a discussion of this problem, see Paul Sheard, "Long-Termism and the Japanese Firm," in Mitsuaki Okabe, ed., *The Structure of the Japanese Economy* (London: Macmillan, 1994), pp. 25–52.

6. In the Anglo-American system, the different stages of monitoring borrowers (ex ante monitoring via the assessment of the credit worthiness of investment projects, interim monitoring via checks of ongoing management behavior, and ex post monitoring via the verification of performance outcomes) are delegated to separate specialized financial institutions. By contrast, in the Japanese main bank system the three stages of monitoring are integrated and delegated exclusively to the main bank. See Aoki Masahiko, Paul Sheard, and Hugh Patrick, "Introductory Overview," in Aoki and Patrick, *The Japanese Main Bank System.*

7. Edwards and Fisher, *Banks, Finance and Investment in Germany.*

8. As a consequence of the purges of top-level corporate executives and *zaibatsu* dissolution, in most leading Japanese firms at this time the top management team consisted of individuals who were promoted from within. For detailed discussion, see Miyajima Hideaki, "The Transformation of Prewar *Zaibatsu* to Postwar Corporate Groups: From Hierarchically Integrated Groups to Horizontally Integrated Groups," *Journal of Japanese and International Economies,* vol. 8 (1994), pp. 293–328; and Miyajima Hideaki, "Senmon keieisha no seiha: Nihon-gata keieisha kigyō no keisei" (The managerial revolution from above: The emergence of the J-Type managerial enterprise), in Yamazaki Hiroaki and Kikkawa Takeo, eds., *Nihonteki keiei no renzoku to danzetsu* (Continuity and discontinuity of J-Type management) (Tokyo: Iwanami shoten, 1995), pp. 99–103.

9. Eleanor Hadley, *Antitrust in Japan* (Princeton University Press, 1970).

10. Miyajima Hideaki, "The Privatization of Ex-*zaibatsu* Holding Stocks and the Emergence of Bank-Centered Corporate Groups in Japan," in Aoki Masahiko and

Hyung-Ki Kim, eds., *Corporate Governance in Transitional Economies: Insider Control and the Role of Banks* (Washington, D.C.: World Bank, 1995), pp. 379–83.

11. Miyajima, "The Transformation of Prewar *Zaibatsu* to Postwar Corporate Groups."

12. Miyajima, "The Privatization of Ex-*zaibatsu* Holding Stocks and the Emergence of Bank-Centered Corporate Groups in Japan," pp. 384–85.

13. Ministry of International Trade and Industry (MITI), *Tsūshō sangyō seisaku-shi* (The history of international trade and industry policies), vol. 5: *Jiritsu kiban keiseiki (I)* (The period of economic independence, I) (Tokyo: Tsūshō sangyō chōsakai, 1988), pp. 311–14.

14. Hideaki Miyajima, "Bank-Centered Corporate Groups and Investment: The Evidence from the First Phase of the High Growth Era," *Waseda Commercial Review*, no. 369 (July 1997), pp. 33–76.

15. Asai Yoshio, "Shihon jiyūka to kokusaika e no taiō" (Capital liberalization and the response to internationalization), in Nakamura Masanori, ed., *Nihon no kindai-ka to shihonshugi* (Modernization and capitalism in Japan) (Tokyo: Tōkyō daigaku shuppankai, 1992), p. 283.

16. Fujio Yoshida, *Shihon jiyū-ka to gaishi hō* (Capital liberalization and foreign capital law) (Tokyo: Zaisei keizai kōhō sha, 1969), pp. 427–36.

17. Thomas F. Adams and Iwao Hoshii, *A Financial History of the New Japan* (Tokyo: Kodansha, 1972), p. 199.

18. Nihon Kyōdō Shōken Zaidan, *Nihon kyōdō shōken kabushiki gaisha shi* (The history of the Japan Joint Securities Corporation) (Tokyo: Kyōdō insatsu kabushiki kaisha, 1978). D. E. Weinstein stresses that "Japanese banks and firms bought more shares because the government subsidized their purchase through low interest lending." See Weinstein, "Foreign Direct Investment and Keiretsu: Rethinking U.S. and Japanese Policy," photocopy, Harvard University, September 1995.

19. T. Suzuki, *Shōhō to tomoni ayumu* (Retrospective on the Commercial Law) (Tokyo: Shōji-hō kenkyū kai, 1977).

20. Miyajima Hideaki, "Regulatory Framework, Government Intervention and Investment in Postwar Japan: The Structural Dynamics of J-Type Firm-Government Interaction," in Miyajima Hideaki, Takeo Kikkawa, and Takashi Hikino, eds., *Competing Policies for Competitiveness* (Oxford: Oxford University Press, forthcoming).

21. A useful discussion of this subject can be found in Itō Osamu, *Nihon gata kin'yū no rekishiteki kōzō* (Historical structure of Japanese-type finance) (Tokyo: Tōkyō daigaku shuppankai, 1995).

22. General Headquarters Supreme Commander for the Allied Nations (GHQ/SCAP), *History of the Nonmilitary Activities of the Occupation of Japan*, vol. 24: *Elimination of Zaibatsu Control* (Washington, D.C., 1951).

23. They were not, however, involved in equity underwriting even during the prewar period. See K. Shimura, *Nihon shihon shijō bunseki* (Analysis of the capital market in Japan) (Tokyo: Tōkyō daigaku shuppankai, 1978), pp. 259–71.

24. See Teranishi Jūrō, *Nihon no keizai hatten to kin'yū* (Economic development and Japanese finance) (Tokyo: Iwanami shoten, 1982), pp. 418, 422–23.

25. Ibid., pp. 483–93; Kazuo Ueda, "Institutional and Regulatory Frameworks for the Main Bank System," in Aoki and Patrick, *The Japanese Main Bank System*, pp. 89–108; Aoki, "Monitoring Characteristics of the Main Bank System," p. 129.

26. Aoki, "Monitoring Characteristics of the Main Bank System."

27. Fuji Ginkō, *Fuji ginkō hyaku nenshi* (The hundred-year history of Fuji Bank) (Tokyo: Fuji ginkō, 1982), p. 797.

28. "Ginkō-shihai no kyōka to zaibatsu saihensei no hōkō" (The increasing control of banks and the direction of *zaibatsu* reorganization), *Tōyō keizai shinpō,* October 24, 1953, pp. 77–111.

29. For detailed discussion, see Miyajima, "Bank-Centered Corporate Groups and Investment."

30. See ibid.

31. Tetsuji Okazaki, "The Wartime Planned Economy and the Firm," *Journal of Japanese and International Economies,* vol. 7 (1993), pp. 175–203. Okazaki first tested the correlation between the *DR* of the *ROE* for 1920 to 1937 for the prewar period and then 1965 for the postwar period, dividing large corporations into *zaibatsu* line firms and independents. The coefficient of *DR* to *ROE* was higher in the prewar years than in the postwar years.

32. Takeo Hoshi, Anil Kashyap, and David Scharfstein, "Corporate Structure, Liquidity and Investment: Evidence from Japanese Industrial Groups," *Quartery Journal of Economics,* vol. 106 (1991), pp. 33–60. Tobin's *q* is the value of the firm divided by net assets and the proxy for the evaluation of the market for an investment project.

33. One inspiration behind the MOF's drive to improve the capital composition of Japanese firms was the World Bank's conditionality requirements of the 1960s. See Ministry of Finance (MOF), *Shōwa zaisei shi: Shūsen kara kōwa made* (The financial history of Japan: The allied occupation period, 1945–52), vol. 2: *Dokusen kinshi* (Antitrust) (Tokyo: Tōyō keizai shinpō sha, 1992).

34. The increase of Δ*SH-Fin* in the first phase of the HGE is assumed to be the result of portfolio investment of financial institutions.

35. This point is confirmed by the analysis in Hoshi, Kashyap, and Scharfstein, in "Corporate Structure, Liquidity, and Investment." They found that between 1978 and 1982, cash flow constraints on investment were much less severe in companies with close main bank ties than in companies without such ties.

36. For a detailed treatment of the Mazda case, see R. Pascale and T. Rohlen, "The Mazda Turnaround," *Journal of Japanese Studies,* vol. 9 (1983), pp. 219–63. For other

anecdotal evidence, see Paul Sheard, "The Main Bank System and Corporate Monitoring and Control in Japan," *Journal of Economic Behavior and Organization,* vol. 11 (1988), pp. 399–422.

37. Miyajima Hideaki, Yamamoto Katsuya, and Kondō Yasushi, "Sengo nihon no daikigyō nokeru gaibyakuin-haken to kigyō pafōmansu" (Outside appointment and firm performance in postwar Japanese firms), photocopy, Waseda University.

38. Nakamura Takafusa, *Sengo keizai* (Postwar Japanese economy) (Tokyo: Iwanami shoten, 1995), pp. 176–78; Akiyoshi Horiuchi, "Financial Structure and Managerial Discretion in the Japanese Firm: An Implication of the Surge of Equity-Related Bonds," in Mitsuaki Okabe, ed., *The Structure of the Japanese Economy: Changes on the Domestic and International Fronts* (New York: St. Martin's, 1995), pp. 53–80.

39. Yoshio Suzuki, ed., *The Japanese Financial System* (New York: Oxford University Press, 1987), p. 133; Bank of Japan's *Economic Statistics Annual* (Tokyo, 1992). A precondition for this development was a change in the preferences of the nonfinancial sectors (and among households in particular) from favoring low-risk assets to favoring high-interest assets. Japanese households had accumulated considerable assets throughout the HGE, and for this reason it was quite natural for them to become more sensitive to interest rates and to the real interest rate in particular.

40. For a detailed discussion of internationalization, see Suzuki, *The Japanese Financial System,* pp. 49–50; and Takatoshi Ito, *The Japanese Economy* (MIT Press, 1992), pp. 317–21.

41. The criteria were quite complex and diversifed by the kind of bond: secured or unsecured; and straight, convertible bond or bond with warrants. See, in detail, Nomura Securities, *Shin ginkō jitsumu kōza* (New general lectures on banking business), vol. 8: *Shoken* (Securities), 1987.

42. Nakamura, *Sengo keizai;* Takeo Hoshi, Anil Kashyap, and David Scharfstein, "Bank Monitoring and Investment: Evidence from the Changing Structure of Japanese Corporate Banking Relationships," in R. Glenn Hubbard, ed., *Asymmetric Information, Corporate Finance, and Investment* (University of Chicago Press, 1990), pp. 108–10.

43. Hoshi, Kashyap, and Scharfstein identify 1983 as the year in which financial deregulation began to decisively influence corporate finance ("Bank Monitoring and Investment," p. 107). Figure 3-3 basically supports this assertion.

44. John Campbell and Yasushi Hamao, "Changing Pattern of Corporate Financing and the Main Bank System in Japan," in Aoki and Patrick, *The Japanese Main Banking System,* p. 332.

45. I owe the definition of *collateral trustee* to Takeo Hoshi, Anil Kashyap, and David Scharfstein, "The Choice between Public Debt and Private Debt: An Analysis of Post-regulation Corporate Financing in Japan," photocopy, University of California, San Diego, 1993.

46. Teranishi, *Nihon no keizai hatten to kin'yū,* pp. 483–84; Ueda, "Institutional and Regulatory Frameworks for the Main Bank System," pp. 94–96; Okazaki Tetsuji,

"Sengo nihon no kin'yū shisutemu" (The financial system of postwar Japan) in Mor-ikawa Hidemasa and Yonekura Seiichirō, eds., *Kōdo seichō o koete* (Beyond high growth) (Tokyo: Iwanami shoten, 1996), pp. 185–87.

47. Bank of Japan, *Economic Statistics Annual* (1990).

48. Calculation based on *Shūkan kin'yū-zaisei jijō,* appropriate volume. This maga-zine, published annually at the end of June, provides comprehensive information con-cerning loans, deposits, and profits for foreign and domestic operations.

49. Sumitomo Ginkō, *Sumitomo ginkō no rekishi* (A history of Sumitomo Bank) (Osaka, 1985), pp. 73–88; Fuji Ginkō, *Fuji ginkō hyaku nen shi,* pp. 1356–57, 1360.

50. Sumitomo, *Sumitomo ginkō no rekishi,* pp. 111–14.

51. This guidance was called "three-bureau guidance," or *sankyoku shidō,* because it was initiated by three of the ministry's divisions (securities, foreign exchange, and banking). This guidance was retracted in 1993.

52. For instance, Yoshida Kazuo, *Nihongata ginkō keiei no tsumi* (The failure of Japanese-style banking operations) (Tokyo: Tōyō keizai shinpō sha, 1994), p. 120.

53. Ikeo Kazuo, "Zaimu-men kara mita nihon kigyō" (The Japanese corporation from the viewpoint of capital composition), in Kaizuka Keimei and Ueda Kazuo, eds., *Henkaku-ki no kin'yū shisutemu* (The financial system in a period of transformation) (Tokyo: Tōkyō daigaku shuppan kai, 1994), pp. 112–17; Ikeo Kazuo, *Kin'yū sangyō e no keikoku: kin'yū shisutemu saikōchiku no tame ni* (The warning to financial industries: For the restructuring of the financial system) (Tokyo: Tōyō keizai shinpō sha, 1995), pp. 196–98.

54. M. Jensen, "Agency Costs of Free Cash Flow, Corporate Finance, and Take-overs," *American Economic Review,* vol. 86 (1986), pp. 323–29.

55. Miyazaki Yoshikazu, *Fukugō fukyō* (Composite recession) (Tokyo: Chūō kōron sha, 1992), pp. 153–60.

56. Horiuchi, "Financial Structure and Managerial Discretion in the Japanese Firm."

57. Further discussion of this topic can be found in Miyajima Hideaki and Arakawa Yasuhiro, "Kigyō kin'yū no kōzō henka to gabanensu no hen'yō: 1980 nendai ni okeru tenkan" (mimeo, August 1998).

58. Naitō Jun'ichi, "Tekisai kijun no kihon-teki minashi ni tuite (Concerning the fundamental reconsideration for bond issue criteria)," *Kōshasai geppō,* April 1995.

59. Kawakita Hidetaka, "Kabushiki mochiai kōzō no hōkai no mekanizumu" (The mechanism of declining cross-shareholding), *Kin'yū zaisei jijō,* January 31, 1994, pp. 42–47; Takano Makoto, "Kabushiki mochiai no kaishō to kongo no kabushiki hoyū kōzō," *Daiwa tōshi shiryo,* September 1995.

60. Economic Planning Agency, *Keizai hakusho* (Tokyo: Ōkura shō insatsu kyoku, 1996), pp. 360–69.

61. Average figure for 1992 to 1994 as published in the *Economic Statistics Annual* (1996). Jenny Corbett makes the same point using figures for 1989 in "An Overview of the Japanese Financial System," in Nicholas Dimsdale and Martha Prevezer,

eds., *Capital Markets and Corporate Governance* (Oxford: Clarendon, 1994), pp. 310–11.

62. Fuji Sōgō Kenkyūjo, *1992 Nendo tsūshō-sangyō shō itaku chōsa: Mein banku oyobi kabushiki mochiai ni tsuite no chōsa hōkoku sho* (Fiscal 1992 Ministry of International Trade and Industry delegated study: Report on a study of main banks and cross-shareholding) (Tokyo: Fuji sōgō kenkyūjo, 1993).

63. The changes in the cross-shareholding ratios of the six corporate groups from 1985 to 1993 were as follows: Mitsubishi Group 25.2 to 26.1 percent, Sumitomo 25.0 to 24.5 percent, Mitsui 17.9 to 16.8 percent, Fuyō (Fuji) 15.8 to 14.9 percent, Sanwa 16.8 to 16.4 percent, and Daiichi (DKB) 13.3 to 11.9 percent. These figures are based on Toyo Keizai Shinpō Sha, *Keiretsu sōran* (Tokyo, 1987, 1995).

64. "Shōhō kaisei o sakate ni keiretsu no kyōka susumu" (*Keiretsu* strengthened despite revision of commercial code), *Shūkan tōyō keizai,* December 31, 1994, and January 7, 1995.

65. *Keizai hakusho* (1996), pp. 346–53.

66. Securities subsidiaries of banks are still prohibited from underwriting equity. They are also prohibited from serving as the managing bank when a client company of the parent bank is issuing the bond (the so-called main bank regulation).

67. Okazaki Tetsuji, Sugayama Shinji, Nishizawa Tamotsu, and Yonekura Seiichirō, *Sengo nihon keizai to keizai dōyūkai* (The postwar Japanese economy and the keizai dōyūkai) (Tokyo: Iwanami shoten, 1996), p. 319.

68. Keizai Dōyūkai, *Kigyō hakusho: Nihon kigyō no keiei kōzō kaikaku* (White paper on the firm: The structural reform of the management of Japanese firms) (Tokyo: Keizai dōyūkai, 1996). This proposal was initiated by Miyauchi Yoshihiko (Oryx Inc.), one of the most prominent advocates of the elimination of Article 9 of the Antimonopoly Law.

69. Mabuchi Noritoshi, *Kin'yū mochikabu kaisha* (Financial holding companies) (Tokyo: Tōyō keizai shinpō sha, 1996), pp. 87–89.

70. Teranishi Jūrō, "Nihon-gata keizai shisutemu no tenki to kin'yū" (Finance and the turning point of the Japanese economic system), paper prepared for a 1996 conference in Fudan University in Shanghai. Consistent with this perspective, Teranishi is not necessarily supportive of removal of the ban on holding companies.

71. Aoki, "Monitoring Characteristics of the Main Bank System," pp. 138–40.

72. Aoki Masahiko, *Keizai shisutemu no shinka to tagensei* (The evolution and multidimensionality of the economic system) (Tokyo: Tōyō keizai shinpō sha, 1995), pp. 212–20.

73. For further details see Miyajima Hideaki, "Sengo nihon kigyō ni okeru jōtai-izonteki gabanasu no shinka to hen'yō: Logit moderu ni yoru keieisha kōtai bunseki kara no apurōchi" (The evolution and change of contingent governance structure in the J-firm system), *Economic Review* (Hitotsubashi University), vol. 49, no. 2 (April 1998), pp. 97–112; and Miyajima, "Presidential Turnover and Performance in the Japanese Firm: The Evolution and Change of the Contingent Governance Structure under the

Main Bank System," in Daniel Dirks, Jean-François Huchet, and Thierry Ribault, eds., *Japanese Management in the Low Growth Era: Between External Shocks and Internal Evolution* (Berlin: Springer Verlag, forthcoming). Both articles offer new estimates of presidential turnover and firm performance using logit models and more elaborate variables. However, the basic findings reported here are almost the same as these new estimates. The following research addresses similar issues during the time frame of the 1980s: Steven N. Kaplan, "Internal Corporate Governance in Japan and the USA: Difference in Activities and Horizons," photocopy, University of Chicago, 1992; Steven N. Kaplan and Bernadetta A. Minton, "Appointments of Outsiders to Japanese Boards," *Journal of Financial Economics,* vol. 36 (1994), pp. 225–58; Randall Morch and Masao Nakamura, "Banks and Corporate Control in Japan," photocopy, University of Alberta 1992; and Paul Sheard, "Bank Executives on Japanese Corporate Boards," photocopy, Bank of Japan, 1994.

CHAPTER FOUR

The Politics of
Administrative Reform

Lonny E. Carlile

One of the more prominent features of Japanese regulatory reform since the early 1980s has been its association with a "movement" revolving around a series of high-profile official commissions devoted to the promotion of what the Japanese have termed administrative reform (*gyōsei kaikaku*). Established outside the normal ministry-based framework of advisory commissions and councils, these panels have each issued reports whose contents range from hortatory articulations of general principles to detailed lists of specific regulatory modifications. These reports, which have been generally covered widely in the media, have frequently been interpreted as obligatory instructions to the government, as promises of future government action, and as barometers of current official opinion on matters relating to administrative reform. As for the term *administrative reform,* defined by one official government source as "the adaptation of administration to change, the promotion of simplification and

Earlier versions of this chapter were presented before the Political Economy of Deregulation Workshop, Honolulu, April 8–10, 1996; the 1996 Annual Meeting of the American Political Science Association, San Francisco, August 29–September 1, 1996; and the "Japanese Deregulation: What You Should Know" Symposium sponsored by the Japan-U.S. Friendship Commission and the Japan Information Access Project, Washington, D.C., April 4, 1997. I thank David Boling, Konoe Shinsuke, Mindy Kotler, Miyajima Hideaki, Elizabeth Norville, Ōyama Kōsuke, Yul Sohn, Sasaki Takeshi, and Mark Tilton for their comments.

increased efficiency, [and] attaining the trust of the people," it is a term whose meaning roughly encompasses that of the English term *regulatory reform* but with a greater association with the idea of agency reorganization.[1]

This chapter reviews the activities of Japan's administrative reform commissions since the early 1980s. Particular attention is paid to the sociopolitical and economic context within which these commissions operated and to the question of how these commissions affected and were affected by that context.

Rinchō

The concerns that gave rise to Japan's nascent administrative reform movement in the early 1980s were different from those that drove regulatory reform in the United States. In the United States and the United Kingdom regulatory reform was driven by the perceived need to roll back state intervention in the economy and foster competitive markets as a way out of the stagflationary impasse these countries faced.[2] Although concerns about state regulation were also expressed in Japan at the time, the issue did not have quite the same salience that it had in the Anglo-American context. By contrast, a looming fiscal crisis proved instrumental in giving rise to the administrative reform movement.

The deficit in the government's general account had grown sevenfold in nominal terms and from 1.6 percent to nearly 6 percent of GNP between fiscal year 1974 and fiscal year 1980.[3] Driving and sustaining these deficits was an ongoing shift in the relationship among the elite triumvirate of the ruling Liberal Democratic party (LDP), government bureaucrats, and big business. Stimulated by election losses and the imminent prospect of losing majority control of the national legislature's two houses, the LDP sought to mobilize the support of specific, electorally significant societal groups by actively directing and bending bureaucratic initiatives and to appeal to the electorate en masse through an expansion of welfare state provisions. Pork barrel politics, mediation with the bureaucracy on behalf of client groups, and influence over discretionary administrative decisions relating to the allocation of funds and policy enforcement—in essence, *zoku* politics—grew to become primary mechanisms by which the LDP assured that appropriate resources and benefits were channeled to the "right" societal interests.[4]

In an effort to counterbalance these expenditures, corporate taxes were raised several times during the 1970s at the initiative of the fiscally conservative Ministry of Finance (MOF), as were rates for various public utilities. In a culmination of this trend, the government of Ōhira Masayoshi announced its intention to introduce a new value-added tax that would significantly broaden the state's fiscal revenue base. However, the tax proposal proved extremely unpopular and became a major factor in the massive losses sustained by the ruling LDP in the October 1979 general election. It was at this point that a consensus began to emerge among governing elites that increased taxes were no longer a politically acceptable solution to Japan's fiscal crisis and a new approach had to be sought to deal with the deficit problem.

Rinchō and Its Agenda

The focal point of Japan's effort to address the fiscal crisis was the Second Provisional Commission on Administrative Reform (Rinchō) formed in March 1981 and disbanded in March 1983.[5] Despite its superficial resemblance to garden-variety Japanese governmental commissions, the nine-member commission possessed a number of distinguishing features. First, unlike most official Japanese commissions, which quietly issue advice that can be ignored by the agency involved, for a variety of reasons Rinchō maintained an unusually high degree of public prominence. Rinchō was also given a much wider area of inquiry—virtually any issue relating to administrative reform—than is the norm for advisory councils, whose mandates tend to be quite narrow.

Of the five reports that Rinchō issued, its basic report of July 1982 constitutes the most authoritative and comprehensive statement of its goals and principles and can be read as a manifesto of the Rinchō administrative reform movement.[6] The reason for issuing the report (and by extension the basic orientation of the administrative reform movement as a whole) was, according to the text, that changed international, technological, and domestic socio-economic conditions were making Japan's existing administrative structures obsolete. In particular, the shift from the rapid economic growth of the 1960s and early 1970s to the slower growth of the 1980s meant that state resources were no longer expanding as rapidly as before. Circumstances required that the state modify its administrative structure in a way that would economize on fiscal resources while effectively addressing the issues and problems—the report emphasized the need for Japan to play a larger global role and did so almost to the point of ignoring other issues—that were generating increased demands on the state's capacities. The report called on the Japanese state to prioritize its goals, where feasible to replace state functions with "self-help" efforts on the part of private citizens and the private sector, and to make state administration more effective, efficient, and comprehensively coordinated. Rather than descend into "Eurosclerosis" (that is, an overly generous welfare state sapping the vitality of the economy), the commission posited that Japan become a "vigorous welfare society."[7] It then outlined general principles, parameters, and concerns that should guide policy in specific policy sectors—agriculture, social security, education, foreign policy making, defense, land use, energy, and science and technology—with the emphasis on modifying bureaucratic agencies in ways that would result in greater efficiency and effectiveness.

Conventional Anglo-American notions of deregulation figured minimally in the report. The closest approach in the basic report can be found in brief passages in which a concept literally meaning "private sector vitality," *minkatsu*, is introduced, but the meaning implied is closer to privatization or contracting out than deregulation per se.[8] Before the release of the basic report, Rinchō had issued a report on the subject of consolidating licensing authority.[9] Accounts of Rinchō's activities at the time, however, suggest that the report was intended primarily as a public relations device to generate popular support for the administrative reform effort, rather than as a statement of a priority item on the reform agenda.[10] Thus, unlike the debate in the United States and the United Kingdom, as well as unlike the direction the discourse in Japan would later take, in the early phase of the administrative reform movement the deregulatory impetus was overshadowed by the theme of making government administration more cost-effective through such measures as the updating of obsolete regulations, the consolidation of overlapping jurisdictions among bureaucratic agencies, the harmonization of Japanese regulations with international rules, the elimination of regulations wherein administrative costs exceed the value of the gains attained, and greater transparency in implementation.

Rinchō: Politics and Process

Critical to understanding both Rinchō's accomplishments and the limits of Rinchō's reform drive is grasping the logic of the "high-commission" format that was adopted for pursuing administrative reform and of the nature of the coalition that undergirded the Rinchō movement.[11] Rinchō was pursuing goals that went against the grain of what had become the norm in Japanese politics, which as already noted was geared toward expanding the overall scope of state intervention and fiscal expansion via the activities of quasi-autonomous subgovernments driven by *zoku* politicians, bureaucrats from specific agencies, and interest groups (usually producer groups) with a direct interest in a specific area of regulation. Because it was precisely this devolution of initiative and control that had led to the fiscal emergency in the first place, in order to correct the problem some way was needed to circumvent the channels controlled by those three types of groups and restore overall fiscal and administrative discipline. Rinchō was thus designed to be "above" the fray and in a position to articulate and promote general interests that did not have a place within the normal framework of Japanese politics. Yet as an advisory commission with little in the way of real administrative authority outside of the vague requirement that the government take its views into account, there was little a priori assurance that its recommendations would result in anything more than pro forma responses.

Rinchō members in fact went beyond the staid and passive role of typical commissioners and deliberately sought to foster a movement. Key figures in Rinchō used the media for publicizing their particular agenda. The release of Rinchō reports were timed to coincide with specific political and administrative events so that their impact would be enhanced. The commission's chair, Dokō Toshio, a former president of both Toshiba and Keidanren, projected a media image perfectly suited to the message. Despite being part of the country's top corporate elite, Dokō was known for his simple, bonzelike lifestyle—eating meals of inexpensive fried fish and miso soup, cultivating a vegetable garden at his mansion, and eschewing limousines in favor of public transportation—and for that reason seemed to personify the virtues of thrift the commission was seeking for government.

What allowed Rinchō to have in the end a substantive effect on the policy process was the backing it received from a coalition of forces that supported its goal of fiscal retrenchment. The first and most consistently enthusiastic pillar of the Rinchō coalition was Japan's big business community led by the peak business association, Keidanren. The feeling was widespread among the firms it represented that the burden of economic adjustment during the 1970s had been placed on their backs and that the politicoeconomic system, rather than serving as a boost to their endeavors as had been true in the past, was increasingly a drag on their fortunes.

Not surprisingly, fiscal retrenchment was a generally unpopular idea in Kasumigaseki, Tokyo's government district. Two bureaucratic agencies, however, perceived that fiscal retrenchment could be useful in advancing their agendas. One such agency was the MOF, whose officials continued to believe in balanced budgets and were terrified by Japan's mushrooming public debt. In particular, the ministry was anxious to put a cap on the so-called three K accounts—*kome, kokutetsu,* and *kenkō hoken* (rice, the Japan National Railways, and the National Health Insurance). The other agency that came out in favor of administrative reform was the Administrative Management Agency, a small, cabinet-level agency consisting primarily of personnel transferred temporarily from other ministries. It stood to expand its rather limited power and influence as the obvious candidate for overseeing administrative reform. Together, the two agencies constituted the second pillar of the Rinchō coalition.

The third pillar was the LDP politician Nakasone Yasuhiro and his supporters. Nakasone was a member of the generation of LDP faction leaders that rose to prominence during the 1970s. For a variety of reasons, Nakasone had been passed over during a decade when all the other faction leaders had been given the opportunity to serve as prime minister. A neoconservative and hawk, Nakasone had long been critical of what he described as Japan's rudderless drift toward profligacy and had advocated a restructuring of the Japanese state in order to ensure the proper leadership that the country needed in order to survive in a hostile and rapidly changing world. Nakasone had been banished to the normally undesirable position of director of the Administrative Management Agency in the Suzuki Zenkō cabinet that followed in the wake of Ōhira Masayoshi's death in 1980. Once in office, and observing the situational imperatives of fiscal retrenchment closing in, Nakasone began to see the budding administrative reform movement and the yet-to-be-created Rinchō as his ticket to the prime ministership.

The fourth and final component of the coalition backing administrative reform was the conservative wing of the Japanese labor movement. The postwar labor movement had always contained a "constructive" wing, which sought the improvement of its membership's situations through cooperation with management. The relative influence of this wing had expanded steadily throughout the high-growth era of the 1950s and 1960s and by the 1970s had come to dominate the private sector. The corporate rationalization drives of the 1970s deepened the identification of these unions (which were almost invariably enterprise based) with the corporations that employed them and thus to share many of the concerns that had driven their employers to come out strongly in favor of fiscal retrenchment and administrative reform. At the level of movement dynamics, in order to maintain the competitiveness of Japanese industry these unions had restrained wage demands. Unable to pitch militant wage increase demands to gain rank-and-file support, the leadership of this moderate wing of the Japanese labor movement by the late 1970s had come to champion tax cuts as a means of increasing the disposable incomes of workers, a position that fit hand in glove with the drive to cut the costs of government.[12] The public sector unions, however, were at the forefront of resistance to administrative reform, although even among these unions there was significant variation in the terms of resistance.[13]

Each component of the Rinchō coalition occupied a strategic location in the political system and as a consequence each was in a position to serve as a "cell" that could mobilize the most important institutional nexuses of the Japanese policy system. The most visible example of such a cell at work was the five-man committee set up to demonstrate the support of the business community that consisted of representatives of each of the leading big business organs— Keidanren, Keizai Dōyukai, Nikkeiren, the Japan Chamber of Commerce, and the Kansai Keizai Renmei. Nakasone, as a senior figure and faction leader in the ruling party and eventually party president, was in a position to steer the LDP. Within the bureaucracy, the MOF used its powers of the purse over other central government ministries and agencies to keep opposition within Kasumigaseki from getting out of control. Dōmei, the national center representing the private sector–dominated moderate wing of the labor movement, served to isolate its rival, public sector-union–dominated Sōhyō. Big business, the bureaucracy, and the LDP, of course, constituted the classical "elite triumvirate" of Japanese politics, whereas the unions represented the core pillar of Japan's opposition camp.

The Rinchō "process" that ultimately emerged was one in which Rinchō would publicize, through its reports and interactions with the press, concrete "assignments" that the LDP governments were expected to fulfill. Included among the assignments successfully completed were such targets as steady progress on moving toward the elimination of budget deficits, the privatization of Japan's primary public corporations (Nippon Telephone and Telegraph [NTT], Japan National Railways [JNR], and Japan Tobacco), and a freeze on civil servant salaries and agricultural subsidies. As prime minister Suzuki Zenkō found out as a result of his failure to hold down rice price increases in 1982, Rinchō was at times even able to set the stage for the removal of a prime minister. It has also been widely noted that one of the secrets of Rinchō's apparent success was that the commission took care to ensure that the assignments did not go beyond the realm of what was politically feasible, which in practice coincided with those matters directly connected to "fiscal reconstruction without a tax increase" on which there was a consensus across the coalition. Beyond this, and notably in the area of deregulation, progress was minimal.

Reform in Abeyance

During the 1985–93 period the Rinchō-led movement began to falter and eventually lost its ability to impose its agenda on Japanese politics. Two broad developments were involved. One was the tentative achievement of fiscal retrenchment, as indicated by the steady reduction in the government budget deficit from fiscal 1983 onward. This set in motion the natural proclivity of all movements to fissure or reconstitute once their original goals are attained. A second development was the transformation of the macroeconomic and macropolitical environment as the Japanese political economy shifted to the expansionary policy framework that characterized the Bubble years. This shift exacerbated the fissuring that was occurring in the old Rinchō-centered coalition. Still, by establishing the institutional mechanisms for an ongoing administrative reform process, Rinchō had given the movement a momentum of its own that allowed the Rinchō agenda to sustain itself despite marginalization.

The Gyōkakushin

In accordance with a recommendation made in Rinchō's final report, the Provisional Commission for the Promotion of Administrative Reform (Gyōka-kushin I) had been established on May 28, 1983, to carry on the work of advancing the agenda established by Rinchō.[14] It was disbanded on June 27, 1986. Gyōkakushin I was succeeded by two commissions: the New Provisional Commission for the Promotion of Administrative Reform (Gyōkakushin II, April 27, 1987–April 19, 1990) and the Third Provisional Commission for the Promotion of Administrative Reform (Gyōkakushin III, October 31, 1990–October 30, 1993).

All three commissions inherited certain basic features from Rinchō. Like Rinchō, they were established through specific enabling legislation and reported directly to the prime minister. Commissioners were chosen from among representatives of big business, labor, ex-bureaucrats, and the "public interest." The deliberation of specialized topics was delegated to subcommittees. Reports were issued periodically. As in Rinchō, the three Gyōkakushin relied on bureaucrats for staff assistance. If anything, the degree of such dependence increased with the establishment of Gyōkakushin II, as secretariat functions were moved from an office directly under the commission to the newly created Management and Coordination Agency (MCA). Like its predecessor, the Administrative Management Agency, the MCA was heavily reliant on personnel brought over from other ministries and agencies and dependent on their goodwill and cooperation for the success of its efforts. Consequently, the MCA (along with the ex-bureaucrats who sat on these commissions and their subcommittees) served as an institutionalized conduit for, on the one hand, feeding inside information about the activities of the commissions and commission members to concerned ministries and, on the other, for the exercise of ministerial influence.[15]

The Gyōkakushins lacked Rinchō's stature and media presence. This was true even of the Gyōkakushin I, despite the fact that it was headed by the charismatic Dokō. The fissuring of the Rinchō coalition meant that the Gyōkakushins were less able to counteract political and bureaucratic manipulation. Whereas Rinchō was able to define the agenda of Japanese government and politics, the Gyōkakushins tended to take their cues from politicians. A growing disjuncture emerged between the thinking of the commissions, or more accurately the nonbureaucratic members of these commissions, and the policies that were implemented in the name of administrative reform.

The declining significance of the formal government administrative reform commissions was masked somewhat during the life of Gyōkakushin I.[16] Rinchō had already set in motion a series of major reforms: for example, caps on government budget increases; the privatization of NTT, JNR, and the Tobacco and Salt Monopoly Corporation; and increases in social insurance copayments and user fees. As the entity charged with the task of overseeing their implementation, Gyōkakushin I was in a position to take credit for these. In other areas, however, its limitations were clearly evident. One such area was local governmental reform. Rinchō had already put forward administrative reform at the local level as a part of the administrative reform agenda, and Gyōkakushin I adopted this as one of its primary areas of emphasis. A subcommittee on agency delegation functions (a key mechanism of central control over local governments in which local governments are required to perform central government functions) was established shortly after the commission's creation and was followed somewhat later by a second subcommittee specifically charged with developing policies for promoting administrative reform at the local level. However, the effort to restructure central-local government relations sparked resistance on the part of central government bureaucrats generally and on the part of the ex-bureaucrats on the Gyōkakushin commissions and its subcommittees in particular, with the consequence that the resulting proposals were watered down dramatically from what the proponents of reform had originally proposed. Once drafted, recommendations were either ignored or at best addressed with largely cosmetic changes. A Gyōkakushin I proposal for a reduction in the number of special legal entities (*tokushu hōjin*) suffered a similar fate. Although the number of special legal entities decreased slightly (from ninety-nine in 1983 to eighty-seven in 1986, for instance), these reductions typically involved the transfer of the functions of the dissolved entity to a surviving one, or else their reconstitution under a different institutional format.[17]

Under Gyōkakushin II and Gyōkakushin III the issue was less a matter of a lack of progress on the Rinchō agenda than a loss of control over what the commissions deliberated, as these commissions frequently served as pulpits for legitimating the particular policy emphases of the prime minister in power.[18] Thus, in a reversal of Rinchō's insistence on holding the line on expenditures, Gyōkakushin II found itself rubber-stamping the increased spending written into the fiscal year 1986 supplementary budget and justifying state intervention in the real estate market in the form of extensive controls on land transactions.[19] One can find a further illustration of the declining role of the administrative reform commissions as definers of the policy agenda in the fact that these expansionary policies had already been deliberated and justified by a personal advisory organ of the prime minister (the Maekawa Commission) well before they were taken up by Gyōkakushin II. In Gyōkakushin III, examples can be seen in the way that it was assigned the task of drafting reports on such election-oriented pet projects of the Kaifu Toshiki and Miyazawa Kiichi cabinets as how to make Japan a "lifestyle superpower" and Japan's contribution to global environmental policy.

Minkatsu *and the Recovery of "Iron Triangle" Vitality*

As noted earlier, although the *minkatsu* concept was mentioned, it was not elaborated nor actively pursued during the initial, Rinchō-led stage of the administrative reform movement. However, thanks to its adoption by Nakasone as a key policy initiative during his prime ministership (1983–87), by 1984 the term came to occupy a position of prominence in public discussions that rivaled that of "fiscal reconstruction without a tax increase" in its heyday. The way in which *minkatsu* was harnessed by political and bureaucratic interests and placed in the service of ends that differed in spirit from that which Rinchō originally envisioned epitomizes the fate of the administrative reform movement as a whole during the post-Rinchō period.

Minkatsu came to be associated with three types of policies, all of them having to do with the construction industry: (1) the relaxation of land use regulations and building restrictions in order to stimulate private sector real estate development and construction investment; (2) the sale of government land to private sector developers, ostensibly for similar reasons; and (3) multibillion-dollar "third-sector" megaprojects such as the construction of the New Kansai International Airport and the Trans-Tokyo Bay Bridge.[20] At one level, this shift in emphasis was a natural outgrowth of the earlier focus on "fiscal reconstruction without a tax increase." That is, the increased economic activity generated by the relaxation of land use and building standards would, it was argued, eventually generate increased tax revenues. The sale of "surplus" public land generated further revenue that could be used to address the fiscal crisis in much the same way that the privatization of NTT did. The private sector funds that went into third-sector projects represented money that did not have to come out of the public purse. A further, unofficial reason for promoting *minkatsu* may have been to use it as a device to "opening up" Japan's construction market while continuing to exclude foreign participants from major Japanese public construction projects such as the Kansai International Airport project.[21]

As Ōtake Hideo argues, *minkatsu* also marks an important transformation in the political dynamics associated with the administrative reform movement.[22] One aspect of this transformation was a shift in the locus of policy initiative away from *zaikai* and the administrative reform councils. It was Prime Minister Nakasone who was the initiator of *minkatsu*. Concrete *minkatsu* project proposals were put together in consultation with the Ministry of Construction and a coterie of personal advisers. In contrast to their leading roles in the earlier phase, both the big business associations (*zaikai*) and Gyōkakushin found themselves to be reactive latecomers to the *minkatsu* bandwagon. It was not until September of the following year that Gyōkakushin assembled its own *minkatsu* committee. Keidanren did not follow suit until May of 1986. By that time, several major *minkatsu* projects were in the process of being implemented and legislation facilitating such projects was being passed in the Diet.

Unlike fiscal retrenchment, *minkatsu* proved highly popular with the LDP rank and file. Political mediation by the LDP's construction *zoku* in the scramble among construction and real estate firms for a piece of the action illustrates how *minkatsu* served as a vehicle for the revival of *zoku*-style politics under conditions of fiscal restraint.[23] The essential complementarity of the pork barrel instincts of Diet members and of the bureaucratic sectionalism of the various central government ministries and agencies was rediscovered as alliances of Diet members, ministry officials, and local government offices joined forces to promote their pet *minkatsu* projects. This was clearly useful for Nakasone, who was seeking to solidify his initially shaky foothold in the ruling party without sacrificing the support he had gathered by promoting fiscal reconstruction without a tax increase.

Minkatsu in practice had the effect of expanding bureaucratic influence. Rather than creating new "spaces" in which the private sector could give free rein to its vitality, *minkatsu* projects frequently served as cost-effective mechanisms for expanding the scope of both formal and informal regulation. Executive positions in the newly formed third-sector firms tended to be monopolized by ex-bureaucrats. Ministries and agencies used third-sector projects as opportunities to draft new regulations governing procedures for selecting participating firms, to impose new licensing and reporting requirements, and to promulgate ordinances that granted them supervisory oversight over what were de facto "state" projects.[24]

Although it is ironic that "private sector vitality" would end up enhancing the power of the bureaucracy, this result, in some ways, was built into the way that the Rinchō-led movement was pursued. The across-the-board zero and negative "ceilings" imposed by the MOF in the name of fiscal retrenchment on ministry and agency budget requests led to decreases in the monetary values of subsidies. A reduction in subsidy size without a corresponding decrease in the paperwork involved simply meant that more paperwork was required in order to obtain a given amount of subsidy. To make matters worse from this standpoint, new subsidy categories and new regulations and licensing powers continued to be added to the repertoire of Japan's ministries and agencies.[25] Likewise, the privatization of NTT and JNR is often argued to have actually strengthened the regulatory authority of supervising ministries by eliminating the legally sanctioned organizational autonomy of those former public sector corporations.[26]

The macroeconomics and the foreign policy milieu of the period exacerbated these bureaucracy-promoting tendencies. Fiscal retrenchment and slower economic growth in Japan had coincided with a growing government budget deficit and relatively rapid economic recovery in the United States. One outcome of this set of macroeconomic policy programs on the part of these two

economically intertwined nations was a rapid growth in the already chronic
Japanese trade surplus and increasingly severe U.S.-Japan economic tensions.
Japan came under formidable pressure from the United States to stimulate its
economy and to show measurable progress in opening up its market to foreign
goods. In the meantime, the rapid appreciation of the yen that began in the
wake of the September 1985 Plaza Accord provoked recessionary fears inside
Japan and demands that the government take decisive measures to prevent this.
The response was a series of stimulatory fiscal and financial measures that
contributed to a speculative "bubble" and a strong economic boom during the
latter part of the 1980s.[27] With the pressure for administrative retrenchment for
fiscal purposes no longer there, the solidarity and focus of the administrative
reform coalition naturally declined. The booming economy, in turn, gave rise
to numerous opportunities to practice another political forte of the LDP,
namely, pork barrel politics. The program that above all signified the return of
this mode was Takeshita's home village (*furusato*) building program, a rather
ill-defined but nonetheless evocative concept that added a positive gloss to the
practice of sending public works projects and funds to the countryside.

Deregulation

A further irony of the administrative reform movement in Japan was that the
very bureaucratic inertia that Rinchō was ostensibly committed to rooting out
ended up helping to sustain the life of the administrative reform process during
this difficult period and push the movement toward a clearer emphasis on
deregulation. One of the lasting legacies of the Rinchō movement, as noted,
was its creation of the bureaucratic machinery for the promotion of administrative reform. In its final report submitted to the government on March 14, 1983,
Rinchō mandated that a system for promoting administrative reform be established.[28] In addition to calling for a successor commission, it called for the
creation of the institutional machinery to draft and implement a concrete administrative reform program on a continuing basis. The response to the latter
mandate was the government's adoption of the practice of drafting annual pro
forma "administrative reform outlines" (*gyōkaku taikō*).[29] These outlines were
supplemented by the periodic passage of "administrative simplification and
rationalization" bills that mandated minor changes in the structure of the bureaucracy.[30] And whatever the actual nature or aim of the policies a bureaucratic agency or politician might champion, it became de rigueur to grant at least
lip service to the desirability of administrative reform. As these practices

illustrate, perhaps the most important of Rinchō's legacies was to give administrative reform an aura of ideological hegemony that kept the movement alive under adverse circumstances and allowed the Gyōkakushin to refine and extend the agenda first enunciated by Rinchō.

The impetus for deregulation to become a core theme of the administrative reform movement can be traced back to developments in the big business community in 1986. In response to complaints voiced by member firms, Keidanren established an internal subcommittee to look into the reasons why the *minkatsu* projects being implemented were not generating the beneficial results that had been anticipated. The essence of the subcommittee's conclusions was that the deregulatory aspect of *minkatsu* had not been given sufficient emphasis in actual projects.[31] As the discussion of *minkatsu* proceeded inside Keidanren, deregulation quickly came to be perceived as both politically and economically desirable. It was seen as an approach that would simultaneously address several economic challenges then confronting Japan: trade frictions, recession, appreciation of the yen, and rapid technological change. In terms of scope, it began to be seen as something that should be applied across a broad range of sectors, including transportation, energy, distribution, finance, primary industries, and telecommunications.[32] Internally, the Keidanren leadership appears to have also begun around this time a campaign to foster a proderegulation, antibureaucratic climate among its membership.[33]

The opportunity to introduce this new spin into the public policy agenda came in February 1988. Shortly after becoming prime minister, Takeshita Noboru requested that Gyōkakushin II prepare a report on measures that Japan might take in responding to foreign criticism of Japan's closed markets. A subcommittee was dutifully created in February 1988 entitled the Subcommittee on Public Regulations (Kōteki kisei ni kansuru shōiinkai). Chaired by long-time administrative reform activist Sejima Ryūzō, the twenty-five-member committee was dominated by business figures and economists. The output generated by the subcommittee in December 1988 was entitled *Kōteki Kisei Kanwa ni Kansuru Tōshin* (A Report on the Relaxation of Public Regulations).[34]

In framing its recommendations, the report classified regulations into two categories: "economic regulations" (*keizai kisei*) and "social regulations" (*shakai kisei*). The report argued that although the latter were needed in order to ensure the health and safety of the population, economic regulation (regulations that manipulated market entry and exit, supply and demand, price levels, and so on) should be kept to an absolute minimum. According to the report, the guiding principle in economic policy should be "nonregulation in principle and regulation only as an exception" (*gensoku jiyū reigai kisei*), rather than the current tendency toward the reverse. It went on to argue for a complete overhaul of the Japanese regulatory structure in line with these principles and attached a long list of specific recommendations in various areas that spanned the entire economy. This approach, it contended, would contribute directly to the resolution of specific problems facing the nation such as a reduction of the gap between domestic and overseas price levels, industrial adjustment under conditions of an appreciating yen, and a reduction of trade friction.

The report concluded by recommending in rather concrete terms the creation of an institutional arrangement for implementing and overseeing such an overhaul. This was to consist of the following elements:

A. Compilation of an outline plan for the promotion of deregulation.
   1. This should list concrete measures to be taken for attaining the regulatory changes stipulated in this report.
   2. The government should review the implementation of the list's items annually and make modifications as needed based on reports of the individual ministries and agencies.
B. Publication of the results of periodic reviews of progress in the implementation of the plan.
   1. This should include a list of licensing requirements that have been established or eliminated.
   2. A similar list should be compiled for inspection requirements.
C. New regulations' specifications of dates at which time the regulations would no longer be in effect or be reviewed.
D. A wholesale review of administrative procedures with the aim of simplifying them and reducing the burden placed on applicants and recipients.

In preparing the report, the subcommittee appeared to go well beyond what Takeshita had in mind when he requested a plan to deal with trade frictions. In his speech accepting the report (delivered in absentia), Takeshita mentioned very little that related to deregulation. Instead, he expressed his hope that he would see Gyōkakushin II discuss matters that would facilitate his *furusato*-building project. On December 13, 1988, the Takeshita cabinet dutifully passed a resolution that vowed to respect the report "as much as possible." When it came to concrete measures, however, the resolution used such passive terminology as "strive for," "consider," or "reconsider."[35] The rationale for deregulation presented in the Gyōkakushin II subcommittee's report on deregulation and the major proposals it contained became standard for subsequent reports written by the commission and its successor, Gyōkakushin III. Despite lip service, none of the LDP governments pushed very hard for actual implementation.

Administrative Reform Revived

The bursting of Japan's economic bubble made the administrative reform movement a highly topical issue once again. The collapse of stock and land prices as Japan entered the 1990s ushered in a period in which the Japanese economy stagnated at a level of negative or near-zero economic growth. Just as Rinchō's target of ridding the government of its chronic budgetary deficits was reached, the government was compelled to run massive stimulatory budgetary deficits once again. The fiscal situation that emerged was even worse than that which had induced the 1980s administrative reform movement, and Japan's debt level quickly soared to the highest level among the leading advanced industrialized countries. With the official discount rate eventually dropping to 0.5 percent, further lowering of interest rates was not an option. It also became clear around the same time that Japan's vaunted high-tech sectors were lagging behind those in the United States and other countries in such commercially and technologically strategic areas as telecommunications and microcomputers. The high cost of domestic services relative to overseas competitors was becoming a conspicuous drag on the competitiveness of all Japanese firms. Overregulation was widely perceived to be the primary cause in both instances. The worst crisis, however, was to be found in its financial sector, in which the fall of land prices and loose controls had given rise to stunning levels of bad debt that continue to threaten the very viability of the Japanese financial system.[36] Adding to these domestic factors that raised the economic urgency of regulatory reform were demands for deregulation and market liberalization from other countries—with bilateral negotiations between the United States and Japan such as the Structural Impediments Initiative talks of the Bush administration and the Framework talks of the Clinton administration being particularly critical.[37]

The Politics of Reform in a Changed Economic Environment

At the outset, public awareness and interest in deregulation and administrative reform were not very high. The struggles between pro- and antireform elements that were precipitated by the growing emphasis on deregulation in the administrative reform movement occurred well out of the public eye. Under these circumstances it was relatively easy for bureaucrats to undercut meaningful reform proposals and to camouflage their actions with purely cosmetic "reforms."[38] On their part, LDP politicians, who had by now become masters of zoku-style politics, found it well in their interest to go along, if not encourage this obfuscation. Throughout the tenure of Gyōkakushin III there was a noticeable disjuncture between the repeated emphasis on state activism in fostering "rich and rewarding lifestyles" (toyokana seikatsu) on the part of the LDP prime ministers who commissioned its reports and the tenacious insistence by its chairman, Suzuki Eiji, on the need to restructure the bureaucracy in line with the major socioeconomic transformations that were confronting Japan. When Suzuki ended his chairmanship in 1993, he left bitterly resentful of the manipulatory maneuverings of the bureaucracy.[39]

The saga of the proposal to eliminate and consolidate the country's 100 or so special legal entities (tokushu hōjin) illustrates why Suzuki might have come to think the way he did.[40] Special legal entities are a category of public corporations established by law outside of the regular central government ministry and agency structure. They are widely regarded as conduits for exercising bureaucratic power and influence and sources of postretirement, or "descent from heaven" (amakudari), landing spots. According to an inside account of the staff of the Mainichi Shinbun, an "interim report" was drafted by a subcommittee of Gyōkakushin III in the spring of 1993 that specifically called for the elimination of thirty-four special legal entities as a step that would contribute to both deregulation and fiscal consolidation. This proposal was met with a boycott of commission proceedings by executives of the special legal entities and a number of key ministries. Influential LDP politicians, including the later prime minister Hashimoto Ryutarō, were mobilized by the bureaucrats to put pressure on the commissioners.

Outside of the formal meetings, commission members were bombarded with incessant "explanations" by bureaucrats of why a proposal to abolish this or that tokushu hōjin was misguided. Perhaps most ironic of all, the vice director of the MCA, the agency serving as the secretariat for the commission, allegedly met personally with Okuno Seisuke, an influential boss in the LDP's powerful administrative and fiscal policy subcommittee, and induced him to engineer a full-fledged LDP phalanx against the plan. According to a Mainichi account, MCA staff members rewrote the commission's draft in order to eliminate any mention of the number of entities to be eliminated as well as any other language that might formally commit the bureaucracy to action. Similar bureaucratic subterfuges were directed against the proposals for a substantial devolution of power to local government put forward in a Gyōkakushin III subcommittee on decentralization.[41]

Public interest in reform began to grow between 1989 and 1990. The break was the Recruit Scandal, in which a huge number politicians from both the LDP and the opposition parties, high-level bureaucrats in the labor and education ministries, and the president of NTT were implicated.[42] During 1990 to 1991, the apparent anachronistic and dysfunctional character of the country's politicoadministrative system was further highlighted by Japan's snail-paced effort to define a role for itself in the Gulf War and the post–cold-war world order.[43] However, despite a degree of spillover into the administrative reform and deregulation issue areas, the bulk of public debate focused on "political reform" in the sense of modifying election and campaign rules.

If these had been official Japan's only missteps, the LDP and the bureaucracy might have been able to weather the public disillusionment of the post-Recruit, post-Gulf period with politicians taking the heat and only a few cosmetic changes that would leave the status quo intact. However, during 1991 and 1992 the Japanese public and the world became aware of a truly stunning set of scandals, revelations, and incidents—the Sagawa Affair, the securities payoff scandal, the Kōmintō incident, the arrest of LDP king maker Kanemaru Shin and the Zenecon Scandal, the JSP's retro-unchic "cow walk" over the price-keeping operation (PKO) bill, to name just a few—that, collectively and precipitously, pulled the rug out from under the public's confidence in big business and the elite bureaucracy and caused the already low level of trust in politicians to drop even further. Just how bad the situation was is illustrated by the fact that it induced prominent members of the Takeshita faction—the very faction that had most benefited the system of *zoku* politics—to bolt from the faction and subsequently leave the LDP in the name of political and administrative reform. As is well known, this move paved the way for the party's loss of its parliamentary majority and the establishment of the reformist non-LDP coalition government under Hosokawa Morihiro in August 1993.[44]

Hosokawa and the Hiraiwa Commission

The brief Hosokawa administration probably constituted Japan's greatest opportunity to date to realize a broad program of regulatory reform.[45] The Hosokawa government and its reform platform were extremely popular with

the public as reflected in the high levels of support for the government regis-
tered in public opinion polls. The fall of LDP governance disrupted the iron
triangle networks that sustained *zoku*-based administrative processes. Journal-
ists suggest that bureaucrats were steeling themselves for a major change in
their status and mode of operations. As it turned out, however, the Hosokawa
government chose to concentrate on electoral reform before tackling administrative reform. Major action on the issue of administrative reform was put on
hold, and deliberation of the subject was delegated to an independent advisory
commission attached to the prime minister's office. Popularly known as the
Hiraiwa Commission, it was asked to report back at the end of the year with
concrete suggestions as to how the government should proceed. In the interim,
the bureaucracy discovered that it was perhaps not as vulnerable as initially
feared. Most of the new cabinet ministers, especially those who had come from
the former opposition parties, were complete novices to governmental office
and it quickly became clear that the bureaucracy was adept at controlling the
agenda to forestall any impetus for reform.

The work of the Hiraiwa Commission, the actions of the Hosokawa government in the brief period following the commission's submission of its report in December 1993, and the fall of the Hosokawa cabinet the following
spring were important in establishing the framework for the subsequent politics of deregulatory reform. The Hiraiwa Commission's relative institutional
independence (comparable with Nakasone's Maekawa Commission) and the
fact that the membership of the Hiraiwa Commission was heavily stacked in
favor of vocal proponents of a thorough neoconservative reform combined to
give their arguments for deregulatory administrative reform unusual clarity
and force. In addition, the renewed public interest in the reform process that
had been generated by the emergence of a non-LDP government encouraged
widespread media coverage of the commission's activities. Despite the commission's commitment and the publicity received, insider accounts make it
clear that even this commission was not immune from the effects of bureaucratic pressures.[46]

The most important contribution of the Hiraiwa Commission's report to the
evolution of the administrative reform movement was its outlining of a machinery for furthering deregulation. (It might be noted here that its proposals
were not completely new; many of its ideas had been expressed in proposals
put forward by Gyōkakushin II and III.) First, it called for the creation of a
deregulation promotion headquarters headed by the prime minister to oversee a
wholesale review of Japan's regulatory structures. It then went on to mandate

the drafting of a five-year deregulation action program during fiscal year 1994. Third, it called for the creation of an independent organ to make suggestions for improving the content of the plan and to monitor its implementation. Fourth, the Office of Trade Ombudsman and the MCA's administrative inspection functions were also to be mobilized on behalf of deregulation. Finally, the report called for the annual publication of a deregulation white paper that would help sustain public awareness of the deregulatory process.[47] These basic points were incorporated into Hosokawa's state-of-the-nation speech before the Diet and in the government's annual administrative reform outline released on February 15, 1994, thereby formally committing the government to their fulfillment.[48]

The Action Plan

The Hosokawa government, however, fell before much concrete action could be taken. The completion of the Hiraiwa Commission's assignment was left to the short lived, minority Hata Tsutomu cabinet and the LDP–Social Democratic Party (SDPJ)–Sakigake (Harbinger Party) government under Murayama Tomiichi (July 1994–January 1996). Most of the work of drafting the action plan was undertaken under the purview of the latter cabinet. A formal action plan listing 1,091 specific items of deregulation in eleven separate categories was formally adopted on March 31, 1995. The plan's date of completion was later moved up as part of a package of emergency economic measures, effectively turning the plan into a three-year plan.[49]

The adoption of the deregulation action program marks an important transformation in the evolution of the administrative reform movement. This program extended the locus of action "downstream"—that is, from one centered in the deliberations of various governmental and quasi-governmental advisory commissions to the policy formulation activities of line ministries and agencies. Given the short life spans of the Hosokawa and Hata cabinets, one can only speculate as to how the deregulation and administrative reform movement might have unfolded had the ostensibly proreform coalition they represented had a chance to implement the Hiraiwa Commission's suggestions. It seems clear that the intent of the core members of the Hiraiwa Commission was to have the cabinet-level promotion headquarters and the independent review agency take the initiative in formulating concrete deregulatory proposals and in overseeing implementation, although the commission's report ended up being watered down to some extent as a result of pressure from the bureaucracy.[50] Given the formal platform and the proclivities exhibited under the Hosokawa government, there is good reason to believe that an attempt would have been made to move the deregulation process in this direction, although given the structural weaknesses of the coalition one would have to be skeptical about its ability to pull it off in the face of strong bureaucratic resistance. What is clear, though, is that under the three-party Murayama-Hashimoto coalition governments the process of drafting and implementing the action plan began to diverge from what was originally envisioned.

In a nutshell, the deregulation "process" built around the action plan became one in which the bureaucratic agencies with regulatory authority over a given sector became the primary determinants of the measures that would be included in the action plan.[51] Despite an overlay of hearings ostensibly designed to provide public and foreign input and review by the Administrative Reform Committee (not to be confused with the subsequent Administrative Reform Council [ARCounc]), an independent committee assigned the task of advising and monitoring the process, the core of the process involved the MCA's Administrative Management Bureau's collecting proposals for deregulation from the respective ministries and agencies and compiling these in a massive table that constitutes the plan's substantive content. This did not mean that input from the Administrative Reform Committee and from nongovernmental and foreign sources were necessarily fated to be ignored, but it did mean that any deregulation that went into the plan would be drafted according to terms dictated by the respective ministries and agencies. Not surprisingly, the latter showed a distinct preference for incremental changes that preserved the status quo with respect to regulatory authority. There was also a tendency to emphasize the *number* of deregulatory items irrespective of their significance. These, it might be noted, often consisted of promises to "consider" (*kentō suru*) an item or some other course of de facto nonaction. As a consequence, the deregulation action plan represented not a plan in the usual sense of the term but an ongoing tally of those deregulatory measures the ministries and agencies were willing to entertain.

Political Parties as Agents of Administrative Reform?

Another way the administrative reform movement was transformed after 1993 involved the emergence of political parties as critical actors in their own right. Party politics had not been particularly important in determining the scope and direction of the administrative reform movement under LDP single-party rule. When politicians were involved in the process, they tended to do so within the context of the intraparty politics of the LDP.[52] The nature of their involvement began to change in the summer of 1993. Indeed, in a number of instances, the positions that a particular party took on these issues became an important part of a party's identity. For instance, the New Frontier party (NFP; Shinshinto), which was established in December 1994 and which became the second largest political party behind the LDP, distinguished itself by its association with the laissez-faire-oriented neoconservative philosophy of its leader, Ozawa Ichirō.[53] A small party with only two dozen or so Diet members in both houses at its peak, Sakigake represented a premier example of a party building its identity around the championing of administrative reform.

The LDP, which remained the single largest party in the Japanese Diet despite losing its majority, was a mixed bag. On the one hand, with its heavy contingent of *zoku* politicians, the LDP was a consistent source of resistance to reform initiatives. At the same time, it did contain strong advocates of radical regulatory reform such as Koizumi Jun'ichirō. The party leadership, in turn, was forced by popular opinion, economic crisis, business association pressures, and the calculus of coalition government to commit the party, often kicking and screaming, to a proadministrative reform stance. The SDPJ, which traditionally billed itself as the protector of the weak against the ravages of unchecked state monopoly capitalism, also suffered from similar internal divisions over regulatory reform. This internal incoherence was alleviated somewhat during September 1996, when the moderate, more proreform elements bolted from the party to join with exiles from Sakigake to form the Democratic party (Minshutō).

The experiences of the LDP-SDPJ-Sakigake coalition governments under the SDPJ's Murayama Tomiichi (July 1994–January 1996) and the first Hashimoto Ryutarō cabinet (January–September 1996) help to highlight how partisan stances became a factor in the regulatory reform process. When the triparty coalition government was first formed, for instance, it was Sakigake's strong insistence on the inclusion of administrative reform as a priority item in the three-party coalition agreement as a quid pro quo for its participation that led to a formal commitment on the part of the Murayama government to continue the Hosokawa and Hata governments' deregulation program. The increased significance of party stances in the policymaking process, however, did not necessarily result in an increased output of regulatory reform measures that could be implemented. Instead, the procedures for governmental decision-making adopted by the coalition had the paradoxical effect of simultaneously raising the visibility of reform issues while virtually guaranteeing the frustration of major reform initiatives.

In contrast to the Hosokawa and Hata coalition governments, which tended to make decisions in top-down fashion via negotiations among high-level officials of the parties in the ruling coalition, the Murayama and Hashimoto cabinets that followed adopted a more decentralized approach reminiscent of policymaking under LDP single-party rule.[54] The work of discussing policy and drafting recommendations was delegated to various coordination conferences (chōsei kaigi) and project teams (some of which were referred to as work teams). Each of the nineteen coordination conferences was assigned the task of deliberating policy relating to a specific central government ministry or agency, whereas more than two dozen or so project teams were organized around major policy issues of the day—for example, the administrative reform and the religious corporations law. In each instance, the three parties were represented in proportion to the number of seats they held in the Diet, which meant that the LDP representatives outnumbered those of the other parties by a wide margin.

The decisionmaking process typically began with deliberation of a given issue at the level of the work team and with an attempt to forge a consensus at that level. An issue would then make its way up through a governing party policy adjustment conference (yotō seisaku chōsei kaigi), a ruling party executive council (yotō innai sōmukai), and the ruling party caretaker's conference (yotō sekininsha kaigi), and ultimately to a parley of the leaders of the respective parties. A typical scenario was one in which Sakigake or the SDPJ would launch a reform initiative only to see it quashed by opposition from LDP politicians defending the status quo on behalf of a ministry or agency (or at times union opposition mediated by the SDPJ).[55] One consequence of this process was a growing level of popular frustration over the official regulatory reform movement and great skepticism overseas about Japanese government intentions.

The Hashimoto Gyōkaku

During 1996 there was a noticeable shift in the character of the demands and proposals being put forward in the name of administrative reform. As one source aptly describes the resulting situation, "The national debate over administrative reform [now] goes beyond the number of regulations that the government imposes and the size of the bureaucracy to more fundamental aspects of the government's structure."[56] Prominent examples include proposals to re-organize the Ministry of Finance, shift the MCA's bureaucratic oversight func-tions to the Diet, secure freedom of information legislation, and devolve central government power and financial resources to local governments. The debate in effect moved upstream to a concern with overhauling both the institu-tional structure of the Japanese government bureaucracy as a whole and the essential practices and procedures associated with it, or what one proponent labels "reforms for the sake of promoting reform."[57] The most vocal partisan proponents of institutional overhaul were the Democratic party and Sakigake, whereas *zoku*-type politicians inside the LDP and legislators with ties to public sector unions were the most active opponents.[58]

Japan's continuing economic stagnation, incessant scandals, and snail's-paced progress toward deregulation were all factors that contributed to this shift in the focus of the administrative reform debate. Equally important, however, was a more purely political factor. Under Japanese constitutional rules, Prime Minister Hashimoto had to call a Lower House election before the summer of 1997. With an election looming, the various political parties were motivated to establish distinctive identities and a presence in the public eye, and administrative reform was perceived to be an excellent vehicle for doing this. Inside the coalition Sakigake, and to a lesser extent the SDPJ, began to press all the more firmly for visible progress on administrative reform. In the opposition camp, the NFP too continued to attack the governing coalition over its failure to attain meaningful reform. The formation of the Democratic party under a platform built around a concept of "reinventing government" added further fuel to the fire. Encircled by partisan advocates of administrative reform and spurred by proreform elements inside the LDP, both Hashimoto and the LDP leadership had little choice but to join the chorus.

The election was called during the summer of 1996, and the actual balloting took place on October 20. The LDP gained a substantial number of seats in the so-called administrative reform election while its coalition partners suffered major reductions. As a consequence, developments inside the LDP and the party's relationship with the cabinet, bureaucracy, and interest groups became more important in shaping the course of Japanese administrative reform than at any time since the fall of single-party majority governance in the summer of 1993. The LDP's gains did not constitute, however, a return to the modes of governance that characterized the heyday of LDP single-party rule. Although consisting exclusively of LDP ministers, the second Hashimoto cabinet, which was formed following the election, was a minority cabinet. The fact that the

LDP did not have a parliamentary majority in either house of the Diet meant that Hashimoto and his lieutenants needed to gain the support of other parties in order to pass a piece of legislation.[59] What this meant in practice was that the prime minister and the LDP leadership (which was dominated by backers of the coalition with the SDPJ and Sakigake) continued to solicit the support of its now extracabinet coalition partners on key issues and attempted to reflect the concerns of its coalition partners in the party's internal policymaking process. This was often an extremely delicate task, for there were influential figures in the party who were calling for an abandonment of the linkup with the SDPJ and Sakigake in favor of a renewed conservative majority (presumably forged through a coalition with the NFP or the incorporation of Diet members currently affiliated with the NFP). External partisan stances and concerns were thus reflected in LDP and government policy, but within a potentially fragile political framework. Inside the LDP there was an incessant tug-of-war between demands for an extensive and radical program of deregulation and administrative reform and entrenched *zoku* tendencies.

Given this context, it is not surprising that Prime Minister Hashimoto devoted considerable attention to efforts that would project the appearance of movement in the area of administrative reform. Hashimoto's vehicle for doing this came to be labeled the Hashimoto administrative reform program (Hashimoto *gyōkaku*). The program began to take shape in the latter half of 1995 as Hashimoto unfolded his eventually successful campaign to take over the presidency of the LDP from his predecessor, Kōno Yōhei. In this campaign, Hashimoto pitched administrative reform and deregulation as means to revive the dormant Japanese economy while at the same time stressing the need to assist small, regionally based businesses in the process of structural adjustment and to preserve employment.[60] Similar ideas were expressed in his state-of-the-nation address given in January 1996. During the late spring and early summer, Hashimoto repeatedly emphasized the need for a thoroughgoing administrative reform process and announced that his party would develop its own program for attaining it.

The challenge for Hashimoto was to get the party, despite its close alignment with bureaucratic interests, behind a credible administrative reform agenda. The vehicle that Hashimoto chose for realizing this goal was the party's administrative reform promotion headquarters (established in November 1995). Hashimoto made it a point to personally attend this new organization's meetings during the spring and early summer of 1996. After a period of internal bickering, the essential parameters of the Hashimoto administrative reform program were ironed out in a document released by the administrative reform promotion headquarters on June 18, 1996, and subsequently approved by the party organizational hierarchy.[61] The party, in turn, used the resulting program as a core platform in the campaign leading up to the October general election.

Having featured the Hashimoto reform program so prominently in their campaigning, Hashimoto and the LDP leadership were, of course, under great pressure to give it some substance after the election. In reconstituting the triparty coalition that had supported his first cabinet, Hashimoto agreed to submit legislation to the Diet in January 1997 that would lead to a major reorganization of the MOF and its powers along with a bill that would result in the elimination and consolidation of special legal entities, as well as to prepare a package of administrative reform bills for submission to the Diet by 1998.[62] To counteract *zoku* resistance, senior figures with influence inside the party and in *zoku* circles were placed in positions in which they would be forced to push for administrative reform measures. For example, Mitsuzuka Hiroshi became finance minister and Mutō Kabun became head of the MCA. Hashimoto also established a high-profile commission, the ARCounc (Gyōsei Kaikaku Kaigi), to generate public interest and support for administrative reform. Finally, the reform program itself was reconstituted as a six-point package involving or-ganizationally distinct efforts in the following areas: administrative reform, fiscal reconstruction, social security reform, economic restructuring, financial system reform (often referred to as Japan's "Big Bang"), and educational reform.[63]

During 1997, it was the work of the ARCounc that drew intense press scrutiny and constituted the de facto core of the Hashimoto reform program. Structurally, the ARCounc was distinguished by the directness of its links with the prime minister. Unlike previous councils in which a reporting relationship was used to create a firewall between an advisory council and the prime minister or minister initiating an inquiry, Hashimoto personally chaired the ARCounc and was reported to have actively led the discussion on occasion. In terms of its agenda, the ARCounc with few exceptions stayed within the track laid out for it by the LDP's administrative reform promotion headquarters. The item of the greatest substance on the ARCounc agenda was the reshuffling of the functions of the central government's ministries and agencies, but also discussed were related organizational issues such as adoption of a British-style agency system and strengthening of the oversight powers of the prime minister. Conspicuously absent from the initial agenda were two items that had figured prominently in earlier administrative reform deliberations and which were also

being championed by reformist elements both inside and outside the LDP—
that is, the reform of special public corporations and the reform of the postal-
savings system. Because the postal-savings system represented a major source
of funding for pork barrel projects and subsidies to special interests, and the
special legal entities constituted important conduits for administering such
projects and subsidy disbursements, both, it might be noted, were issue areas in
which reform could directly affect the delivery of pork barrel benefits that were
so much at the heart of traditional LDP politics.[64] These potentially explosive
issues were claimed by the LDP administrative reform headquarters.

Despite the implicit division of labor just outlined, conflict and controversy
were not completely absent from the ARCounc and its deliberations. At the
outset, for instance, there were tensions between the bureaucrats in the council's secretariat, who were pushing for a rigidly systematic approach centered
around presentations by representatives of the ministries and agencies, and
those inside the council who wanted a more free-flowing debate. Even more
controversial were a number of debates stemming from the content of the
interim report. As illustrated in the experiences of earlier administrative reform
councils, midterm reports often supply important turning points in the council
deliberation process. The release of an interim report provides affected interests an opportunity to scrutinize the direction of council debate, and this
scrutiny then sets in motion a process in which council proposals are "adjusted" to fit political realities. This was certainly the case in the deliberations
of the ARCounc.[65] The highpoint of freewheeling discussion was reached just
prior to the preparation of the council's midterm report in August. In the
process, a number of proposals were included in the ARCounc's interim report,
apparently with the approval of Hashimoto, that clearly went beyond what was
envisioned in the version of the Hashimoto reforms certified by the LDP's
administrative reform promotion headquarters.[66] Most controversial by far
among the proposals was that calling for the privatization of the postal-savings
and insurance systems. The release of the interim report set the stage for a
classic *zoku*-led protest campaign orchestrated by the Ministry of Posts and
Telecommunications, associations of postmasters, and the postal workers
union, leading to the abandonment of the original proposal. Other specific
proposals suffered a similar fate with the result that the final report of
the ARCounc released during the first week of December 1997 was a relatively "safe" document with a solid base of support.[67] As of the time of
this writing, legislation to revamp the central government bureaucracy along
the lines recommended by the ARCounc had just made its way through the

Diet. The new legislation mandates that at the turn of the century the existing twenty-two ministries of the central Japanese bureaucracy will be consolidated into a structure of twelve ministries and a vastly expanded prime minister's office, an arrangement presumably better suited to the needs of the new age. As critics of the reform have maintained, however, the result involves a reshuffling of state functions and almost no net reduction in the overall size of the Japanese state. Systematic reform of the practices of bureaucratic administration that are so critical in sustaining Japan's system of discretionary and politicized bureaucratic administration still awaits the emergence of a constellation of political forces capable of pushing such a program forward.

Conclusion

As the preceding discussion has demonstrated, regulatory reform in Japan has been framed by an official administrative reform movement centered around the activities of a series of governmental commissions unattached to any specific ministry or agency. The contrast between the tremendous amount of time and energy that has gone into producing the mountain of reports issued by these commissions over the past decade and a half and the modest levels of regulatory reform actually achieved in Japan would appear to suggest that the format has not been a particularly efficient means of attaining regulatory reform. Why, one might legitimately ask, has a "movement" of this sort survived so tenaciously? Is it strictly institutional inertia that accounts for this? Official claims to the contrary, these commissions have not been strictly neutral, disinterested players analyzing issues from an academic standpoint. As the preceding sections of this chapter elucidate, their actions have been both attuned to and affected by the economic and political context in which they have operated.

Perhaps most fundamental is the way in which the structure of the Japanese political system creates a need for an institutional arrangement such as that of these commissions to promote regulatory reform. As analysts of Japanese politics have noted, the state bureaucracy and its often highly informal regulatory behavior pervade Japanese economy and society, and by the same token this pervasive state presence is also one characterized by a tendency toward fragmentation as a consequence of a high degree of sectionalism among bureaucratic agencies and a capturing of regulatory policy by the sectional interests of the bureaucrats, ruling party politicians, and associated interest groups. Meaningful deregulation in any given sector is unlikely to be produced in a milieu of this sort, for it would in most instances undercut the interests of the "iron triangles" associated with the subgovernments that produce policies under normal circumstances. For this reason a system of this sort virtually mandates the creation of an organ outside the normal channels of subgovernmental politics to articulate and promote regulatory reform, and it is also for this reason that those who do come to have an interest in promoting regulatory reform find it advisable to use these specially created commissions as a vehicle for promoting their particular agendas.

The very fact that the commissions are created outside the normal institutional structure of policymaking means, however, that they do not control the levers of power and authority that drive policy in the Japanese system and cannot unilaterally impose their recommendations. Thus, if commission recommendations on regulatory reform are to reach the implementation stage, it is necessary to gain the backing of individuals, groups, and interests that do have access to institutionally based power and authority in the system. The relative success of the original Rinchō in attaining its agenda of fiscal retrenchment without a tax increase through the previously described Rinchō coalition offers a case in point. The failure of the Gyōkakushin to realize its proposals once that coalition crumbled provides a counterillustration.

The tenuousness of the movement's connection to the levers of institutionalized policymaking authority in the Japanese system explains the stop-go character of the visibility and impact of the Japanese administrative reform movement, and to date it is this dimension of the development of the movement that has been the most conspicuous. Another point that emerges out of the material presented in this chapter, however, is that the movement has had a cumulative aspect. This is in what might be termed the "ideological" dimension. Although severely constrained in their ability to ensure that their recommendations are implemented, the administrative reform commissions have managed to establish a considerable degree of ideological legitimacy. Substantively, there has been over time a deepening and expansion of the issues and proposals being put forward by the movement, as the progression from a focus on fiscal retrenchment to deregulation and then wholesale administrative overhaul illustrates. And although this influence on the part of the movement remains primarily ideological in nature—and for that matter one that coexists with strong mercantilist tendencies—there are signs that it is beginning to have an impact on "real" politics as illustrated by the emergence of political parties who have built their identities around regulatory reform, the 1996 "administrative reform" election, and, most recently, the overhaul being pursued under the guise of the Hashimoto reform plan. In the end, however, progress on promoting and implementing administrative reform will inevitably be sporadic at best until an appropriate vehicle can be established in the arena of Japanese party politics that can translate the ideological support into a systematic and sustained reconstitution of the Japanese state and its practices.

Notes

1. From the home page of the Management and Coordination Agency, April 19, 1997, World Wide Web URL http://www.somucho.go.jp/gyoukan/kanri/a_00.html.

2. Steven K. Vogel, *Freer Markets, More Rules: Regulatory Reform in Advanced Industrialized Countries* (Cornell University Press, 1996), pp. 43–50, for the United Kingdom; and James W. McKie, "US Regulatory Policy," in Kenneth Button and Dennis Swann, eds., *Age of Regulatory Reform* (Oxford: Clarendon, 1989), pp. 33–35.

3. Ito Takatoshi, *The Japanese Economy* (MIT Press, 1993), p. 168.

4. Ellis S. Krauss and Jon Pierre, "The Decline of Dominant Parties: Parliamentary Politics in Sweden and Japan," in T. J. Pempel, ed., *Uncommon Democracies: The One-Party Dominant Regimes* (Cornell University Press, 1990), pp. 226–59; Kent Calder, *Crisis and Compensation: Public Policy and Political Stability in Japan, 1949–1986* (Princeton University Press, 1988), pp. 214–26. In addition to acting as a pressure for fiscal expansion, these developments promoted a conspicuous deepening and broadening of state oversight over various sectors of society. The most commonly used indicators of this expansion are the flood of new legislation during this period and, of course, the mushrooming of subsidies and fiscal expenditures.

5. Rinchō was the second provisional commission in light of the fact that it was preceded by a first commission on administrative reform established in 1962 and disbanded in 1964.

6. "Gyōsei kaikaku ni kansuru dai sanji tōshin: Kihon tōshin" (Third report on administrative reform: Basic report), in Rinchō Gyōkakushin OB Kai, ed., *Rinchō gyōkakushin: Gyōsei kaikaku 2000 nichi no kiroku* (Rinchō and Gyōkakushin: A record of 2,000 days of administrative reform) (Tokyo: Gyōsei kanri kenkyū sentaa, 1987), pp. 165–249.

7. Ibid., p. 170.

8. Ibid., p. 167.

9. "Gyōsei kaikaku ni kansuru dainiji tōshin: Kyoninka tō no gorika" (Second report on administrative reform: The rationalization of licensing, etc.) (February 10, 1982), in Rinchō Gyōkakushin OB Kai, *Rinchō gyōkakushin,* pp. 154–64.

10. For instance, Maki Tarō, *Shōsetsu dokō rinchō* (Dokō's Rinchō: A novel) (Tokyo: Kadokawa shoten, 1986), pp. 178–84; Ōtake Hideo, *Jiyūshugiteki kaikaku no jidai: 1980-nendai no nihon seiji* (The age of liberal reforms: Japanese politics in the 1980s) (Tokyo: Chūō kōron sha, 1994), p. 85.

11. Based on Masumi Junnosuke, *Contemporary Politics in Japan* (University of California Press, 1995), pp. 408–17; Daiichi Ito, "Policy Implications of Administrative Reform," in J. A. A. Stockwin, and others, eds., *Dynamic and Immobilist Politics in Japan* (University of Hawaii Press, 1988), pp. 77–105; Ōtake, *Jiyūshugiteki kaikaku no jidai;* Iio Jun, *Min'eika no seiji katei: Rinchōgata kaikaku no seika to genkai* (The political process of privatization: The accomplishments and limits of Rinchō-style reform) (Tokyo: Tōkyō daigaku shuppankai, 1994); Leon Hollerman, *Japan Disincorporated* (Stanford, Calif.: Hoover Institution Press, 1988); and Shumpei Kumon, "Japan Faces Its Future: The Political Economics of Administrative Reform," *Journal of Japanese Studies,* vol. 10, no. 1 (1984), pp. 143–63.

12. Lonny E. Carlile, "Party Politics and the Japanese Labor Movement: Rengo's 'New Political Force,'" *Asian Survey,* vol. 24 (July 1994), pp. 301–16; Lonny E. Carlile, "*Sōhyō* versus *Dōmei:* Competing Streams of Labour Movement Strategy in the Era of High Growth in Japan," *Japan Forum,* vol. 6 (October 1994), pp. 145–57.

13. Mike Mochizuki, "Public Sector Labor and the Privatization Challenge: The Railway and Telecommunications Unions," in Gary D. Allinson and Yasunori Sone, eds., *Political Dynamics in Contemporary Japan* (Cornell University Press, 1993), pp. 181–99.

14. "Gyōsei kaikaku ni kansuru daigoji tōshin" (Fifth report on administrative reform) in Rinchō Gyōkakushin OB Kai, *Rinchō gyōkakushin,* p. 266.

15. Mainichi shinbunsha shuzai han, *Kasumigaseki shindorōmu: "Kan'eki" kokka no uragawa* (The Kasumigaseki syndrome: Behind the scenes in the "bureaucracy-enriching" state) (Tokyo: Mainichi shinbunsha, 1994), pp. 114–15.

16. For a review of developments during Gyōkakushin I, see Rinchō Gyōkakushin OB Kai, *Rinchō gyōkakushin,* pp. 67–117; Iio, *Min'eika no seiji katei,* pp. 105–15.

17. For discussion, see Namikawa Shino, *Zukai: Gyōsei kaikaku no shikumi* (An illustrated guide to the mechanics of administrative reform) (Tokyo: Tōyō keizai shinpō sha, 1997), pp. 59–62.

18. The official versions of the activities of Gyōkakushin I can be found in Rinji Gyōsei Kaikaku Suishin Shingikai Jimutshitsu, ed., *Gyōkakushin: Zen shigoto* (The Gyōkakushin: Complete works) (Tokyo: Gyōsei, 1990), pp. 11–19. For Gyōkakushin III, see Rinji Gyōsei Kaikaku Suishin Shingikai Jimushitsu, ed., *Dai sanji Gyōkakushin teigenshū: Shin jidai no gyōsei kaikaku shishin* (Collection of recommendations of the Third Gyōkakushin: Directions for administrative reform in a new era) (Tokyo: Gyōsei Kanri kenkyū sentaō, 1994), pp. 7–21.

19. Otake Hideo, "The Rise and Retreat of Neo-liberal reform: Controversies over Land Use Policy," in Allinson and Sone, *Political Dynamics in Contemporary Japan,* pp. 242–63.

20. See Lonny E. Carlile, "'Industrial Policy' and Organized Business on the Other Side of the Developmental State: The Japanese Construction Industry, 1967–1987," CAPRI Special Series 3 (Vancouver, B.C.: Institute of Asian Research, University of British Columbia, 1993).

21. See, for instance, Ellis Krauss and Elizabeth Coles, "Built-in Impediments: The Political Economy of the US-Japan Construction Dispute," in Kozo Yamamura, ed., *Japan's Economic Structure: Should It Change?* (Seattle: Society for Japanese Studies, 1990), pp. 333–58.

22. Ōtake, *Jiyūshugiteki kaikaku no jidai,* pp. 189–238.

23. For detailed discussion of the political economy of the Japanese construction industry, see Brian Woodall, *Japan under Construction: Corruption, Politics, and Public Works* (University of California Press, 1996).

24. Miyaji Soshichi, "Nejimagerareru! 'Minkan katsuryoku'" (It's being distorted! "Private sector vitality"), *Trace,* December 1, 1985, pp. 2–4.

25. See Miyamoto Ken'ichi, *Hojokin no seiji keizaigaku* (The political economy of subsidies) (Tokyo: Asahi shinbunsha, 1990), pp. 27–38.

26. Vogel, *Freer Markets, More Rules,* pp. 137–66.

27. For details, see Yukio Noguchi, "The 'Bubble' and Economic Policies in the 1980s," *Journal of Japanese Studies,* vol. 20 (Summer 1994), pp. 291–329.

28. "Gyōsei kaikaku ni kansuru daigoji tōshin," in Rinchō Gyōkakushin OB Kai, *Rinchō gyōkakushin,* p. 266.

29. For dates and titles of these administrative reform outlines, see *Gyōsei no kanri to sōgō chōsei* (The management and comprehensive coordination of government administration) (1995), pp. 305–10.

30. *Kisei kanwa suishin no genkyō* (The current status of deregulation) (1996), appendix 4, contains a list of dates and formal titles of these laws.

31. Keidanren, "Kisei kanwa ni kansuru yōbō (chūkan torimatome): Kihontekina kangaekata" (Requests concerning deregulation [interim assessment]: Basic thinking) (March 31, 1988), in *Keidanren geppō,* vol. 36 (May 1988), pp. 8–11.

32. See the summaries of sector-specific proposals listed in *Keidanren geppō,* vol. 36 (May 1998), pp. 12–22; as well as the articles in the series "Kisei kanwa no suishin o motomeru" (We seek the promotion of deregulation) published in that journal in 1988 and 1989.

33. On this point, see the various issues of *Trace* published during this period.

34. Reproduced in Rinji Gyōsei Kaikaku Suishin Shingikai Jimushitsu, *Gyōkakushin,* pp. 369–92.

35. "Sōri to gyōkakushin iin to no kondan ni okeru naikaku sōridaijin aisatsu" (Remarks of the prime minister at discussions between the prime minister and Gyōkakushin commissioners) (December 19, 1988), ibid., pp. 533–35.

36. Gavan McCormack, *Afterbubble: Fizz and Concrete in Japan's Political Economy,* Japan Policy Research Institute Working Paper 21 (Cardiff, Calif.: Japan Policy Research Institute, June 1996); Ulrike Schaede, "The 1995 Financial Crisis in Japan,"

Japan Information Access Project Deregulation Forum Paper (Washington, D.C.: Japan Information Access Project, February 1996).

37. Leonard J. Schoppa, *Bargaining with Japan: What American Pressure Can and Cannot Do* (New York: Columbia University Press, 1997).

38. For an illustrative case study involving the MOF and the securities industry, see E. B. Keehn, "Virtual Reality in Japan's Regulatory Agencies," in Harald Baum, ed., *Japan: Economic Success and Legal System* (Berlin and New York: Walter de Gruyter, 1997), pp. 321–30. For a nuanced discussion of the dynamics of Japanese bureaucratic politics in the late 1980s and early 1990s, see Muramatsu Michio, "Patterned Pluralism under Challenge: The Policies of the 1980s," in Allinson and Sone, *Political Dynamics in Contemporary Japan*, pp. 50–71.

39. Nihon keizai shinbunsha, *Kanryō: Kishimu kyodai kenryoku* (Bureaucrats: Giant power creaking) (Tokyo: Nihon keizai shinbunsha, 1994), pp. 15–16. At the time of Gyōkakushin III's formation in 1990, chairman Suzuki Eiji vowed that there would be "no sacred cows" in the commission's deliberation of administrative reform. It is worthy of note that there was some degree of resistance to the selection of the outspoken Suzuki. See Hayabusa Nagaharu and Namikawa Shino, *"Kasumigaseki" ga habamu nihon no kaikaku: "Toyokana kurashi" gyōkaku an wa donoyōnishite honenuki ni saretaka* ("Kasumigaseki" prevents Japan's reform: This is how the "fulfilling lifestyle" administrative reform proposal was undercut) (Tokyo: Daiyamondo sha, 1993), pp. 4–7.

40. Account based primarily on Mainichi shinbunsha shuzai han, *Kasumigaseki shindorōmu*, pp. 92–104.

41. Nihon keizai shinbunsha, *Kanryō*, pp. 15–16; Mainichi shinbunsha shuzai han, *Kasumigaseki shindorōmu*, pp. 104–12.

42. Taro Yayama, "The Recruit Scandal: Learning from the Causes of Corruption," *Journal of Japanese Studies*, vol. 16 (Winter 1990), pp. 93–114; Peter J. Herzog, *Japan's Pseudo-democracy* (Folkestone, Kent: Japan Library, 1993), pp. 175–88.

43. Jiro Yamaguchi, "The Gulf War and the Transformation of Japanese Constitutional Politics," *Journal of Japanese Studies*, vol. 18 (Winter 1992), pp. 155–72.

44. Ōtake Hideo, "Forces for Political Reform: The Liberal Democratic Party's Young Reformers and Ozawa Ichiro," *Journal of Japanese Studies*, vol. 22 (Summer 1996), pp. 269–94; Chalmers Johnson, *Japan: Who Governs? The Rise of the Developmental State* (New York and London: Norton, 1995), pp. 212–31; Herzog, *Japan's Pseudo-democracy*, pp. 188–95, 268–70.

45. This conclusion is based on the accounts presented in Mainichi shinbunsha shuzai han, *Kasumigaseki shindorōmu*, and Nihon keizai shinbunsha, *Kanryō*.

46. Nakatani Iwao and Ōta Hiroko, *Keizai kaikaku no bijon: "Hiraiwa repōto" o koete* (A vision of economic reform: Beyond the "Hiraiwa Report") (Tokyo: Tōyō keizai shinpō sha, 1994), pp. 116–88, passim.

47. Keizai Kaikaku Kenkyūkai, "Kisei kanwa ni tsuite (chūkan hōkoku)" (On deregulation [interim report]) (November 8, 1993) ibid., appendix 1.

48. Sōmuchō, *Kisei kanwa suishin no genkyō* (July 1995), pp. 176–78.

49. For the plan and a detailed official review of the deregulation process, see Sōmuchō, *Kisei kanwa suishin no genkyō* (July 1995). Subsequent editions of this deregulation white paper contain the amended versions resulting from the annual review process.

50. For "insider" details on developments in the Hiraiwa Commission, as well as the commission's interim and final reports, see Nakatani and Ōta, *Keizai kaikaku no bijon*.

51. For a description of the formal institutional mechanisms involved, see Sōmuchō, *Kisei kanwa suishin no genkyō* (1995), pp. 58–64.

52. It was true that the Democratic Socialist party and the Clean Government party, both small opposition parties, backed legislation stemming from the Rinchō initiatives of the mid-1980s and that the Socialist party, reflecting the interests of the public sector unions backing it, opposed legislation such as that which privatized Japan's public corporations. However, under an LDP majority, the eventual passage of such legislation was a foregone conclusion and none of the non-LDP parties played a significant role in formulating administrative reform proposals.

53. Ichiro Ozawa, *Blueprint for a New Japan: The Rethinking of a Nation* (Tokyo: Kodansha, 1994). The NFP was formed out of an amalgamation of several preexisting parties with radically different organizational structures and bases of electoral support. In practice, therefore, it inherently housed a variety of contradictory views on regulatory reform.

54. For a discussion and analysis of the decisionmaking processes in these cabinets, see Nakano Minoru, "Seikai saihen ki no rippō katei: Henka to renzoku" (The legislative process during a period of political realignment: Change and continuity), *Leviathan*, vol. 18 (1996), pp. 71–95; Nihon keizai shinbunsha, *"Renritsu seiken" no kenkyū* (A study of "coalition government") (Tokyo, 1994).

55. For a critique along similar lines focusing primarily on foreign policy, see Mikuriya Takashi, "Jishasa 'kettei sakiokuri' no kōzō" (The structure of LDP-SDPJ-Sakigake "decision postponement"), *Chūō kōron*, March 1996, pp. 62–71.

56. Jon Choy, "Administrative Reform in Japan: Tokyo Confronts Downsizing," *JEI Report*, March 7, 1997, p. 8.

57. Kan Naoto, *Nihon daitenkan* (Japan in transformation) (Tokyo: Kōbunsha, 1996), p. 110.

58. On the Democratic party and its positions, see Igarashi Fumihiko, *Korega minshutō da: Jiritsu to kyōsei no shimin chūshin gata shakai e* (This is the Democratic party: Toward a society based on self-reliance and community) (Tokyo: Taiyō kikaku shuppan, 1996). For Sakigake, see its policy platform, which was available April 1997, World Wide Web URL http://www.coara.or.jp/07E~sakigake/pol/taikou#K1.

59. Thanks to a steady trickle of defecting Diet members from the NFP and other parties, the LDP did eventually regain its majority in the Lower House by late 1997. However, the party still did not have a majority in the Upper House, and for that reason the Hashimoto government continued to require the support of its coalition partners.

60. Hashimoto Ryūtarō, "Bappontekina gyōsei kaikaku ni shidōryoku o hakki" (Showing leadership in comprehensive administrative reform), *Jiyū minshu,* no. 523 (October 1996), pp. 44–54.

61. Jiyu minshu tō Gyōsei Kaikaku Suishin Honbu, "Hashimoto gyōkaku no kihon hōkō ni tsuite" (On the basic direction of the Hashimoto administrative reform), June 18, 1996, World Wide Web URL http://www.sphere.ad.jp/idp/saisin/saisin-12b.html.

62. Makoto Sato, "Hashimoto Taking a Shaky Helm," *Nikkei Weekly,* November 4, 1996, pp. 1, 4.

63. Outlined in Ministry of Foreign Affairs, "Reforms and the Creation of a New Era Society: The Six Reform Packages of the Hashimoto Administration," n.d., World Wide Web URL http://www2.nttca.com:8010/infomofa/domestic/6reforms.html.

64. See Kent E. Calder, "Linking Welfare and the Developmental State: Postal Savings in Japan," *Journal of Japanese Studies,* vol. 16 (Winter 1990), pp. 31–61.

65. For a detailed account, see Mukaidani Susumu, "Yūsei min'eika hidaruma no kōbō" (The fiery fight over postal services privatization), *Bungei shunjū,* vol. 75 (December 1997), pp. 110–25. See also "Meisō no butai ura: Kensentsu-Nagatachō e kanbu o sōdōin, gikan mo hashiru," *Asahi shinbun,* November 20, 1997.

66. The ARCounc's interim report could be accessed (January 15, 1998), World Wide Web URL http://www.kantei.go.jp/jp/gyokaku/0905nakaho-01.html.

67. The ARCounc's final report could be accessed (January 15, 1998), World Wide Web URL http://www.kantei.go.jp/jp/gyokaku/report-final/.

CHAPTER FIVE

The "Illiberal" Roots of Japanese Financial Regulatory Reform

Elizabeth Norville

Japan has undertaken a dramatic restructuring of the regulatory arrangements in its financial sector in recent decades. Since the mid-1970s, the authorities have liberalized interest rates, relaxed international capital controls, permitted firms to offer a much broader range of products and services, and removed some of the functional divisions within the financial services sector. Most recently, the government's "Big Bang" reform scheme announced with great fanfare in late 1996 promises radical liberalization of all aspects of Japan's financial regulatory system. If all goes according to this plan, Japan will be the home of "free, fair, and global" financial markets by the year 2001.

The considerable fallout from the bursting of the asset bubble, including Japan's mountainous bad-debt problem and endless spate of financial scandals, has reinforced the view that ineluctable pressure to enhance market efficiency is driving Japanese regulators to adopt an Anglo-American–style regulatory regime. Arguing along these lines, two analysts wrote in 1994 that Japan's financial sector was becoming "a highly competitive, market-based financial system where government regulation focuses on prudential regulation for system safety and protection against various forms of moral hazard, while leaving the allocation of financial resources to the marketplace."[1] Also reflecting widespread sentiment, another Japan watcher has pronounced the developmental

I thank Katsuhiko Hiyama and Tu-Nga Nguyen for valuable research assistance.

state dead. He argues that the Ministry of Finance (MOF) in particular has veered off in an "antidevelopmental" direction, "retarding growth, fighting vainly against market trends, and acting selfishly to protect its vested interests."[2] Day-to-day press accounts of the 1990s similarly paint the picture of a grueling sumo-wrestling match between the MOF and the marketplace. And for many, the battle appears to be over. Certainly the failures of large Japanese financial institutions in 1997 suggest that the MOF may have finally lost its grip, succumbing to the ferocious disciplinary bind of the marketplace.

Is Japan truly becoming a liberal pea in an increasingly open global financial pod? At this historic juncture in Japanese financial history, it is important to maintain proper perspective on Japanese financial regulation and the reform process. Here I suggest that the "revisionist" paradigm, which assigns the state a critical role in guiding the economy, continues to shed the best light on the process of financial restructuring in Japan. Financial regulatory reform in Japan is not simply about establishing fair and transparent rules that will allow the full swing of the market mechanism in order to maximize efficiency. Rather, it is first about the state's ongoing attempts to shape market forces along lines that will enrich and empower Japan. Second, the reform story is about the MOF's dramatic efforts to maintain bureaucratic discretion over the collection and dispersal of Japan's considerable wealth.

An elaborate administrative apparatus for consultation and coordination with the private sector has given the finance ministry substantial infrastructural powers with which to penetrate and centrally coordinate the activities of financial firms. The traditional "convoy fleet system" of governance captures the MOF's dual role as master and patron of Japan's private financiers. The hierarchic organization of finance in Japan has inspired the image of a warship escorting a convoy of ships. The MOF has customarily set the course and ensured that all financial institutions proceeded in lockstep. Under the convoy system, the weakest ships in effect determine the pace of the entire fleet. As economist Yukio Noguchi comments, "Many people think the objective of the Japanese government is the promotion of large corporations in strategic industries. But I see it as protection for low-productivity sectors."[3]

Consistent with the revisionist perspective, this chapter probes the notably "illiberal" strategic rationale behind Japanese financial regulatory reform and the peculiarly Japanese style of carrying out regulatory change. I suggest below that Japanese financial liberalization reflects an aggressive attempt by the MOF to harness the waves of the global product cycle. That is, MOF bureaucrats have hammered out industrial adjustment policies pragmatically, flexibly, and gradually in response to rapidly changing patterns of national comparative advantage in the world's financial service sector. In tracing this process, I identify three phases of industrial development, each associated with a distinct constellation of regulatory arrangements designed to manipulate the flow of Japanese capital toward strategic ends. Japan's "infant" financial industry graduated to the "immature international" phase of development at the end of the 1970s. Presently, a push is under way to carry Japanese finance into the next stage, "mature internationalization." This is the express purpose of the current Big Bang.

The "Infant Industry" Phase

Japan's strategic circumstances following World War II led regulators to reconstruct a new financial system on the foundations of the wartime regulatory regime. They sought to devise a financial system that would both channel Japan's scarce capital toward the development of export-oriented heavy industry at low cost and maximize government control over financial institutions and markets. Japan's military reliance on the United States also influenced the financial mobilization effort. Specifically, the Korean War spurred development of industrial finance arrangements in Japan as U.S. demand for Japanese products for this cold war effort intensified the need to pool investment capital.

Several design features of the newly constructed regulatory apparatus facilitated Japanese aims. First, the regulators in the MOF assigned banks the most prominent role in the financial intermediation process. To cope with the country's capital shortage, they evolved a system of bank "overloans." Special borrowing privileges from the Bank of Japan allowed the nation's twelve city banks to extend more credit than they acquired from deposits or their capital base. In turn, corporations borrowed from these banks beyond their ability to repay. The regulators possessed ultimate control over lending decisions in this system of interdependencies among industry, finance, and the government. To supplement this lending arrangement, the government created the Japan Development Bank and the Export-Import Bank to subsidize favored investment and export sectors. The substantial funds for these public banks came from Japanese households, whose savings were channeled through the nation's extensive postal-savings system to the Fiscal Investment and Loan Program for dispersal to these and other public financial institutions.

Second, beyond the bias toward credit over capital markets, the regulators established a system with a high degree of functional segmentation. Japan's Article 65 of the Securities Transaction Law, the equivalent of the U.S. Glass-

Steagall Act, separated securities houses and Japanese banks. Four securities firms dominated the industry, whereas the more significant, banking sector was subdivided into different types of institutions with highly specialized activities. Besides the twelve city banks, the industrial finance system was dominated by one foreign exchange bank, three long-term credit banks specializing in long-term industrial lending, and seven trust banks responsible for managing trusts and pension funds. Heavy restrictions on product markets curtailed entry and exit into the "sacred territory" of each industrial segment. Each cartelized industrial segment was headed by a lead firm. This segmentation around highly structured markets was intended to give order and stability to the financial system and to enhance the MOF's administrative guidance.

Third, the regulators instituted tight controls on the rates offered by various financial instruments in order to keep the cost of capital at bargain-basement levels for industry. Households earned low interest rates on their savings deposited in banks and the postal-savings system, wheras industry borrowed money at artificially low rates. Controls on capital costs stimulated "excess" demand for capital and permitted the regulators to ration capital toward favored industrial sectors.

Finally, the financial regulators instituted an extremely tight system of supervision over foreign exchange. The Foreign Exchange and Foreign Trade Control Law (1949) provided the legal framework for the bureaucratic prohibition of all external transactions except for those that could be shown to have positive consequences for the Japanese economy. The shortage of foreign exchange and the need to protect Japanese industry encouraged the establishment of these restrictions. By insulating the domestic financial system, such capital controls facilitated the high degree of functional specialization of markets and institutions and the suppression of the price mechanism.

The results of Japan's tightly regulated financial system in this first infant industry phase were impressive. The regulatory arrangements greatly reinforced the hierarchic pattern of governance associated with the convoy system and gave the MOF nearly unlimited discretion over the flow of funds. The exceptionally high rates of savings, industrial productivity, and overall economic growth equated with Japan's "economic miracle" all indicate that the banking system was a highly effective mechanism for collecting domestic savings and channeling them into industrial development. Through intensive capital investment, Japan's government and business elite shifted the country's industrial structure as a whole through the global product cycle, as reflected in the shift in the composition of exports from lower to toward higher value-added products and the movement in Japan's trade and current account from chronic deficits to chronic surpluses. It took the country only about two decades to reverse its global financial position from a debtor-borrower nation to a creditor-lender nation. In sum, the MOF deserves very high marks on both the state "capacity-building" and "effectiveness" counts of strategic success during this era.

The "Immature Internationalization" Phase

Catching up to the West economically introduced a whole new set of strategic imperatives that worked to push Japan into the immature international phase of financial development. Prompted by the macroeconomic and industrial concerns detailed here, the MOF began to support the overseas expansion of Japanese financiers at the outset of the 1980s against a backdrop of extensive protection at home. Although some modest internal opening did occur in Japan before the loosening of capital controls, domestic market liberalization generally lagged behind external liberalization. This fundamental order of financial liberalization was deliberate. On the promotional side, the MOF sought to encourage the international competitive development of the financial sector by exposing Japanese firms to market forces in relatively less regulated markets abroad. On the protective side, the MOF preferred to delay the opening of financial markets at home until Japanese institutions had honed their competitive skills. The MOF appreciated the risk of perpetuating domestic protection. If a home cannot keep up with the liberalization process abroad, financial institutions and markets will migrate to locations with more congenial regulatory settings.[5] Regulatory competition with more advanced financial sectors has thus been a key force pushing Japan down the path of financial liberalization.

The Macroeconomic Dimension: Saving for the Future

Financial market liberalization became an important avenue to macroeconomic security for Japan beginning in the 1970s. Unlike in the United States, where the country's external payments position is essentially a by-product of other policies, the Japanese actively pursue international payments goals. Japan's industrial mobilization had paid off on the country's balance of payments. By the early 1970s, Japan had achieved a current account surplus and essentially settled its small international debt, moving the nation into the international investment position of "young creditor." Long-term projections about Japan's future investment needs and savings rates in the twenty-first century provided a rationale for perpetuating, if not increasing, disequilibrium in the nation's international accounts. Since Japan reached young creditor status, the MOF has employed, sequentially, two basic methods for maintaining and expanding Japan's strategically attractive international macroeconomic position. Both strategies would require financial liberalization.

In the early 1970s, and during the first oil crisis in particular, the MOF avoided balance-of-payments adjustment through deficit spending. Expanding government debt, as is frequently recognized, became the spur that set the process of Japanese financial liberalization in motion.[6] To better facilitate its own borrowing needs in the mid-1970s, the MOF initiated regulatory reform in the government bond market. However, the MOF was never much enchanted with the Keynesian solution to the problem of excess savings and soon turned to an alternative strategy for maintaining the country's current account surplus. The shift to a capital export strategy had significant implications for financial regulatory policy.

At the end of the decade, the MOF reiterated its credo of fiscal austerity and began to tighten its belt. Given the domestic rates of savings and investment in Japan fiscal consolidation meant a substantial buildup of surplus capital, and under these conditions, continued economic growth became dependent on foreign absorption of Japan's surplus. Even without the expenditure-dampening effects of the MOF's fiscal consolidation program, various financial policies put in place during the high-growth era would have encouraged economic expansion based on foreign, rather than domestic, investment. Through its tax policies and its financial treatment of land, the MOF effectively blocked investment opportunities at home and in doing so contributed to the expansion of Japanese capital formation internationally.[7] Throughout the 1980s, the MOF stood as a major bastion of resistance as Japan's trading partners increased pressure on the country to reduce its current account surplus through domestic demand-led growth. Those charged with overseeing Japan's economic performance pointed to changing national demographics as a threat to economic growth in the future that had to be alleviated now by generating excess national savings and lending them abroad.

The breakdown of the MOF's mechanism for financing debt resulted in some modest domestic financial reforms in the 1970s. The redirection of Japan's excess savings abroad in the 1980s led to a much more significant liberalization chapter in Japanese financial history that was geared toward internationalization. The passage of a new Foreign Exchange and Foreign Trade Law in 1980 altered the basic regulatory principle that all international transactions were to be "prohibited, unless excepted" to the new presumption of "free in principle, unless excepted." The law more or less ratified regulatory changes that were already underway and signaled a further relaxation of foreign exchange controls. In particular, the MOF began progressively to lift the limits on the foreign portfolio investments of institutional investors (table 5-1).

Japan's bilateral relationship with the United States played a critical role in shaping the course of Japan's evolution as a young creditor nation in the 1980s. At the same time that Japan graduated to the position of young creditor, the international investment position of the United States uncoincidentally began to degenerate.[8] As the United States descended deeply into debt, the strength of the dollar as the world's top currency became an important source of leverage for securing external financing and avoiding macroeconomic adjustment. The United States additionally took initiatives to tear down the restrictive international financial order it had constructed after World War II.[9] U.S. moves to sustain its chronic balance-of-payments deficit created opportunities for Japan to further improve its external payments position. Japan's external surplus expanded well beyond its 1970s range, and the growing surplus was accompanied by a tremendous expansion in the country's long-term capital exports. A significant share of those funds was invested in the United States. Through the 1980s Japanese investors put $20 billion to $50 billion a year, mostly in the form of portfolio investments, in U.S. financial markets.[10]

Official pronouncements aside, both Japan and the United States showed more interest in financing than in adjusting to the imbalance in their respective international accounts.[11] The Yen-Dollar Agreement of 1984, which essentially codified the mutually attractive lender-borrower arrangement between the United States and Japan, constitutes a significant piece of evidence to support this claim. Ironically, whereas the official rationale behind these United States–initiated financial negotiations was to correct the external payments imbalances of the two countries, the financial liberalization measures adopted by Japan under the 1984 agreement, as the Japanese team anticipated, had the opposite effect of reinforcing the imbalance.

The systemwide macroeconomic effect of this bilateral interplay was the formation of a new mechanism for external payments financing in the international monetary system. This new international regime represents a continua-

Table 5-1. Regulations on Foreign Investment by Japanese Institutional Investors, 1980–89

Upper limits on the ratio of foreign securities holding to total assets (%)

Date	Life insurance	Casualty insurance	Loan trusts and jointly managed money trusts	Pension trusts	Postal life insurance	Trust fund bureau
Total assets at the end of 1988 (in trillions of yen)	92.4	19.6	37.3	17.7	39.9	209.4
Situation in 1980	10	10	0	0	0	0
January 1981	10	10	0	10	0	0
May 1983	10	10	0	10	10	0
February 1986	10	10	1	10	10	0
March 1986	25	25	1	10	10	0
April 1986	25	25	1	25	10	0
June 1986	25	25	3	25	10	0
August 1986	30	30	3	30	10	0
April 1987	30	30	3	30	10	10
June 1987	30	30	3	30	20	10
February 1989	30	30	5	30	20	10

Source: Mitsuhiro Fukao, "Liberalization of Japan's Foreign Exchange Controls and Structural Changes in the Balance of Payments," *Bank of Japan*, September 1990, p. 45.

tion of the petrodollar recycling regime of the 1970s to the extent that private markets have continued to serve the function of creating international liquidity.[12] The key differences between the two regimes concern the source of finance, the type of borrower, and the nature of financial intermediation involved. Under the petrodollar recycling regime, OPEC nations supplied finance to numerous developing countries via foreign banks in London. That is, OPEC countries deposited their excess funds with foreign financial institutions, who in turn transferred them abroad at their discretion. Under the more recent regime, both the world's major lender and borrower were advanced industrial countries, and Japan's surplus tended to flow directly to the United States through Japanese financial institutions.

Promotion Policies for Financial Internationalization

To understand the strategic roots of Japanese financial reform, one must consider the strong preference in Japan for maintaining Japanese control over the allocation of the country's surplus. In light of the relative backwardness of the Japanese financial sector, the MOF and the financial institutions it regulated were confronted with the daunting task of internationalizing quickly so that Japanese financiers, not foreign ones, would be equipped to intermediate the transfer of Japan's excess savings abroad.

In an adaptation of the product cycle theory of foreign investment, Terutomo Ozawa suggests that "followers" are motivated to set up plants in more advanced countries in order "to capitalize on market conditions that they cannot enjoy at home such as the innovation-conducive atmosphere and the technological resources of advanced markets."[13] Like Japanese manufacturers in high-technology fields, the Japanese financial sector has had good reason to move offshore in order to gain access to the abundant technological resources of the U.S. financial industry. Although often viewed as an infrastructural industry, the financial service sector has in fact become an important lead sector in the international political economy in its own right.

Two important trends have in recent years intensified the competitive race in financial services: convergence and globalization.[14] Convergence refers to the erosion of traditional boundaries separating financial markets. It is associated with the twin developments of disintermediation, which refers to the shift of financial activities away from banks, and securitization, the increased use of securities instruments rather than loans. This blurring of traditional lines of business is rooted in a number of factors, including increased uncertainty in financial markets, regulatory barriers within market segments, and new tele-communications technology. In combination, these factors have heightened competitive pressures in the financial services sector and have put a premium on financial innovation. The proliferation of financial innovations has meant that traditionally distinct financial products have become close substitutes for one another, accelerating competition between different types of financial institutions. This dynamic has spurred the financial liberalization process across the advanced industrial world.

Globalization refers to the expansion of links between domestic and international financial markets, and it is largely an outcome of competitive deregulation. The post World War II growth of international manufacturing trade and investment, the development of new financial instruments, and technological advances in telecommunications and other high-technology fields have driven states to reduce financial regulatory barriers in order to capture a larger share of the growing international financial activity. The growth of Euromarkets has been a particularly significant source of competitive pressure on financial regulators. These "offshore," formally unregulated markets have been hothouses for financial innovations and have set the standards of efficiency for international competition.

Since the early 1980s, the "financial revolution" has threatened to leave the Japanese behind and since that time, the Japanese financial sector has been strongly motivated to catch-up technologically with the more mature financial industries of the United States and England. Behind the eagerness of Japanese financial firms to learn financial techniques that offer better ways to manage exchange and interest rate risks has been their need to follow their manufacturing clients abroad. At a more fundamental level, the Japanese financial sector was committed to performing the recycling function in the new international balance-of-payments financing regime. Lagging far behind their financial counterparts in the United States and Britain, Japanese financial institutions stood to lose this prerogative unless they learned how to operate competitively in international financial markets.

In the face of these multiple pressures the MOF actively supported the internationalization of the Japanese financial sector. With the blessing and support of the regulators, Japanese banks, securities houses, and life insurance companies have all flocked abroad to the world's top financial centers since the early 1980s. The overseas operations of Japanese banks expanded from 299 to 913 between 1980 and 1988. During the same period, securities houses more than tripled their foreign presence, expanding their offshore units from 65 to

196.[15] Japanese brokers channeled so much money from Japanese institutional investors into U.S. Treasury bond markets that the Federal Reserve Bank granted Japan's bigger securities houses primary dealer status in the late 1980s. External liberalization also led Japanese life insurers to become both important portfolio and direct investors in the United States after 1980. The foreign operations of the top ten Japanese life insurers (*seiho*) grew from virtually none in 1980 to eighty-four in fiscal year 1990.[16]

The Case of the Seiho

Establishing offshore operations in New York and London may be seen as an industrial offensive on the part of Japanese *seiho* hoping to gain competitive ground in the international arena. Rather than let the international market mechanism decide how the industry would be restructured, the MOF actively sought to "rationalize" the international process. A brief overview of the off-shore movement of *seiho* serves to illustrate the general strategy of catch-up undertaken by the financial sector during the 1980s, the peak period of "immature" internationalization.

The MOF encouraged life insurers to make certain types of portfolio and direct foreign investments in the United States beginning in the early 1980s. With the industry managing approximately 17 percent of Japanese personal savings, the regulators saw the *seiho* as an extremely important conduit for channeling Japanese savings into foreign investments. As a fund manager in a leading Japanese life insurance company stated in reference to an episode in the late 1980s when the MOF persuaded the *seiho* to buy U.S. treasury bonds against their own inclinations: "The ministry's banking bureau feels that Japan should recycle capital, but they don't have any money. So they look to the fat people even if there are low returns and high risk."[17] Although the overlap of public and private interests was not always complete, Japanese insurers generally had plenty of their own reasons for foreign expansion, including the need to find outlets for their burgeoning assets, the need to maintain overseas clients, and the desire to gain skills in "innovators'" markets.

The internationalization of the Japanese life insurance industry through the decade clearly bore the mark of patronage regulation. At home, the finance ministry kept life insurers tightly wrapped in a bundle of government regulations. Principle areas of business regulation included licensing, prohibitions on "noncore" business, strict regulations on financial and investment activities, accounting rules, and regulations on domestic affiliate companies. On the

Table 5-2. Overseas Subsidiaries of the Top Japanese Life Insurers (as of the end of FY 1987)

Function	Companies in rank order	Subsidiary name	Location	Date established
Real estate subsidiary	Nippon Life	Nissei Realty	New York	April 1, 1981
		NLI Properties Canada Inc.	Toronto	October 1, 1986
	Dai-ichi Life[a]	Dai-ichi Seimei America	New York	May 14, 1981
	Sumitomo Life	Sumitomo Life Realty (N.Y.), Inc.	New York	November 12, 1982
	Meiji Life	The Meijiseimei Realty of America Inc	New York	July 28, 1981
	Asahi Life	Asahi International Ltd	Atlanta	May 1, 1981
	Mitsui Life	Mitsui Seimei America Corporation	New York	August 29, 1983
	Yasuda Life	Yasuda Realty America Corporation	New York	June 27, 1980
	Taiyo Life	Taiyo Life Realty of America, Inc	New York	July 7, 1987
	Chiyoda Life	Chiyoda Life Realty of America, Inc.	New York	December 1, 1986
Insurance subsidiary	Nippon Life	Nissei Life America, Inc.	New York	August 1, 1984
	Dai-ichi Life	Dai-ichi Seimei Service (U.S.A.)	New York	June 3, 1985
	Sumitomo Life	Sumitomo Life Insurance Agency America, Inc	New York	June 4, 1986
	Meiji Life	Pacific Guardian Life Insurance Company Ltd.	Honolulu	August 3, 1961
		The Meisei International Services of America Inc.	New York	April 3, 1987
		The Meijiseimei Insurance Services of California Inc.	Los Angeles	February 11, 1988

Investment advisor/subsidiary				
Nippon Life	NLI BOT Asset Management		New York	March 7, 1984
	NLI Sheason Lehmon Hutton Ltd		London	May 19, 1987
Dai-ichi Life	Dai-ichi Seimei Fund Management		New York	August 22, 1986
Sumitomo Life	Sumitomo Life Ivory Asset Management (H.K.) Ltd.		Hong Kong	April 3, 1987
Meiji Life	The Meijiseimei Asset Management of America		New York	April 9, 1985
	The Meijiseimei International London		London	August 10, 1987
Asahi Life	Asahi Life Investment Europe Ltd		London	January 1, 1982
	Asahi America Inc.		New York	October 1, 1984
	Asahi Life Investment Hong Kong Ltd.		Hong Kong	March 18, 1988
Mitsui Life	Mitsui Life Asset Management America Corporation		New York	August 8, 1986
Yasuda Life	Yasuda Life International (London) Ltd.		London	November 6, 1986
Taiyo Life	Taiyo Asset Management of America Inc.		New York	April 24, 1986
	Taiyo Life International (U.K.) Ltd.		London	January 13, 1988
Chiyoda Life	Chiyoda Life Asset Management of America Inc.		New York	October 1, 1986
	Chiyoda Life Europe Ltd		London	August 18, 1987

Source: "The Seiho," Financial and Investment Committee, Life Insurance Association of Japan, September 1988.

a. Subsidiary of Dai-ichi Seimei Fund Management

insurance side of the business, premiums and dividend rates for the entire industry were also set by the MOF.

From this protected platform, the MOF promoted the industry's offshore business activities in the more open regulatory environment of the United States. The MOF's mechanisms for coordinating the internationalization of the Japanese life insurance industry in the 1980s are consistent with the general pattern of regulatory policymaking in the financial sector. Multilayered regulatory controls gave MOF bureaucrats a great deal of discretion in managing their client industries. The Insurance Industry Act provided the statutory basis for regulation. Supplementary ordinances issued by the cabinet gave the MOF additional regulatory authority. The lion's share of industry regulation, however, came from administrative guidance through written notifications and oral instructions.

The cartelized nature of the *seiho* enhanced the authority of the finance ministry. Compared with the United States, where there are some 2,000 life insurance companies, there are only 25 life insurance firms in Japan.[18] The MOF possessed an elaborate and routinized consultative framework for discussing regulatory issues with the industry. The Life Insurance Council (Hoken Shingikai) provided an official forum for formulating industrial policy. Leading firms also had day-to-day informal contacts with ministry officials. "Liaisons" from top firms would routinely spend several hours a day with MOF officials exchanging ideas and information. It was customary for the MOF to dispense information and advice to the lead firm, Nippon Life Insurance, which in turn transferred the information to the trade association for its dissemination to other companies.[19] A number of "study groups" constantly discussed regulatory issues.

The overseas march of Japanese insurers to the United States had three salient features. First, the *seiho* arrived in the United States in an orderly drove. Consistent with the convoy approach, the MOF laid out the basic parameters for internationalization and ensured that all financial institutions proceeded in lockstep. Once the ministry gave them the green light to expand into U.S. markets, firms in an industrial segment initiated their foreign expansion more or less in rank order. The leading insurers arrived in quick succession temporally, with the lead firm typically establishing the first foreign operation in each type of business the finance ministry allowed. Table 5-2 lists the foreign subsidiaries of the top Japanese life insurers in three functional categories through fiscal year 1987. The table classifies companies within each category according to their rank ordering in the industry.

Second, the overseas thrust of the *seiho* seemed a bit premature in light of the extreme backwardness of the sector, suggesting that mounting external pressures pushed them abroad long before they were prepared to compete in open markets. The industry's strict regulatory environment at home must be cited as a chief cause of the unfortunate reputation Japanese life insurers established in the international financial community during the 1980s as fat and a little dull. The *seiho* had lots of capital but completely lacked sophistication in the ways of the wide and fast-paced world of international finance when they roamed abroad.

Besides the high degree of bandwagoning behavior and lack of preparation, the *seiho*'s external advance proceeded with an eye toward knowledge acquisition. Because of the risks and opportunities associated with international finance, it became imperative for the *seiho* to become more sophisticated technically. A particularly important avenue for developing much needed financial expertise and knowledge about global markets was to establish links with U.S. securities houses. In April 1987 Nippon Life Insurance purchased a 13 percent share of Shearson Lehman Brothers Incorporated. Later that year, Yasuda Mutual Life Insurance Company bought an 18 percent share in the broker Paine Webber Group. The linkup was not expected to yield any immediate financial rewards, but rather was aimed at helping Japanese insurers gain valuable expertise. Such tie-ups were not allowed in Japan at the time, although insurers anticipated that they would be in the future. The regulators sought to protect insurers at home until they gained the requisite skills for operating in a more competitive domestic market.

The Consequences of External Liberalization

Did regulatory change during the immature international phase of development significantly further Japan's strategic agenda? Japan's external financial liberalization met the effectiveness criterion of strategic success to the extent that it served some key military and macroeconomic objectives. On the geopolitical front, Japanese financing of the U.S. budget and external payments has worked as a superb mechanism for stalling politically unwelcome burden-sharing in Japan's military relationship with the United States. The MOF undertook its capital recycling program at the same time that the Reagan administration launched an ambitious fiscal policy of military Keynesianism. Unfettered by regulatory restrictions, Japanese institutional investors became highly valued participants in U.S. Treasury bond auctions. The military strategic significance of Japanese portfolio investment in U.S. government bonds has not been lost on Japan's financial regulators. I borrow the label "Economic SDI" from Oba Tomomitsu, vice minister of the MOF during the early 1980s, who coined the term to capture the geopolitical dimension of U.S. and Japanese financial integration in the 1980s. Oba uses wordplay to imply that Japanese capital exports to the United States represented a "strategic defense initiative" (SDI) for Japan: that is, Japanese savings, used to finance the U.S. deficit, contributed directly to Japanese security, because they helped pay for Japan's defense.[20]

Besides rewarding Japan geopolitically, external financial opening brought about its intended macroeconomic results. Economic SDI allowed both Japan and the United States to avoid taking more drastic internal and external adjustment measures. Japanese regulators were able to maintain the desired macroeconomic imbalance between savings and spending. Externally, the Japanese supply of finance to the United States contributed to both macroeconomic and trade diplomacy between the two nations. The MOF's use of its informal regulatory controls to manipulate capital flows to the United States has been a key dimension of bilateral currency management. On the trade policy front, the external payments financing arrangement prevented much more severe trade measures for redressing the current account imbalance. And growing U.S. financial dependence gave Japan a new source of leverage in the bilateral relationship. Most significant, the acceleration of capital exports, supported by Japan's burgeoning trade surpluses, made Japan a very rich net creditor nation. The country began the 1980s with $11.5 billion in net foreign assets and closed the decade with $400 billion.[21]

In contrast to these geopolitical and macroeconomic successes, the MOF did not accomplish important industrial policy aims through its promotion of capital exports. It is fair to say that the MOF's effort to guide the financial sector through the global product cycle did not yield much fruit in terms of technology acquisition. A number of analysts have disparaged the capital-for-technology deals. For instance, based on their interviews with Japanese bankers and MOF officials, Mark Scher and Schon Beechler conclude that "to achieve internationalization, Japanese banks set up overseas branches in their major markets of New York, London, and Hong Kong, naively believing that the purchase of overseas assets would automatically result in the diffusion of knowledge and information back to the parent. This time banks found their expectations of acquiring badly-needed Western information and skills generally disappointed."[22] Eugene Dattel largely blames the finance ministry for what he believes is the failure of the overseas operations of Japanese financial institutions to "acquire skills or knowledge effectively, despite having had years of experience abroad. This rendered them unable to compete, either in new areas in Japan or overseas. The coveted technological or analytical knowledge was not absorbed or transferred to Japan, nor integrated within the corporation."[23]

In the case of Japan's life insurers, the immature internationalization phase may have yielded some technology transfer, but the cost was high. As a manager in Nippon Life's United States–Europe department states: "It is an undeniable fact that we suffered from substantial foreign exchange losses on our direct investments from an economic point of view. However, there are other unquantifiable but important factors that we cannot neglect, such as gaining technical knowledge, developing human resources, gathering information and constructing human networks."[24] Solvency problems within the industry during the 1990s provide sobering evidence that asset and liability management techniques in the industry are still weak and that the *seiho* have not been optimal recyclers of Japanese capital. Overall, it is fair to say that the United States maintained the competitive edge in financial engineering and the Japanese have been unable to "catch up."

The Failings of Patronage Regulation

Although external liberalization compelled a degree of regulatory loosening in Japan's domestic financial markets through the dynamic of competitive deregulation, it did not bring about any fundamental procedural change on the home front. The liberalization of market rules in Japan has mostly worked to sustain, and even bolster, the MOF's administrative powers. As would become painfully evident in the 1990s, the perpetuation of patronage-style financial regulation has seriously hampered the competitive development of Japanese financial institutions and jeopardized the health of the Japanese economy more generally.

The lifting of capital controls in the 1980s exposed the Japanese financial system to a host of international competitive pressures. To keep the "hollowing" threat at bay, the MOF relaxed market controls on all key dimensions of the old regulatory regime. The worldwide trend away from bank lending and the increased use of securities instruments put pressure on the regulators to develop the neglected capital market side of the financial system. The strengthening of the securities markets and institutions in turn generated pressures to relax the strict functional differentiation between industry segments. The MOF indicated its intentions for desegmentation in the early 1980s and deliberations about what shape the desegmentation should take began in 1985. The authorities also slowly but surely liberalized rates on financial instruments. The liberalization of deposit interest rates moved incrementally from large time to small time deposits through the decade. Finally, in the 1980s the MOF liberalized the range of products and services financial institutions were allowed to offer.

These market rule changes provided the MOF with new sources of leverage for inducing private sector compliance. First, financial liberalization enhanced the MOF's licensing authority as a source of power over the financial sector. As Steven Vogel states in reference to desegmentation, "The ministry itself would retain the discretion to determine the timing and the extent of cross-entry. . . . They effectively created a new queue for the all-important license for new subsidiaries. They knew well that they could make or break financial institutions depending on how they determined the order and timing of entry, and how they defined the scope of business in which the new subsidiaries could engage."[25] Second, liberalization further empowered the MOF by putting a premium on access to new regulatory information. The informal and opaque nature of MOF governing procedures means that financial institutions would go to great lengths to stay in the MOF's information loop, because being cut out of it could have serious repercussions for business. Thus, ironically, financial liberalization did not mean the retreat of the MOF from the marketplace.

There are a number of negative side effects associated with heavy state intervention in the marketplace for developmental purposes, which have long been recognized by revisionists. Prominent among these are "bureaucratic red tape, oligopoly, a political[ly] dangerous blurring of what is public and what is private, and corruption."[26] These unfortunate trade-offs are acceptable only as long as the developmental state achieves national strategic objectives. The MOF successfully promoted industrial expansion and maintained an orderly and stable financial system for decades. Recently, however, the MOF has combined ineffectiveness with inefficiency, oligopoly, and corruption, and the result has been a full-blown legitimacy crisis for the ministry.

Until the 1990s, the MOF's reputation for skillful guidance of the Japanese financial sector was intact. Between 1986 and 1990 the finance ministry warded off the recessionary effects of a soaring yen. Historically low interest rates of 2.5 percent contributed to the doubling, then tripling, of Japan's stock and property values. The famed asset bubble fueled the internationalization process, as Japanese corporations flooded the world with portfolio and direct investments. By Japanese Ministry of Construction calculations, Japan was in the financial position to purchase the whole of the United States four times over during the bubble years.[27] When the risks of the financial mania became apparent, the central bank, at the bidding of the MOF, began to deflate the bubble by raising interest rates. The abrupt end of the easy money era in turn led to the collapse of asset prices. The Tokyo Stock Exchange took a huge tumble and almost crashed in the summer of 1992, as the Nikkei average dropped from its 1989 high of 38,915 to less than 15,000. Likewise, the price of land has declined rapidly. By 1997, land prices were down 80 percent from their 1991 high.[28]

The bursting of the asset bubble is the proximate cause of a financial crisis of untold proportions and the longest recession in Japan's post–World War II history. In the 1990s, the evidence was everywhere that the MOF was fallible and even corrupt. Blame for Japan's deflated stock market and mountain of bad loans has been placed squarely on the lap of the finance ministry. The media feeding frenzy surrounding MOF mishaps has not let up since the crisis began. In the wake of the loss compensation scandal during the summer of 1991, the *Economist* reported that "the world's largest single source of capital and one of its three top financial centres is riddled with crookery, [and] has been supervised by the blind or the complacent."[29] The MOF's troubles seemed to snowball in the mid-1990s. Daiwa Bank's New York branch lost $1.1 billion in late 1995 and an employee was jailed for criminal activities that allegedly spanned more than a decade. The Daiwa Bank scandal exposed a number of weaknesses in the management of Japanese banks, as well as in the MOF's disclosure practices.

Although some view the MOF's efforts to engineer a "soft landing" for Japan's ailing financial community as preferable to shock therapy and a "hard landing," the ministry's management of the financial crisis has mostly drawn criticism. In the late 1980s the MOF's ability to prevent the Tokyo Stock Market from crashing was widely praised in global financial circles. The similar rigging of stock prices through price-keeping operations (PKOs), drew negative attention as evidence of Japan's backward collusionary regulatory practices in the 1990s. The bailout of seven insolvent housing loan companies (*jūsen*) created controversy, as taxpayers were targeted in MOF aid schemes. The *jūsen* represent only 15 percent of Japan's nonperforming loans, however, and the MOF's bigger headache has been to try and formulate rescue plans for financial institutions holding the other 85 percent of the bad debt total. The

MOF, which has notoriously understated the bad loan problem, admitted in January 1998 that Japanese banks hold approximately 76 trillion yen in bad loans, or 12% of their total loans and loan guarantees, which is 3.5 times as much as the MOF announced in September 1997.[30] In March 1998 the government allocated 30 trillion yen of the public's money to boost the capital of Japan's wobbly financial institutions. To make this measure politically palatable, proponents of the rescue plan had to sell taxpayers the idea that they were primarily interested in protecting depositors, investors, and policyholders and not in shoring up the weak financial institutions themselves.

Toward Mature Internationalization?

Japan's financial crisis and consequent economic stagnation, widely believed to be rooted in the country's traditional financial regulatory arrangements, have precipitated significant initiatives to push the financial sector into the "mature international" phase of development, which is characterized by a very high degree of market freedom for financial players both externally and at home. The regulators, who face the schizophrenic agenda of introducing more stability and more competition into the financial marketplace simultaneously, are feeling increasing pressure to tip the balance away from protective policies toward policies that will promote the competitive development of the financial sector. As economist Heizō Takenaka states: "Stabilization efforts should only be judged successful when the bad habits of banks, long protected by a market that allowed insufficient disclosure practices and the convoy system to flourish, are removed."[31] The following discussion of recent changes and continuities in Japan's financial regulatory regime suggests how far down the road the country has gone in the financial arena toward the institutions associated with liberal capitalism.

In November 1996, Prime Minister Hashimoto announced plans to undertake a sweeping reform of the country's financial system by the year 2001. Japanese banks, securities houses, and insurers were given fair warning to prepare for immersion into a market-driven domestic financial environment. For several months before its announcement the Big Bang reform program was nothing more than a pledge to revive the Tokyo market through structural reform with a five-year deadline. In June 1997, the five deliberation councils that have long been charged with hammering out the country's financial liberalization program unveiled some specific liberalization measures and a de-

Table 5-3. Big Bang Liberalization Measures

Date	Measure
December 1997	Investment-trust companies allowed to sell their products at banks.
March 1998	Financial institutions allowed to establish holding companies.
April 1, 1998	Revised Foreign Exchange and Foreign Trade Control Law takes effect, allowing companies and individuals to make foreign-exchange transactions without government authorization.
	Securities companies to be allowed to freely set commissions on securities trades of more than ¥50 million.
In fiscal 1998	Requirement for government licensing of securities brokerages to be eliminated.
	Banks to be allowed to sell their own investment trusts.
	Securities companies to be allowed to expand asset-management services.
In fiscal 1999	Banks to be allowed to issue straight bonds.
By end of 1999	Securities companies to be allowed to freely set commissions on securities trades of any size.
In second half of fiscal 1999	Barriers keeping banks, trust banks, and securities companies from entering one another's markets to be removed.
March 2000	Insurance companies to be allowed to enter banking sector.
March 2001	Banks and securities companies to be allowed to enter insurance sector.

Source: "Holding Companies at Core of Push toward Conglomerates," *Nikkei Weekly,* March 30, 1998.

tailed timetable. Market rule changes will proceed at an accelerated pace along well-established lines. Table 5-3 outlines the liberalization timetable for the Big Bang.

Market-opening legislation under the Big Bang includes the revision of the Foreign Exchange and Foreign Trade Control Law, which took effect on April 1, 1998. Although extensive reporting requirements remain, the new law removes the licensing requirement for foreign activities. The lifting of restrictions on foreign exchange transactions has led investors to shift yen-denominated savings into foreign currency instruments, especially dollar ones, offering higher returns. The ability of capital to migrate more freely overseas can be expected to hasten steps at home to increase efficiency and spur innovation in order to stave off the ever-present "hollowing" threat. Internally, the Big Bang is geared toward bringing Japanese financial institutions and markets up to world-class standards. Competition in home markets is expected to heat up following the removal of barriers to entry into different market segments. Banks and securities companies will first be allowed into each other's traditional lines of business in fiscal year 1999. The insurance sector's traditional domain will be opened up further by the end of 2001. The lifting of the ban on financial holding companies in March 1998 promises to contribute to greater efficiency in the development and sales of financial products, as financial institutions move to conglomerate. The reforms also aim to intensify competition domestically by giving financial institutions the liberty to offer new products and services, and to freely set all forms of commission.

Beyond the market rules, traditional governance arrangements in the regulatory regime have become important targets of reform. Loud and sweeping criticism of the finance ministry's mismanagement of the financial system has led to administrative reform legislation designed to break up the MOF's excessive concentration of power. The first revisions to the Bank of Japan Law in a half a century took effect in early 1998. The reorganization and procedural changes are designed to give the central bank more autonomy from the finance ministry, which traditionally keeps the Bank of Japan (BOJ) on a tight leash. Besides seeking to curb the MOF's power over monetary policy, administrative reforms have sought to diminish the MOF's control over financial institutions. The Financial Supervision Agency (FSA) was established midway through 1998 to license, supervise, and inspect financial institutions. This new independent regulatory body will house the Securities Exchange Surveillance Committee (SESC), which was established in 1992 to monitor the securities industry. The MOF retains its financial "planning" function, which it will tentatively carry out through a new bureau that combines the banking and securities bureaus.

Reforms introduced to change the method of financial oversight in Japan stand to eviscerate the MOF's patronage function, if they ever gain momentum. The MOF itself ceaselessly publicizes the need to replace "administrative guidance," its most cherished discretionary tool, with transparent and formal methods of supervision. Assuming the MOF follows through, its announcement in June 1998 that it would abandon all administrative "notifications" represents significant movement toward more formal and less opaque governance.[32] Similarly, the recent "prompt corrective action" reform, which requires lenders to meet explicit capital adequacy ratios and threatens punishment for those who do not, represents movement toward "harmonization" with international standards.

The extent to which the new flurry of reform legislation will actually bring about the devolution of MOF discretionary power and produce a method of arms-length regulatory supervision of Japan's financial players remains to be seen. At this point, the changes appear to be mostly cosmetic. The less than successful effort by MOF detractors to set up an independent regulatory agency along the lines of the U.S. Securities Exchange Commission (SEC) points to the MOF's formidable resistance to deep-seated change. The SESC began operation in 1992. If the SESC does in fact work like the independent U.S. SEC, then we should have by now witnessed some significant shift away from informal, opaque, and highly discretionary regulatory procedures toward formal, legalistic, transparent ones with equal regard for small and large investors in the securities business. Instead, we have the "*sōkaiya* scandal." By late 1997, all of the big four brokerage houses—Nomura, Daiwa, Nikko, and the Yamaichi, along with the Dai-Ichi Kangyo Bank—had become embroiled in a corporate extortion scandal. Each firm admitted to paying off a corporate racketeer in 1995 to compensate him for losses in discretionary investment accounts. The MOF, which had lobbied hard to keep the fledgling SESC both "in house" and hamstrung resourcewise, came under fire for its failure to uncover the illicit payments to a well-known corporate racketeer.

Even as chronic bad performance and the taint of corruption steadily erode public trust in the MOF, the ministry has continued to exhibit a remarkable ability to defang reform legislation. From a narrow self-interest perspective, MOF bureaucrats are certainly concerned about shrinking retirement prospects (*amakudari*) associated with procedural reforms. More than 200 MOF retirees had executive positions at Japanese financial institutions in 1997.[33] But to reduce their motivations to personal gain clearly misrepresents the ambitions of MOF bureaucrats. From a strategic vantage point, the MOF has battled ferociously to maintain its capacity for steering Japanese funds to public ends. Most of the staff for the new financial inspection agency will come from the ministry, and the FSA might very well function to help MOF accomplish its industrial policy goals. In the words of one member of the Diet, "Under the guise of devolving power, what's really being created is nothing but a subsidiary of MOF, which will actually extend MOF's empire rather than reducing it."[34] Within weeks after its establishment, the FSA was assigned the leading role in the government's latest scheme for cleaning up the banking crisis. Under the bridge-bank scheme announced in July 1998, the FSA will have the power to declare financial institutions "bankrupt" and to take over their operations, extending loans to healthy borrowers and disposing of bad loans. If the FSA cannot find merger partners to take over the state-run bridge bank, the state would assume ownership.[35]

Because the bridge-bank plan takes a harder line toward troubled banks, the MOF claims this scheme represents a significant departure from the convoy system, a recent focal point of reform. Compared with the organizational overhaul of the MOF, cracks in the convoy system have much more effectively stripped the MOF of its traditional patronage function. The MOF has historically come to the rescue of troubled financial institutions through a variety of means, including the coordination of mergers. The *Nikkei Weekly* reports that the MOF and BOJ arranged most of the 280 mergers that occurred between smaller Japanese financial institutions between 1955 and 1994, the majority of which were bailout mergers.[36] The financial crisis has now widened the gap between strong and weak financial institutions and put pressure on the MOF to allow the weak, who are holding back the entire convoy, to fail.

It is thus highly significant that in 1995 and 1996, the MOF departed from its "no failure" principle by allowing several smaller financial institutions with insolvency problems to close. During this period the MOF continued to insist that no top twenty financial institutions would close. Then came the failures of Hokkaido Takushoku Bank (number 16) and Yamaichi Securities Company (number 4) in November 1997, suggesting that either the MOF had come around to the Darwinian survival of the fittest mentality, or was simply unable to arrange bail-outs. The MOF's herculean efforts to provide a safety net for weak Japanese financial institutions should give pause to convergence theorists. Compared with regulatory reform elsewhere, the finance ministry has worked aggressively to minimize the pain for industrial players. For example, it was clear in 1995 that Nippon Credit Bank (NCB), one of Japan's three long-term credit banks, needed a merger to survive. However, the MOF's behind-the-scenes approaches to several Japanese financial institutions, including the International Bank of Japan, Dai-Ichi Kangyo, and Tokyo-Mitsubishi were rebuffed. It is unclear how hard the MOF pushed, because the MOF is sympathetic to the desire of healthier financial institutions to gird themselves for the Big Bang. In the end, the President of NCB, a former top MOF official, was pleased when the finance ministry found a *foreign* white knight, Banker's Trust.

Table 5-4. Major Linkages between Japanese and Foreign Financial Institutions

Date	Institutions	Linkage
April 1997	Nippon Credit Bank and Bankers Trust New York Corp.	Cross-shareholding, cooperation in securitizing assets in Japan.
July 1997	Long-Term Credit Bank of Japan and Swiss Bank Corp.	Cross-shareholding, forming alliance on investment banking, asset management, and private banking.
	Nikko Securities Co. and Smith Barney International Inc.	Setting up joint venture for wrap accounts.
December 1997	Merrill Lynch & Co. and failed Yamaichi Securities Co.	Acquisition of branches, hiring of personnel.
February 1998	GE Capital Services Inc. and Toho Mutual Life Insurance Co.	Setting up joint venture to sell insurance through Toho's branches.
March 1998	Meiji Life Insurance Co and Dresdner Bank	Setting up joint venture for asset-management services.
June 1998	Nikko Securities Co and Travelers Group Inc.	Capital investment, comprehensive cooperation.

Source: "Financial Realignment Picks Up Speed," *Nikkei Weekly,* June 8, 1998.

The trend toward strategic alliances between weak Japanese financial institutions and competitive foreign ones is likely to continue as a survival tactic for troubled Japanese financial institutions who clearly need foreign skills in order to compete in more open domestic financial markets. Like NCB, the troubled Long-Term Credit Bank established a foreign linkup in anticipation of Big Bang reforms. In July 1997, LTCB Securities Company agreed to establish a joint venture with SBC Warburg Japan Limited, a part-Swiss, part-British securities firm.[37] Japanese life insurers and securities companies have also established tie-ups with stronger foreign firms in order to survive in Japan's increasingly competitive domestic financial markets. The alliance between the U.S.-based Travelers financial conglomerate and Nikko Securities Company announced in June 1998 provides the most significant indication so far of Japan's receptiveness to foreign penetration. Under this partnership, Salomon Smith Barney, a business unit of Travelers, becomes the largest shareholder in Japan's third-largest securities company with a 25 percent equity stake. Salomon will essentially takeover Nikko's investment-banking and international operations.[38] The merger promises to compel further realignment of the Japanese financial sector. Table 5-4 summarizes recent business alliances between Japanese and foreign financial institutions.

The recent bankruptcies and the significant strategic role assigned to foreign institutions in the financial restructuring process represent an important break from the past. With Japan's financial crisis pushing the economy into a deflationary spiral, making the Japanese regulators and financial institutions reach out in desperation for foreign support, the prospects for the demise of the convoy system have certainly increased. In exchange for its $2 billion intervention to help rescue a plummeting yen in June 1998, the United States exacted a pledge from Finance Minister Matsunaga Hikaro to abandon efforts to keep weak banks afloat. Whether Japan will in fact resort to such "shock therapy" remains to be seen. All eyes are on the newly announced merger between Sumitomo Trust & Banking Company and the troubled Long-Term Credit Bank as a litmus test of the government's resolve to pull the plug on life support mechanisms for ailing Japanese banks.[39]

Conclusion

As 1998 unfolds, confidence in the MOF's ability to handle the financial crisis is in short supply. It is widely believed that the MOF's failure to provide early treatment for the problem allowed Japan's financial crisis to fester, that the financial mess is now largely beyond the MOF's control, that a financial meltdown is imminent unless more drastic measures are taken to restructure the financial sector, and that sooner is better than later. Borrowing the widely used cancer metaphor to describe the situation, one close observer of the financial scene in Japan comments, "The MOF and Japanese industry have been hoping for a soft landing ever since the bubble burst. Sort of like a doctor who treats a cancer victim by giving him some pain-killer to make him comfortable, but is too afraid to take drastic action, like surgery or chemo to try to heal the patient."[40]

 Taking drastic measures to restructure Japan's ailing financial system necessarily means allowing the market mechanism, rather then bureaucrats, determine the nature and timing of industrial adjustment. The radical solution would require the liberalization of all layers of the Japanese financial regulatory regime, from its market rules, to its traditional governing practices, to its philosophical foundations.[41] In this chapter I have argued that financial reform has not penetrated as deeply as many commentators have suggested. Although regulatory reform has brought about a major liberalization of rules, it has just begun to make a dent in the traditional procedures for making and implementing financial regulation in Japan. The Japanese regulators are unlikely to allow a messy and abrupt industry shakeout. Cartelization will remain the rule, as the MOF seeks to consolidate the financial sector into larger and stronger financial groupings.

Conflicting governmental imperatives will ensure that reform of Japan's patronage-style regulatory arrangements will not proceed in a linear fashion, but rather that it will continue along its zigzag course. Like financial regulators everywhere, the MOF must steer a course between efficiency and stability. For the ultra-conservative MOF, a little shock therapy at one point is likely to be followed by efforts to ease the pain at another. For example, before the "prompt corrective action" reform even took effect, the MOF began backpedaling on this new set of accounting rules. With a credit crunch threatening to exacerbate Japan's financial woes, in December 1997 the MOF announced a one-year grace period for banks unable to meet the new standards by April 1, 1998. Unlike regulators in Anglo-American–style regulatory regimes, the MOF must furthermore strike a balance between effective governance and state capacity. The financial crisis brought the tension between the MOF's interest in the economic well-being of the nation and its more local concern with maintaining bureaucratic power into sharp relief. These contradictory aims have made the MOF ambivalent about fundamental procedural changes that promise to undermine its authority in the course of strengthening the financial system. In carrying out further financial reforms, the key challenge for the MOF will be to render Tokyo a more attractive center for international financial transactions without compromising the regulatory authority of the MOF unduly and without sacrificing much ground in the marketplace to foreign competition.

Of all the dimensions of the Japanese financial regulatory regime, the ideational bedrock is least susceptible to change. In Spring 1997, amidst great pessimism about Japan's economic circumstances, a leading member of the MOF's international faction, provided the following statement about the purpose of financial regulatory reform: "As we have done for the 130 years since the Meiji Restoration, we will quickly absorb what needs to be absorbed and become fully competitive with the Anglo-Saxon and other systems. In sectors such as automobiles, semiconductors, and machine tools we are fully competitive. It is in areas such as finance and information that we need to concentrate our efforts to catch up. The Tokyo Big Bang is a series of reforms to restructure our financial system and institutions to achieve such goals in the area of finance."[42] A more doctrinal statement of product cycle evolution is hardly possible. The MOF can hope to reclaim some of its legitimacy if the Big Bang reform policies, in fact, help Japan catch up with the West.

Although core principles of action have endured, some fundamental norms of government-business cooperation have been violated with increasing regularity. The transition to a more competitive market environment under crisis circumstances has created huge strains in the relationship between the MOF and private financial institutions. Healthier members of industrial groupings, who do not wish to support their ailing brethren, have challenged the MOF's traditional methods of oversight. More significant, the MOF's failure to rescue private financial institutions, especially big ones, constitutes a serious breach of social contract. The MOF has now carried out the threat implicit in the Big Bang to let the market punish inefficient firms. This life-or-death authority enhances the MOF's informal power over troubled financial institutions. However, the MOF's abandonment of the "no failure" principle should quickly speed up the development of self-help attitudes in the private sector.

The search for autonomy from the regulators led the president of a Japanese securities company in early 1998 to wonder out loud if the securities industry should continue to finance twenty-two semi-governmental securities organizations. They are a bit of a frill to maintain at a time when securities firms are trying to cut costs and reorganize for the Big Bang, especially when they know the golden days of MOF protection are over.[43] Just as the old arrangement of protected market segments provided a sanctuary for securities firms, these industry organizations have offered sanctuaries for retiring MOF bureaucrats. To openly discuss cutting them off constitutes a direct affront to the political authority of the MOF.

Semi-governmental organizations are but one of numerous types of public-private arrangements for informally coordinating industrial policy in the Japanese financial system. The after-hour entertainment of MOF officials by private financial institutions is another such mechanism. The arrest of two MOF bank inspectors in January 1998 for allegedly accepting lavish entertainment in return for favors, notably information about the timing of bank inspections, further promises to further undermine the administrative culture of cooperation in the future.[44] This scandal, which led to the resignation of the finance minister, has made MOF liaisons in the private sector think twice before inviting MOF officials for weekend golf trips. In short, a chain of mutual "un-accommodation" is emerging between the MOF and private institutions, and it has struck a blow at the Japanese creed of order, hierarchy, groupism, and informal governance. Still, the fundamental commitment to an illiberal ethos remains, and regulatory reform has a long way to go before the Japanese financial system looks just like ours.

Notes

1. Editors' preface in Hugh T. Patrick and Yung Chul Park, eds., *The Financial Development of Japan, Korea and Taiwan: Growth, Repression, and Liberalization* (New York: Oxford University Press, 1994), p. v.

2. David L. Asher, "What Became of the Japanese 'Miracle,'" *Orbis*, Spring 1996, p. 233.

3. "No Easy Reform Options for Japan," *Oriental Economist*, March 1997, p. 2.

4. For one of many good overviews on the subject, see Koichi Hamada and Akiyoshi Horiuchi, "The Political Economy of the Financial Market," in Kozo Yamamura and Yasukichi Yasuba, eds., *The Political Economy of Japan*, vol. 1: *The Domestic Transformation* (Stanford University Press, 1987), pp. 223–60.

5. The dynamic of "competitive deregulation" is a much-discussed phenomenon in the study of financial liberalization. Empirical data support the thesis that business and capital tend to migrate to the most open financial regulatory environments. The lifting of capital controls across the advanced industrial world has thus compelled regulators toward further financial reform. See, for example, Eric Helleiner, *States and the Reemergence of Global Finance: From Bretton Woods to the 1990s* (Cornell University Press, 1994), pp. 166–68.

6. See Edward Lincoln, *Japan: Facing Economic Maturity* (Brookings, 1987), pp. 130–277; Thomas F. Cargill and Shoichi Royama, *The Transition of Finance in Japan and the United States: A Comparative Perspective* (Stanford, Calif.: Hoover Institution Press, 1988), pp. 107–20; Robert Alan Feldman, *Japanese Financial Markets: Deficits, Dilemmas, and Deregulation* (MIT Press, 1986); and James Horne, *Japan's Financial Markets: Conflict and Consensus in Policymaking* (London: Allen & Unwin, 1985), pp. 46–73.

7. These financial policies persist to the present day. See R. Taggart Murphy, "Don't Be Fooled by Japan's Big Bang," *Fortune*, December 29, 1997.

8. During the same period that Japan has evolved as a young creditor, the United States has proceeded rapidly through the latter phases of the balance-of-payments cycle—first consuming part of its investment income (1971–81), then drawing down on its international assets (1982–84), and finally coming full circle as a net debtor country borrowing from abroad (1985).

9. For a comprehensive account of the breakdown of international capital controls established under Bretton Woods, see Helleiner, *States and the Reemergence of Global Finance*.

10. Richard Koo, "Japan and International Capital Flows: A New Challenge," (Nomura Research Institute, April 1991), p. 1.

11. States face two fundamental options for coping with an external payments imbalance. They may adjust to it or they may finance it. Concerning the liquidity-adjustment trade-off, C. Fred Bergsten has noted that "Liquidity and adjustment are perfect substitutes. An infinite supply of liquidity obviates any need for adjustment, and a perfect adjustment process obviates any need for liquidity." Quoted in Gerald M. Meier, *Problems of a World Monetary Order* (Oxford University Press, 1974), pp. 146–47.

12. For an account of the shift from the Bretton Woods financing regime to the petrodollar recycling regime, see Benjamin Cohen, "Balance-of-Payments Financing: Evolution of a Regime," in Stephen Krasner, ed., *International Regimes* (Cornell University Press, 1983), pp. 315–36.

13. Terutomo Ozawa, *Multinationalism, Japanese Style: The Political Economy of Outward Dependency* (Princeton University Press, 1979), p. 53.

14. This brief overview of the financial service revolution is based on Richard McGahey, Mary Malloy, Katherine Kazanas, and Michael P. Jacobs, *Financial Services, Financial Centers: Public Policy and the Competition for Markets, Firms, and Jobs* (Boulder, Colo.: Westview Press, 1990), pp. 77–182.

15. Data from George Tavlas and Y. Ozeki, "The Japanese Yen as an International Currency," International Monetary Fund, January 1991, p. 2. Cited in Eric Helleiner, "The Challenge from the East: Japan's Financial Rise and the Changing Global Order," in Philip Cerney, ed., *Finance and World Markets* (Brookfield, Vt.: Edward Elgar, 1993), p. 6.

16. This overseas expansion has tapered off dramatically, and at last count in 1997 the total for the top ten insurers was ninety-one representative offices, foreign branches, and subsidiaries. "Kaisha shinshutsu kigyo soran '97, kaisha betsu hen" (Data book on Japanese firms operating overseas, 1997) (Tokyo: Tōyō keizai shinpō sha, April 1997).

17. Elizabeth Norville, interview with manager in the international planning department of a major Japanese life insurance company.

18. This number decreased by one following the MOF's closure of Nissan Mutual Life Insurance Company in April 1997. This was the first insurance company bankruptcy in fifty years.

19. Elizabeth Norville, interview with manager in Nippon Life Insurance planning division, July 1993.

20. Elizabeth Norville, interview with Oba Tomomitsu, November 9, 1988.

21. For data on Japanese gross and net external assets, see Bank of Japan, *Balance of Payments Monthly*.

22. Mark Scher and Schon Beechler, "The Internationalization of Japanese Financial Institutions: What Went Wrong?" Paper prepared for the Annual Meeting of the Association for Japanese Business Studies, January 1994, p. 9.

23. Eugene Dattel, *The Sun That Never Rose: The Inside Story of Japan's Failed Attempt at Global Financial Dominance,* (Chicago: Probus, 1994), p. 43.

24. Personal correspondence, January 1998.

25. Steven K. Vogel, *Freer Markets, More Rules: Regulatory Reform in Advanced Industrial Countries* (Cornell University Press, 1996), p. 185.

26. Chalmers Johnson, *MITI and the Japanese Miracle* (Stanford University Press, 1982), p. 30.

27. Asher, "What Became of the Japanese 'Miracle,'" p. 216.

28. "Japan's Fate Remains Unsettled; A Quick Guide to Some Scenarios," *Wall Street Journal,* Interactive Edition, December 24, 1997.

29. "Japan in the Dirt," *The Economist,* August 17, 1991, p. 11.

30. "Japanese Banks Hold 76 Trillion Yen in Problem Loans: MOF," Nikkei Net, Nihon keizai shimbun electronic information service, January 13, 1998.

31. "Analysts Predict Stagnant Japanese Economy," Nikkei Net, Nihon keizai shimbun electronic information service, January 12, 1998.

32. "Japan MOF Lifts Notices to Financial Institutions," *Wall Street Journal,* Interactive Edition, June 8, 1998.

33. "Agency to Take Staff, Power from Ministry," *Nikkei Weekly,* December 29, 1997, and January 5, 1998, p. 15.

34. "Breaking Up Is Hard to Do . . . Especially for the Ministry of Finance," *Oriental Economist,* May 1997, p. 5.

35. "Japan LDP Official: Government Panel Approves Bank Plan," *Wall Street Journal,* Interactive Edition, July 2, 1998.

36. "Japan's Financial Convoy System Approaches the End of the Road," *Nikkei Weekly,* July 8, 1996, p. 1.

37. Yasumasa Shimizu, "Bank Braces for Lessons From Foreign Partner," *Nikkei Weekly,* November 17, 1997.

38. "Financial Realignment Picks Up Speed," *Nikkei Weekly,* June 8, 1998.

39. "Bank Merger: A Long-Term Gain?" *Nikkei Weekly,* June 29, 1998.

40. Personal correspondence, December 18, 1997.

41. *Regime* here refers to the domestic "principles, norms, rules and decision-making procedures around which actor expectations converge." Stephen Krasner, "Structural Causes and regime Consequences: Regimes as Intervening Variables," in Krasner, *International Regimes,* p. 1.

42. Eisuke Sakakibara, "The Once and Future Boom," *The Economist,* March 22, 1997, p. 89.

43. "Amakudari muyo!?" (No more descent from heaven!?), *Nihon keizai shimbun,* January 18, 1998, p. 11.

44. "Japan's Finance Ministry Raided: Two Arrested in Bribery Scandal," *Wall Street Journal,* Interactive Edition, January 27, 1998.

CHAPTER SIX

The Policymaking Process behind Petroleum Industry Regulatory Reform

Kōsuke Ōyama

The petroleum-refining industry is a typical case of Japanese regulatory reform. Reforms were carried out in both 1986 and 1996 that superficially appeared to liberalize a market characterized by high prices and few imports. In both instances, however, new restrictions on imports limited genuine market competition. In the mid-1980s, petroleum refiners and users successfully blocked the introduction of refined petroleum product imports into Japan by using a new law that was cynically touted as "market-opening"—the Provisional Measures Law on the Import of Specified Refined Petroleum Products (Refined Petroleum Import Law)—to limit the right to import to domestic refiners. By the mid-1990s, however, the refiners' political strength had weakened, they were unable to prevent the law's expiration, and as a result their monopoly over petroleum product imports was weakened. The 1996 law did increase competition and reduce refined petroleum prices somewhat, but prices

I thank Katsunori Tanisaki and Michael C. Lynch for their useful ideas, comments, and kind help with editing. Mark Tilton, Lonny Carlile, Elizabeth Norville, Yul Sohn, Hideaki Miyajima, Mindy Kotler, Margaret McKean, and three blind referees gave me useful comments. I also thank Richard J. Samuels and Kenneth A. Oye for their support in my research as a visiting scholar at the Center for International Studies at MIT in 1996–97.

continue high by international standards. Imports have again not increased, due to new technical standards introduced to block imports and to new restrictions on which companies are allowed to import. This pattern, which produces a modest increase in competition but maintains high prices and restrictions on new entrants, is typical of Japanese deregulation. Similar patterns can be seen in the limited deregulation of airline and taxi fares, telecommunication services, and permits for new large stores The key reason for the feigned reform of 1986 was international pressure to open the Japanese market. The reason for its failure was opposition by virtually all powerful interests, including not only producers, politicians, and bureaucrats, but industrial users as well. The success of the very modest 1996 reform was due to the leadership of the Hosokawa government in pushing for deregulation. The 1996 reform was limited in its impact because producer interests and bureaucrats were still nervous about wide-open liberalization and because the Japanese concept of deregulation is itself quite limited. This chapter explains what made the reforms possible and looks at regulatory and other factors that continue to block imports and domestic market change.

Deregulation in Western countries means to abolish or diminish governmental regulation of private firms, but (as pointed out in chapter 1) in Japan the commonly used term *kisei kanwa* means only to relax them. This difference in meaning is exacerbated by the fact that although the Japanese definition of deregulation is narrow, the actual practice of regulation is quite broad, encompassing not only formal measures such as requirements for licenses or reporting of business activities, but also informal measures such as administrative guidance or self-regulation by industry associations. And Japan's regulatory reform looks different depending on whether it is viewed from within Japan or from abroad. In the United States and Europe the primary hope for Japanese regulatory reform is that it will open markets to imports by bringing Japanese trade practices closer to international standards.[1] By contrast, although *kisei kanwa* has become a fashionable term recently in Japan, most Japanese want stability and do not want radical reform because they fear it would increase unemployment. Regulatory reform has a range of economic and political meanings; I use it here in its broad sense to include informal measures by both bureaucrats and trade associations. The point of this discussion of the conflicting meanings of deregulation in Japan and many Western countries is that petroleum deregulation appears a success in Japan because the goals of relaxing regulation are so limited. By Western standards, it would appear that little meaningful deregulation has been achieved.

Japan's Petroleum Industry Structure and the Regulatory System

Regulatory reform in Japan's petroleum industry is particularly challenging because the industry is unusually fragmented and many small firms depend on existing regulations to stay in business. Most of the world's oil companies are vertically integrated, meaning that a single corporation carries out both the upstream activities of discovering and pumping crude oil and the downstream activities of refining and distribution.[2] But as table 6-1 shows, most of Japan's oil companies are engaged only in refining and sales.

There are four types of petroleum companies in Japan: (1) wholesalers (*motouri kaisha*), (2) refining and wholesale companies (*seisei motouri kaisha*), and (3) special agents (*tokuyakuten*), which are distribution companies that operate service stations and often sell to (4) retailers, which own and operate individual or small service stations.

Wholesalers do not have the upstream sectors that make big profits for the big international oil companies, or "majors." But some majors, such as Esso Eastern, Caltex, Mobil, and Shell, have operated in the Japanese oil refining and wholesale market through joint ventures with Japanese companies. Because they are inefficient, profits are low despite high prices. The special agent and retail firms are mostly small, and there are more gasoline stations relative to demand in Japan than in the United States or Europe. Not only does fragmentation reduce profits because of the lack of economies of scale, but it also means that there is a lack of powerful management centers that can make the painful cuts that might create economies of scale. Although wholesalers sometimes own service stations, the stations are managed by special agent firms, so wholesalers have less control over their distribution networks than do the European or American refiners. Much of the unique character of Japan's market can be explained by regulatory controls over competition.

The Ministry of International Trade and Industry (MITI) has applied many forms of regulation to the oil industry in order to ensure stable supplies of what is considered a strategic resource. The present regulatory system was shaped by the Petroleum Industry Law, which was enacted in 1962 and which has largely accomplished its objective of maintaining a stable supply of refined petroleum.[3]

The Petroleum Industry Law is an excellent postwar example of the use of licensing to establish diffuse government control over industry, a practice Sohn's chapter details for the prewar petroleum and auto industries. The law

Table 6-1. Structure of Japan's Petroleum Industry and Regulation, 1962 to the Present

Stage of production	Companies	Associations	Government: The Petroleum Department of the ANRE
1. Crude oil production, export	Majors, other companies	OPEC Sekiyu Kōdan (JNOC)	Development Division
2. Import, refining, wholesale	Importers, refiners, wholesalers	Sekiyu Renmai (PAJ)	Planning Division, Refining Division, Petroleum Reserve Division
3. Distribution	Dealers (agents), gas service stations	Zensekiren	Distribution Division
4. Consumption	Consuming firms	Consumer organizations	Director-General's Secretariat, Energy Conservation and Alternative Energy Policy Division

Source: Ōyama Kōsuke, *Gyōseishidō no seiji keizaigaku* (The political economy of administrative guidance) (Tokyo: Yūhikaku, 1996), p. 231.

requires permits to establish refineries or to purchase equipment for them and requires notification of sales and imports. The bureaucracy has successfully used these policy tools as leverage to suppress competition and maintain a domestic refining industry. As a result, the petroleum refining industry is said to be "privately owned and operated, but publicly managed."[4] The industry is regulated by a panoply of laws. The Petroleum Supply and Demand Balance Law and the Emergency Temporary Law for Stabilizing the Nation's Livelihood, often called the "Two Petroleum Laws in Case of Emergency," created emergency plans for disruptions in the oil supply and price jumps. The Petroleum Stockpiling Law constructs a stockpiling plan for normal, undisrupted times. The Quality Assurance Law attempts to guard against "excessive competition" (which both Mark Tilton and Yul Sohn discuss in chapters 7 and 2, respectively) and to ensure quality of gasoline and light oil by prohibiting service stations from selling substandard products.

Table 6-2 lists the large variety of forms of regulation in the petroleum industry. Regulation occurs at all stages of the production and distribution chain (importation, refining, wholesale and retail distribution, and consumption) and at various levels of market actors' decisionmaking process (market entry, investment, production, consumption, and pricing). There is a whole range of levels of government power implicit in various forms of regulation. Some parts of the regulatory procedure, such as requirements for notification (*todokede*) or registration (*tōroku*), represent information gathering on the part of the government. Notification announces to the government events such as birth, death, or marriage, whereas registration records legal events or relationships such as the creation of a patent or the entry of a medical doctor or lawyer into a profession into the public record. Information gathering, of course, enhances the state's understanding of markets and its ability to regulate them. Other forms of regulation allow the state to direct firm behavior. Direction (*shiji*), guidance (*shidō*), and recommendation (*kankoku*) represent formally noncompulsory advice. (The difference among these terms is a technical legal question and depends on the individual case.)

As Sohn points out in chapter 2, however, these formally noncompulsory forms of advice can be in practice compulsory through linkage to other forms of regulation, notably licensing. He notes that licensing represents government permission for activities that are otherwise prohibited. It is notable that licenses for new investment have been made automatic if already existing plants are running at at least 80 percent of capacity. But the refining companies themselves require ongoing licenses, and it is plausible that refiners could fear the bureacuracy manipulating the 80 percent of capacity standard if it wanted to deny a license (for instance, down times for cleaning might or might not be counted as idle production time). Licenses are also required for importation of certain petroleum products. Reflecting the nationalist orientation of petroleum industry policy, foreign firms are required to get permission to invest and are limited to equity stakes under 50 percent.

In addition, various procedures require cooperative planning, for example, supply and stockpiling by industry and the state. This represents not compulsion by the state but rather leadership. Other forms of regulation represent industry self-governance, notably the monthly setting of standard prices, or state support for industry self-regulation, such as the publication of sales prices.

The 1986 Refined Petroleum Import Law in principle allowed free imports of petroleum products and appeared to represent a major change in Japan's regulatory system. It was enacted in response to pressure from Western nations to open the market to the large volume of refined petroleum products beginning to come out of new refineries in the Persian Gulf region. But the devil is in the details: the Refined Petroleum Import Law restricted the right to import to companies that had refineries in Japan by requiring companies to have domestic production, stockpiling, and quality control capacity. The upshot was that in fact refined petroleum product imports did not increase and actually later decreased because of the Gulf crisis of 1990.[5]

The Refined Petroleum Import Law expired on March 31, 1996, and the Stockpiling Law and the Gasoline Sales Law were also amended at that time. The expiration of the Refined Petroleum Import Law shifted the emphasis of Japan's petroleum policy somewhat from stability toward efficiency. The petroleum industry has come under scrutiny during discussions of the need for deregulation in recent years because of the industry's extreme inefficiency and high prices. Prices for gasoline are of course high in both Europe and Japan because of high taxes, but the pretax price was much higher in Japan. In March 1993 gasoline cost 62 yen per liter in Japan, 20 yen per liter in the United States, and 25 yen per liter in Europe.[6] Thus the pretax price was triple the U.S. price and two and a half times the European price. Japanese public opinion came to support petroleum product imports and greater distribution efficiency in order to push down gasoline prices. However, there was still recognition that Japanese petroleum supplies are inherently vulnerable because Japan imports almost all its petroleum and depends on the Middle East for 80 percent of its imports.

Table 6-2. Required Licenses, Registration, and Other Forms of Regulation in the Petroleum-Refining Industry, 1962 to the Present

Level of market actors' decisionmaking process	Importation, refining, wholesale distribution	Retail distribution[a]	Consumption
Market entry	Notification for import and wholesale firms Registration of firms that want to import certain specified items such as gasoline under the 1986 Refined Petroleum Import Law Licensing of refining firms Required permission for investment by foreign capital (limited to under 50%)[b]	Registration of gasoline sales[a]	. . .
Investment	Licensing of refining facilities investment (*automatic licensing,*[c] but pre-existing facilities should have a utilization rate above 80%)	. . .	
Supply-and-demand adjustment	Notification of production plans (*administrative guidance on gasoline production quotas for crude oil handling and stockpiling of kerosene abolished,* but replaced with a committee to do quarterly market surveys) Government recommendation for changes in production plans Recommendation on quality	Prohibitions on selling low-quality gasoline Regulations on quality control personnel and on analysis of gasoline Recommendation and guidance on reducing gasoline waste Direction on gasoline storage Guidance on gasoline distribution relationships	Restrictions on oil use Provision of consumer information Quotas and rationing oil in emergencies

	Planning of stockpiling	Quotas and rationing of petroleum shipments in emergencies	
	Notification of production, sales, and import quantities	Regulations on bookkeeping	
	Notification of stockpiling plan	Inspections of facilities and reports	
	Standards for stockpiling volumes		
	Quotas and rationing of petroleum refining in emergencies		
	Regulations on bookkeeping		
	Inspections of facilities and of written reports		
Price	Setting of standard prices (prices set on monthly basis through industry self-governance)	Recommendation on sales prices	. . .
		Publishing of sales prices	
	Subsidization of domestic refiners from tariffs on imported C-grade heavy oil[d]	Rules from Fair Trade Commission, such as bans on postsales price adjustment	
	Publishing of sales prices		
	Regulation of exports (export of certain items under government watch)		

Source: Ōyama Kōsuke, *Gyōseishidō no seiji keizaigaku* (The political economy of administrative guidance) (Tokyo: Yūhikaku, 1996), p. 231.

a. The Special District System was abolished in March 1996.
b. Items in parentheses are based on informal guidance.
c. Italicized items represent reforms implemented under the Deregulation Action Plan of 1987–92.
d. The Tariff Quota System on imported C-grade heavy oil was abolished in March 1993.

The 1996 reform moved somewhat away from emphasis on stability in favor of encouraging greater efficiency. It relaxed restrictions on imports by allowing the Refined Petroleum Import Law to lapse and encouraged more efficient distribution by abolishing the Specified District System (Shitei Chiku Seido), which prohibited newcomers from entering specified districts in which there were already many gasoline stations, such as downtown areas. At the same time, however, requirements were maintained that importers continue to stockpile for seventy days under an amended Stockpiling Law and that importers and retailers manage the quality of their imports in order to maintain good condition of their imported products. MITI announced that specifications for both gasoline and diesel fuel would be tightened even more by 1999, a move likely to shut the Japanese market further to imports.[7] Thus, although superficially anyone can import gasoline into Japan, unusual product specifications and stockpiling requirements in effect protect the domestic market from imports. And as we saw in table 6-2, the reform left intact the wide range of regulatory tools for intervening in the marketplace.

The best way to understand the impact of regulatory changes on the Japanese refined petroleum products market is to compare it with that of Europe, where the product mix is similar to Japan's.[8] European countries have ample access to imported petroleum products, either from global markets through Rotterdam or from individual European national refining industries. Countries such as France that have opened their markets to imports have seen their prices fall. But Japan is unlikely to import much because the only firms likely to be able to meet the onerous stockpiling and quality requirements besides the refiners are Japanese trading companies and the National Federation of Agricultural Cooperative Associations (Zennō). The new importers have accounted for only 5 percent of Japan's gasoline, kerosene, and gas oil imports since the lapse of the Refined Petroleum Import Law and are unlikely candidates for revolutionizing the petroleum products market in the future with large quantities of cheap imports.[9]

Prices in Japan have not been influenced by international prices as much as in European countries such as France or Germany, but reforms in Japan have begun to bring prices down gradually and steadily. The pretax gasoline price fell to 47 yen per liter by March 1997 despite flat crude oil prices and a slight depreciation of the yen. This was still double the U.S. pretax price of 23 yen per liter and three-quarters higher than the U.K. pretax price of 27 yen per liter.[10] Throughout the postwar period MITI has used administrative guidance to keep prices down for kerosene, which is seen as a necessity for home heating, but industry was allowed to set high prices for gasoline, which has been seen as a luxury. Kerosene prices too remain high by international standards, although they have recently decreased slightly: 46 yen per liter pretax, compared with 35 yen per liter in the United States, 23 yen per liter in the United Kingdom, 29 yen per liter in France, and 25 yen per liter in Germany.[11]

The unusual fragmentation of the Japanese gasoline retail sector makes consolidation difficult, for both political and firm-level reasons. In European countries (except Italy) urban populations have spread into the suburbs and people now do much of their shopping at large shopping centers or hyper-markets, which include gasoline stations. In Japan large shopping centers may also spread in the suburbs and small towns but will likely provide less of an impetus to change to a more efficient distribution structure than in Europe. In Europe, unlike Japan, the number of gasoline stations has been decreasing and the sales volume per station has been increasing. In France, where restrictions on new gasoline stations were discontinued in 1985 (as they were just recently in Japan as well), gasoline stations have rapidly shut down and consolidated. But whereas oil-refining companies own and manage many gasoline stations in Europe (except Italy), in Japan the gasoline stations that oil companies own are managed by special agent or retail firms. As oil-refining companies do not have the management authority to close individual gasoline stations, the rationalization of petroleum distribution will not proceed as easily in Japan as in Europe. Furthermore, opposition to layoffs among the 400,000 workers employed in special agent firms, retail firms, and gasoline stations, and the difficulty of obtaining land to build larger gasoline stations, will impede the transition to a more efficient distribution system.

The Policy Process Leading to Passage of the Refined Petroleum Import Law

The decade from 1986 to 1996 was characterized by import restriction and domestic market regulation but also by a move toward limited regulatory reform. (See figure 6-1 for policy processes at work before 1986.) The 1996 expiration of the Refined Petroleum Import Law has increased competition and reduced prices somewhat. Why did MITI and the petroleum industry allow the law to expire? Who favored reform and who opposed it? How was the conflict of interests resolved? The reason protectionism lost out to some degree in the 1990s was a combination of foreign pressure and the growing domestic power

Figure 6-1. The Policy Process Associated with the Enactment of the Refined Petroleum Import Law, 1986

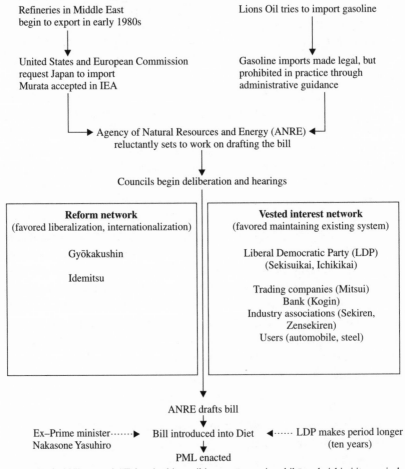

Source: Tanisaki Katsunori, "Tokutei sekiyu seihin yunyū zantei sochihō no haishi ni itaru seisaku kettei katei" (The policymaking process toward the abolition of the refined petroleum import law), graduation thesis, College of International Relations, University of Tsukuba, January 1996, p. 66.

of the deregulation movement, led by the opposition prime minister Hosokawa Morihiro. The reason the reform did not go further than it did was the continued strength of producers and bureaucrats and the fundamental weakness of the deregulation movement's goals.

As is often the case with important policy changes in Japan, foreign pressure was the prelude to the enactment of the 1986 Refined Petroleum Import Law. In response to the start-up of export-oriented refineries in the Middle East in the early 1980s, the United States and the European Community asked Japan to open its markets in order to take in its proper share of the new production. MITI minister Murata Keijirō agreed, and domestic laws were modified to formally admit imports. In fact, however, MITI used administrative guidance to prevent Japanese outsiders to the petroleum industry from importing gasoline. This became widely publicized when Lion's Oil Company tried to import gasoline but was blocked by MITI threats to have financial institutions cut off Lion's financing.[12] Clearly, Japan needed to make deeper reforms if its petroleum market was to become truly open to imports.

Bowing to foreign pressure, the Agency of Natural Resources and Energy (ANRE) agreed to consider import liberalization, but reluctantly. ANRE director Nono'uchi Takashi believed that energy security was more important than international cooperation. A number of oil industry forces constituted a powerful protectionist coalition. The main petroleum firms, the Petroleum Association of Japan (Sekiyu Renmei), the National Federation of Petroleum Commercial Association, and the National Federation of Petroleum Cooperative Association (Zensekiren), were firmly opposed to liberalization. The Liberal Democratic party (LDP), which was the ruling party at the time, created a new Petroleum Problems Research Council, made up of Diet members with special interests in and ties to the petroleum industry. There were also other subgroups tied to specific interest groups such as the Sekisuikai, headed by Sasaki Yoshisuke, and the Ichikikai, headed by Esaki Masumi. These groups advocated protecting the existing structure of the domestic refining system, strongly opposed the import of refined oil products, and led the fight to dissuade LDP leaders from permitting imports. The iron triangle of politicians, the bureaucracy, and industry was strong and firmly against imports.

Debate over liberalization proposals took place within the Petroleum Council of the ANRE, which has the function of interest adjustment among the various parties involved in the petroleum market. An expanded subcommittee of the council heard testimony from scholars and other persons concerned with the issue of imports. The council itself was opposed to the import of refined oil products. One distinctive feature of the deliberation was that the actors that one would suppose would favor liberalization in fact opposed it. Trading companies such as Mitsui and Company, Limited, which stood to gain from handling imports, opposed rule changes that would allow themselves to import and said that only wholesalers should be allowed to import. Banks such as the Industrial Bank of Japan said government support should be used to build up wholesalers' profits, and industrial users such as the automobile and steel industries, as well as consumer groups, said that maintaining quality controls that were unusually strict by international standards was more important than lowering prices.[13]

There were voices in favor of reform, but they were weak. The Deregulation Subcommittee of the Provisional Commission for the Promotion of Administrative Reform (Gyōkakushin I) recommended that imports be liberalized, and the Idemitsu Corporation, a reform advocate within the oil industry, said imports of refined petroleum products would actually enhance Japan's energy security. Prime Minister Nakasone Yasuhiro engaged in a show of market opening by moving up the implementation date of the Refined Petroleum Import Law from April to January 1986, although this did not mean that Nakasone actually supported the law or favored import liberalization.

As something of a compromise among the conflicting interests, the ANRE permitted refined petroleum product imports on its own authority but drafted a bill that actually limited imports to existing refiners. Imports were limited to firms that had domestic refining facilities, could do stockpiling, and could manage quality. Thus the regulations did not in fact permit any new importers but protected existing vested interests. Furthermore, although the ANRE bill was to last five years, Tateuchi Yasuoki, president of the Petroleum Association of Japan, and Nippon Oil Company, Limited, wanted to make it permanent, and LDP Diet members such as Tahara Takashi and Watanabe Hideo actively supported them. Based on this support, the law was later extended to a total of ten years.

The Policy Process That Allowed the Refined Petroleum Import Law to Expire

Between the initial passage of the Refined Petroleum Import Law and the deliberation that lead to its expiration in 1996, the protectionist coalition became weaker and reformers stronger. The most important factor in strengthening the advocates of reform was the formation of the Hosokawa Morihiro coalition government, which excluded the LDP (see figure 6-2). The creation of the Hosokawa administration on August 9, 1993, quickly led to a review of the Refined Petroleum Import Law. Hosokawa needed fast results because his base of support was people without party allegiance. He relied heavily on

Figure 6-2. The Policy Process Associated with the Abolition of the Refined Petroleum Import Law, 1996

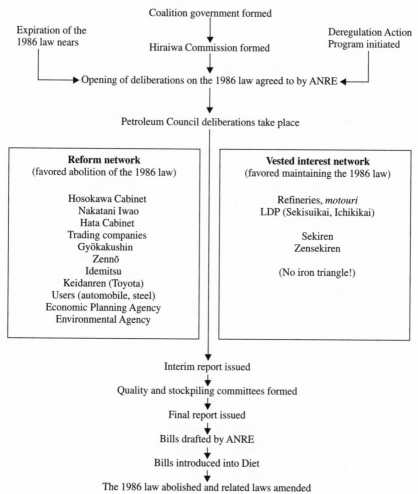

Source: Tanisaki Katsunori, "Tokutei sekiyu seihin yunyū zantei sochihō no haishi ni itaru seisaku kettei katei" (The policymaking process toward the abolition of the refined petroleum import law), graduation thesis, College of International Relations, University of Tsukuba, January 1996, p. 67.

expert advice, much as had former prime minister Nakasone. In late August, Hosokawa established the Economic Reform Study Committee as a private advisory body reporting to him, installed Hiraiwa Gaishi, president of the Federation of Economic Organizations (Keidanren) as chairman, and hand-picked its members. By pulling business leaders into the economic reform group, he attempted to garner business support for his government. Hosokawa expected the Hiraiwa Committee to recommend bold regulatory reform to deal with the negative effects of the appreciation of the yen. He tried to support the committee's efforts by instructing government ministries to formulate concrete plans for regulatory reform and ordering ministries to take an active role in pushing the process forward. The Hiraiwa Committee advised that such basic economic activities as entry into new markets, investment in manufacturing plants, importing, and price setting should be free in principle and regulated only in exceptional cases. Regulation of the petroleum industry should be kept to a minimum, except in emergency situations. In November 1994, MITI responded that it would allow trading companies and some other firms to begin importing petroleum products and that it would reexamine the Refined Petroleum Import Law.

One key member of the council, Professor Nakatani Iwao of Hitotsubashi University, wanted to scrap the Refined Petroleum Import Law completely. He was on a number of policy councils and spoke out vociferously in favor of reform. He argued that the committee should look after the economic welfare of society as a whole and complained that most proponents of regulatory reform only favored it in theory while opposing doing away with regulations that protected their own interests. Although his proposals were not completely accepted, they eventually led to the lapse of the Refined Petroleum Import Law. The opening of the market to gasoline imports, an act this law was thought to represent, became a symbol of regulatory reform. The subcommittee of the Hiraiwa Committee charged with writing the report was made up of Gyōten Toyo'o and Miyazaki Isamu, who were ex-bureaucrats; Kobayashi Yōtarō, who was from a private firm; and Nakatani Iwao, who was intended to support the prime minister's reform position. Nakatani writes that trying to push his views on the committee was futile. "Since everyone seemed to be behind me, I stated my position in radical terms. But although they went along with me to a point, after that they rejected what I had to say and would not take me seriously. I had this feeling over and over while participating in the drafting committee. It was like being up against a solid metal wall."[14]

The Hosokawa administration's regulatory reform campaign created a general legitimacy for regulatory reform. The term regulatory reform won a prize from a publisher, Jiyū Kokuminsha, for the newest and most popular word in 1993, and actors who had previously opposed refined petroleum imports now came to favor them. User industries, along with trading companies, the Agricultural Cooperative Associations, and Idemitsu, now demanded that the Refined Petroleum Import Law be abolished but that the government still regulate the stockpiling and quality of petroleum products. The Economic Planning Agency argued in favor of scrapping the Refined Petroleum Import Law and the Gasoline Sales Law because they were responsible for Japan's extraordinarily high gasoline prices, while the Environment Agency warned that the government should be careful to regulate the benzene content in gasoline. The ANRE switched sides and now favored letting the Refined Petroleum Import Law lapse.

The idea of regulatory reform now had the high ground, and opponents of market liberalization found themselves isolated and discredited. Most refinery and wholesale companies, the Petroleum Association of Japan, the National Federation of Petroleum Commercial Association, and the National Federation of Petroleum Cooperative Associations demanded that the Refined Petroleum Import Law be continued, but wider business circles did not back them up. Keidanren was generally in favor of regulatory reform. Diet members belonging to the Sekisuikai or Ichikikai in the LDP, which was an opposition party at the time, had lost influence and did not get involved in defending the Refined Petroleum Import Law.

The Advisory Committee for Energy, which discusses Japan's broader energy policy, established the Basic Policy Directions subcommittee in September 1993. It sought ways to adapt to the changes in the international energy environment brought about by the end of the cold war and rapid economic growth in the developing countries and it reexamined policies to ensure stable supplies of petroleum, natural gas, and nuclear power. The committee recommended (1) tackling energy problems in a holistic way in order to stabilize energy supply and demand, (2) managing energy policy in a cooperative, international fashion in order to best achieve security and environmental goals, and (3) making the energy supply system more flexible in order to increase efficiency.[15]

Does Regulatory Reform Help Japan Move to a Postpetroleum Energy Strategy?

The theme of this book is the question of whether the Japanese government is willing to allow greater freedom for the market. The refined petroleum products market is certainly an apt case for examining the hesitant and partial granting of greater market freedoms. However, I must here make something of a digression from the main theme of the book and argue that in the case of energy, in some respects even *stronger* government regulation is called for, in order to promote legitimate security and environmental goals.

It is important for Japan to make petroleum industry efficient and to bring prices down to international levels. But at the same time, we need to examine the relationship between regulatory reform and environmental problems for the coming generations. How does regulatory reform in the petroleum industry affect Japan's overall energy strategy, and in particular how does it help Japan move away from the use of petroleum, whose overuse appears to be gradually causing global warming? Oil industry regulatory reform has had the positive effect of shifting from an emphasis on producer interests and market stability toward more emphasis on consumer interests and efficiency. But short-term market efficiency will not wean Japan away from the environmentally damaging use of petroleum, and regulatory reform has had the negative effect of hindering Japan's conversion to new, safe, and renewable forms of energy.

The United States and Europe have begun a conversion from large, concentrated operations managed by suppliers, such as petrochemical complexes and nuclear power plants, to a new system of small, dispersed operations managed by users, such as co-generation and energy–self-sufficient houses. This type of energy conversion is connected to conversions of social organization from the centralized state to the community, from corporations to nonprofit and nongovernmental organizations and to individuals, and from an industrial to a postindustrial society. The most important problem in Japan's energy strategy may be how Japan can come to a consensus on the value of energy system conversion combined with social conversion and how to achieve it politically. In the United States and Europe, unlike in Japan, small, dispersed energy systems based on demand-side management tend to be achieved through community-based experimental social systems.[16]

The Japanese energy system is currently oriented to large suppliers. The Advisory Committee for Energy has produced "Long-Term Energy Supply and Demand Outlooks," which always exaggerate demand, and government regulators encourage power companies and refineries to build sufficient capacity to meet projected demand.[17] Instead, energy policy should aim at discouraging demand increases and at shifting supply from large producers to small, local sources. Many are saying that establishing autarky in the area of "food, energy, and water" is a historical necessity. Uchihashi Katsundo, for instance, argues that fewer nations are choosing to depend on other nations for such essentials as food and energy, that countries should be wary of opening their agricultural markets, and that countries should attempt to maximize food and energy self-sufficiency.[18]

The main obstacles to shifting to new and renewable sources of energy such as photovoltaic power generation, solar thermal energy, and electric vehicles is high cost; that is, they are technologically but not commercially feasible. The problem is that the "social costs" from continued use of fossil fuels and nuclear power are not reflected in market prices but may become very heavy over the long term. If a consensus on the need to shift away from fossil fuels and nuclear power can be reached, the problem is then how to internalize social costs within energy prices. Some measures that have successfully offered financial incentives to encourage a shift away from petroleum and toward safer energy sources are tax credits in the United States, Standard Offer 4 in California, the energy tax in Denmark, and the Electricity Purchase Act or Ahen Model in Germany.[19]

The recent regulatory reform in the refined petroleum products field may have mixed effects on the environment and on Japan's energy security. Although on the positive side regulatory reform may encourage electric companies to buy electricity from more diverse sources or promote co-generation, on the negative side cheaper imported gasoline may hinder efforts to reduce our use of fossil fuels. Japan should not deregulate energy blindly but instead should use regulatory reform to further its overall energy strategy. As in the United States and Europe, we should not wait for the day when new energies are commercially feasible but should use subsidies or regulation of corporate behavior in order to foster them.

Conclusion

The petroleum industry is useful for understanding the political conditions that have promoted reform and for understanding that even cases of "successful" deregulation in Japan leave the bureaucracy and industry considerable power to restrict competition and keep prices high. The industry has experienced both formal regulatory reform, with the lapse of the Refined Petroleum Import Law, and also reform at the level of administrative guidance, through the regulatory reform action program.[20] The key to the regulatory reform was the leadership of Prime Minister Hosokawa and the shift in power from the vested interest network to the reform network. The impulse of Hosokawa's regulatory reform campaign led to a reexamination of Japan's energy policy and helped bring user groups and the Keidanren into the reform camp. The invigorated reform network ended up stronger than the vested interest network and was able to push through reform.

The lapse of the Refined Petroleum Import Law has produced gradual change in the Japanese oil market. Regulations continue to keep major new importers out of the market, and the fragmented gasoline distribution system is much less equipped to carry out rationalization than the European industry. Pretax Japanese prices have dropped from three times the U.S. price in 1993 to twice the U.S. price by 1997. Broadly speaking, the refined petroleum products case is typical of deregulation in heavily regulated sectors, such as transportation, telecommunications, and finance. There has been significant "relaxation of regulations" (*kisei kanwa*), but the bureaucracy continues to enjoy strong powers to regulate domestic market entry, imports, investment by foreign firms, pricing, and quality standards in ways that restrict domestic competition. At the same time the industry is atypical in that environmental and security requirements are likely to lead to *stronger* regulation. From the perspective of Japan's broader need to shift to nonfossil fuels, there is little benefit from the modestly lower gasoline prices that have resulted from the expiration of the Refined Petroleum Import Law. To achieve the environmental and security goals of conversion and renewable energy sources, Japan will actually need stronger, if reoriented, regulation.

Notes

1. Ōyama Kōsuke, "Japanese Trade Policy and Political System," in Frantz Waldenberger, ed., *The Political Economy of Trade Conflicts* (Berlin: Springer-Verlag, 1994), pp. 45–59.

2. Much of the description of the Japanese petroleum industry in this section draws on Koide Yasuhiro, "Kisei kanwa to wagakuni sekiyu sangyō no shōrai" (Regulatory reform and the future of our nation's petroleum industry), *Enerugii keizai,* vol. 21 (October 1995), pp. 8–26.

3. Imai Ken'ichi, "Sekiyu seisei" (Petroleum refining), in *Gendai sangyō soshiki* (Contemporary industrial organization) (Tokyo: Iwanami shoten, 1976), pp. 61–106, is excellent on the market structure of the petroleum industry; see also Richard J. Samuels, "A Political History of the Japanese Oil Industry," *The Business of the Japanese State: Energy Markets in Comparative and Historical Perspective* (Cornell University Press, 1987), pp. 168–227; and Matsui Ken'ichi and Ōyama Kōsuke, "Sekiyu sangyō seisaku" (Petroleum industrial policy), in Matsui Ken'ichi, ed., *Enerugii: Sengo 50 nen no*

kenshō (Energy: An examination of the postwar 50 years) (Tokyo: Denryoku shimpōsha, 1995), pp. 133–66.

4. There is more competition in the distribution sector, in which there are more small firms, than in the highly concentrated refining sector. See Ōyama Kōsuke, "Gyōseishidō no kisei kanwa" (Deregulation of administrative guidance), in *Gyōseishidō no seiji keizaigaku* (The political economy of administrative guidance) (Tokyo: Yūhikaku, 1996).

5. MITI guided industry not to import products from overseas but to refine crude oil domestically in order to ensure stability of petroleum supplies. Mitsubishi Sōgō Kenkyūjo, *Henbō suru oiru maaketto* (Changing oil market) (Tokyo: Jiji tsūshin sha, 1996), pp.47–48.

6. Economic Planning Agency, ed., *Kōzōkaikaku no tameno keizai shakai keikaku* (Economic and social plan for structural reform) (Tokyo: Ōkurashō insatsu kyoku, 1995).

7. The MITI announcement about gasoline was made in October 1996 and followed an earlier announcement about diesel fuel. "Japan: Tighter Specifications Threaten Products Imports," *Weekly Petroleum Argus,* October 28, 1996, p. 2.

8. The American market, by contrast, is weighted heavily toward gasoline. This section draws heavily on Koide, "Kisei kanwa to wagakuni sekiyu sangyō no shōrai."

9. The trading companies that are beginning to import include Marubeni, Kanematsu, Sumitomo, Itōchu, and Nisshō Iwai. Nakagawa, previously a distributing agent for refiner Cosmo Sekiyu, has also started importing products. "Japan: Tighter Specifications."

10. Petroleum Association of Japan, *Kiseikanwa, kawaru sekiyu, Q&A* (Deregulation: Changing petroleum, Q&A) (Tokyo, October 1997), p. 9

11. Ibid.

12. Frank K. Upham, "The Man Who Would Import: A Cautionary Tale about Bucking the System in Japan," *Journal of Japanese Studies,* vol. 17 (Summer 1991), pp. 323–43.

13. Mitsui Sekiyu owns a 50 percent share of Kyokutō Sekiyu in oil refining with Mobil Sekiyu, and the Industrial Bank of Japan owns small shares of Tōren, which is also owned by Esso Eastern and Mobil Petroleum Company, Cosmo Sekiyu, Japan Energy, Kyūshū Sekiyu, and other companies.

14. Nakatani Iwao and Ōta Hiroko, *Keizai kaikaku no bijon: "Hiraiwa repōto" wo koete* (The vision of economic reform: Beyond the "Hiraiwa report") (Tokyo: Tōyō keizai shimpōsha, 1994), pp. 146–47.

15. See the subcommittee's interim report, *Kyōjin katsu shinayakana enerugii bijon* (A tough and flexible visionary plan for energy) (Tokyo: Tsūshō sangyō chōsa kai, 1994), p. 59.

16. Uchihashi Katsundo, "Jikkenteki shakai shisutemu' no hata" (The flag of "experimental social system"), in *Kyōsei no daichi: Atarashii keizai ga hajimaru* (An earth

based on symbiosis: A new economy emerges) (Tokyo: Iwanami shoten, 1995), pp. 115–70.

17. Shimin Enerugii Keizai Kenkyū Jo, Part 1 of *2020 nen nihon enerugii keikaku* (An energy plan for Japan in 2020) (Tokyo: Daiyamondo sha, 1994).

18. Uchihashi, *Kyōsei no daichi.*

19. These examples are largely from ibid.

20. MITI seems to be reviewing the Petroleum Industry Law now.

CHAPTER SEVEN

Regulatory Reform and Market Opening in Japan

Mark C. Tilton

Despite a long-standing regulatory reform movement, government regulations as well as market rules implemented by private trade associations continue to limit access to the Japanese market. Federation of Economic Organizations (Keidanren) vice chairman Kumagai Naohiko warns that international trust in Japan has weakened because of regulations and other invisible barriers that block trade and investment from overseas.[1] One of the best indicators of the failure of regulatory reform to introduce real competition into Japanese markets is that Japanese prices continue to be far higher than those in other advanced industrialized countries. A 1994 Ministry of International Trade and Industry (MITI) survey of business costs found Japanese prices for raw materials, intermediate goods, and capital goods to be 30 percent higher

Earlier versions of this chapter were presented before the Political Economy of Deregulation Workshop, Honolulu, April 8–10, 1996, and the "Japanese Deregulation: What You Should Know" Symposium sponsored by the Japan-U.S. Friendship Commission and the Japan Information Access Project, Washington, D.C., April 4, 1997, and published as a discussion paper of the Wissenschaftszentrum Berlin. I thank Abo Tetsuo, Michael Beeman, Patricia Boling, Lonny Carlile, Hirowatari Seigo, Kudō Akira, David Leheny, Edward Lincoln, Miyajima Hiroaki, James Nickum, Elizabeth Norville, Kōsuke Ōyama, Arthur Stockwin, Yamazaki Hiroaki, and Yul Sohn for their helpful comments. I also thank Tanya Dresp for her valuable research assistance.

than in the United States, 19 percent higher than in Germany, and 46 percent higher than in South Korea. Prices for services were 51 percent higher than in the United States, 96 percent higher than in Germany, and 475 percent higher than in South Korea.[2] A November 1996 survey by Japan's Economic Planning Agency (EPA) estimated that prices for durable goods in Tokyo were 23 percent greater than New York prices, although 16 percent less than Berlin prices. Clothing and shoes were 68 percent greater than in New York and 8 percent greater than in Berlin, whereas other manufactured goods were 31 and 11 percent greater, respectively.[3] Yoko Sazanami, Shujiro Urata, and Hiroki Kawai concluded from their comparison of Japanese domestic and import prices that nontariff barriers add 174 percent to the prices of tradable goods in Japan. For machinery the "implied nontariff barrier rate," they revealed, was 140 percent, for chemicals 127 percent, and for metal products 60 percent.[4] As of this writing, the weaker yen has reduced the price gap somewhat; nevertheless the gap has lasted well over a decade and it is significant that Japan's prices for tradable goods are far less sensitive to competition from lower-priced imports than prices in countries such as the United States.[5] Hiroshi Iyori and Akinori Uesugi, both former Fair Trade Commission (FTC) officials, have written that "the big disparity in price for many imported products shows that price competition in the domestic market is not necessarily very strong."[6]

To understand why the regulatory reform movement has failed to free the market from these barriers, we need to look closely at the goals of Japanese business and government. Whereas in the United States arguments for regulatory reform point to its benefits for expanding consumer welfare, Japanese advocates of reform have focused on the need to strengthen Japan's international competitiveness.[7] And whereas the U.S. deregulation movement expresses strong faith in fluid markets, Japanese business appears to be comfortable with the power of bureaucracy and business to order markets. The focus of the Japanese regulatory reform movement has been to relax regulations selectively when this will increase the competitiveness of Japanese business. Free market arguments provide useful leverage to make strategic modifications to the inefficient excesses of a heavily regulated system, but it would be a mistake to conclude that the dominant thinking of Japan's business or political leaders is oriented toward wholesale promotion of free competition. As pointed out in chapter 1, the ordinary term that corresponds to deregulation in Japanese, *kisei kanwa,* merely means relaxation of regulations, a much less ambitious goal than deregulation. Rather than an overall opening of markets, we should expect regulatory reform to lead to selective market opening based on a combination of strategic concerns, the political clout of certain factions of business, market factors, and pressure from foreign governments.

Licensing as a Barrier to Competition and Trade

Japanese regulation is based on broad powers held by the bureaucracy that are to an important extent based on licensing authority. According to Funada Masayuki, "the use of regulations is fundamentally different between the U.S. and Japan. In Japan administrators use the system of permits and licenses to pull related firms into their world, and, while regulating them with orders and administrative guidance, nurture and protect the firms and industries. This is what the term 'Japan, Inc.' means."[8] Regulation tends to benefit insiders and prevent market change and is often pointedly directed at importers. Japanese bookstores abound with books that complain about the power of the bureaucracy to impose its will, often in arbitrary, nonsensical ways. For example, an indoor ski run was forced by the Ministry of Transportation (MOT) to spend $10,000 on a wind gauge for a ski lift because regulations stipulated that all ski lifts had to have them, despite the fact that there was obviously no wind inside the building and therefore no legitimate need for a wind gauge. In another case the former captain of a cruise ship that was being taken out of service bought it to use as a floating hotel in Beppu, Kyushu. The MOT first told the company that the ship was no longer really a ship, because it was not registered as one, and that the firm should be licensed by the Ministry of Construction (MOC). The MOC then ordered the passageways widened, the cabins taken out, and the wood paneling replaced with fireproof materials. Without cabins, the company gave up on the idea of running a hotel and decided to turn it into a restaurant instead. At that point the MOT said that because it was still floating it should be licensed as a ship. The extra work required cost 4.5 billion yen (roughly US$40 million) and forced the sale of the ship to a company in China, where it was possible to use it as a hotel.[9] The point of such stories is that licensing authority gives the bureaucracy enormous power even over domestic firms and that there is often no recourse to appealing its decisions.

An executive at one of Japan's top electronics firms recounted an example of how the MITI uses its general power to grant licenses and distribute information to get its way in areas not directly related to a specific license. MITI asked electronics firms to contribute money to a new high-tech information institute, the purpose of which seemed to be mainly to pay high salaries to MITI retirees. Although employees in other parts of the firm argued against wasting company money on the institute, the people directly in charge put money into it anyway because they feared that otherwise MITI at some point might withhold crucial information or permits. The electronics executive went on to say,

> Bureaucrats legally don't have power. But we're still afraid of being called in to present documents over some issue. When I think of being called in to explain something to some bureaucrat who is younger than me, my hands shake. It would be shameful to have to do that. It's not just a matter of money. And bureaucrats can always find something to penalize you over. For instance, you might make some small oversight or mistake that would normally be overlooked, but if you're on the outs with bureaucrats they'll call you in over it. Say, for instance, maybe you were supposed to import 20 percent of your semiconductors and you only imported 19.8 percent. They can find some pretext to fine you.[10]

Licensing powers have been key to restricting the establishment of large discount stores, thus protecting small shops and the domestic manufacturers that sell to them. One of the principal means of preventing the opening of discount stores has been the Large Store Law, created in 1973 to protect small stores from competition. The law requires prospective new store owners to consult with preexisting store owners to get their approval before beginning construction. The applicant must submit complete blueprints, which are normally not accepted in full, requiring new plans to be drawn up at considerable expense and restricting the size and efficiency of the new retail operations. The Large Store Law also restricts the days and hours that big stores can do business and their use of vending machines and advertisements.[11] Although the law has been loosened somewhat, the Japan FTC has complained that it is still a powerful barrier to retail competition and that "regulatory reform efforts have so far not tackled the major problems inherent in the retail sector."[12] Under the Large Store Law, MITI allowed retailers themselves to decide which stores should be allowed to open, thus enabling them to act as cartels.[13] Because of U.S. pressure after 1990, Japan allowed more new discount stores to open. This has led to some significant commercial successes by new discount stores, including major foreign discounters. Toys R Us opened its first store in Japan in 1991 and by the end of 1997 had opened sixty-four. Sales topped 100 billion yen for fiscal year 1997, making it Japan's largest toy retailer. Other big foreign stores such as Office Depot and Sports Authority have also come into the Japanese market. However, Frank Upham notes that although MITI has allowed more stores to open, the approval process continues to be controlled by MITI and the local retailers' associations and remains opaque and unaccountable to the public.[14] Not only are retailers still forced to scale back floor plans to get a license; the local small shop associations also use their influence over the licensing process to informally pressure large retailers to accept other restrictions on their operations. Thus, for instance, although 200 Daiei stores have liquor licenses, fifty of them can only sell imported liquor because of special extra restrictions written into their licenses. The president of Itō-Yōkadō, Suzuki Toshifumi, complains that regulation still represents a major barrier to opening large stores: "Since there are various regulations one can't get enough floor space and parking space into a store to bring in enough customers. The result is that lots of stores have to shut down. If there weren't regulations, it would be possible to build stores with a view to the long term."[15]

One of the practices the FTC has complained about is the use of licensing to limit the entry of new stores. For instance, the MOF uses licenses to limit the number of liquor and tobacco dealers in any given area. New liquor stores must be a certain distance from existing stores, and if the finance ministry, represented by local government officials, thinks there are too many, a lottery is held to allocate a license. To open a supermarket one needs forty-five different licenses, requiring the submission of 200 pages of applications under seventeen different laws. This includes separate applications to different agencies for licenses to sell meat, fish, milk, bread, tofu, pickles, ice cream, cakes, tea, frozen foods, box lunches, and so forth. The Daiei supermarket chain estimates the application process costs 160 million yen (about US$1.2 million) per supermarket.[16]

Obstacles to opening large stores have enabled small stores to hold onto a much larger share of the market than in the United States. In Japan in 1991, stores with one to four employees were 79.4 percent of total retail outlets in contrast to the 44.7 percent accounted for by small shops in the United States in 1989.[17] Restricting discounts has been important for keeping prices high for Japanese manufacturers and limiting access to foreign competitors. Discount stores sell electronics and other goods more cheaply and successfully negotiate for lower wholesale prices. Small shops charge higher prices and in the electronics market tend to be controlled by manufacturers, a unique feature of the Japanese distribution system that makes it harder for importers to break into the market.[18] Itoh Motoshige writes that during the period when the Japanese electronics industry was establishing itself as the world leader by selling large volumes of inexpensive, high-quality products overseas, manufacturers' control of domestic retailers enabled them to act as a "cartel" and charge high prices in the Japanese market.[19] Although the market share of discount stores has risen and that of manufacturer-controlled electronics stores has fallen less than 50 percent in recent years, they are still important for manufacturer profits.[20]

In April 1998 the Diet voted to abolish the Large Store Law and replace it with the new Large Store Location Law (Daikibo Kouri Tenpo Ritchi Hō), effective in the spring of 2000. MITI initiated the drive to replace the law with a less restrictive law in order to placate criticism from the United States and the European Union (EU), and perhaps also as a result of domestic concerns with efficiency and economic growth. The Japan Research Institute (Nihon Sōgō Kenkyūjo) estimates that relaxing regulations on distribution would raise GDP by 1.5 percent.[21] The new Large Store Location Law was originally supposed to reduce barriers to building large stores, but it was heavily criticized by the Central Federation of Societies of Commerce and Industry, Japan (Zenkoku Shōkōkai Rengō Kai), whose members deluged the Liberal Democratic party (LDP) main office and MITI with faxes. According to one young Diet member, "During the summer [of 1997], because of the Upper House elections, it was considered taboo to oppose the will of the small retailers."[22] LDP Diet member Tanaka Kazunori declared that "if the Large Store Law is abolished we can't win the next election."[23] MITI gave in and changed the bill to give local retailers associations an explicit say in decisions about whether to approve the building of new large stores.[24] According to the newspaper *Nihon keizai shinbun,* the final draft of the law was permeated with the interests of the retailers association.[25] According to the Keidanren, "There is fear that the review powers given to local municiapl governments [*chihō jichitai*] will make regulation of new store openings even stricter than under the Large Store Law." The Keidanren complains that the new law continues to give absolute power to administrative guidance.[26]

Not only does the new MITI-sponsored law allow local retailers to block new large stores, the Ministry of Construction (MOC) has also presented a new law to the Diet, the City Planning Law (Toshi Keikaku Hō), which allows city and village governments to restrict the areas in which large stores may be opened. The *Nihon keizai shinbun* comments that "on the surface it looks like a law close to the kind of Western regulation that would promote town development"[27] but that many in the distribution industry are critical of the new law for simply continuing old regulations in a new guise. "There will probably be some municipal governments that use the revised City Planning Law to introduce zoning oriented toward large-scale commercial facilities and facilitate store opening. However, in towns that want to preserve old shopping areas as a tourist attraction or where the local population wants to preserve old-fashioned shopping districts, it is likely that the local autonomous bodies will oppose the building of large stores and will use zoning to shut large stores out.[28]

In short, the regulation of the establishment of large stores is restrictive and opaque, and recent reform will not change this. The laws are flexible enough that they have made it possible for many new large stores to open, but they continue to provide significant protection for small stores. Although the Keidanren has been critical of the protection of small stores, the political power of small and medium-sized firms has blocked attempts to genuinely reform the Large Store Law.

Product Standards That Discriminate against Imports

Another way the bureaucracy favors domestic manufacturers over importers is through discriminatory use of product standards. Standards often fit the strengths and peculiarities of the domestic industry rather than serving any clear public interest in safety or quality. A common problem is that standards require specific designs unique to Japanese manufacturers, rather than fulfillment of performance criteria. For instance, the Construction Standards Law bases standards on traditional Japanese designs; standards for these are not even consistent among different regions of Japan.[29] The construction ministry has revised standards to allow in low-value-added products such as two-by-four lumber but has not introduced broader performance-based changes to allow in many commonly used higher-value-added building materials such as nails or prefabricated housing.

Japan also has many safety standards that both Japanese and foreign critics say are unnecessarily strict and that seem to serve mainly to keep out goods made in countries with more ordinary standards. Such barriers keep out high-pressure gas equipment, boilers, electric equipment, plumbing supplies, laminated wood products, fire protection glass, roofing tiles, timbered housing, and fire-resistant paints.[30]

Jay Tate argues that Japanese standards have greater power to block imports than do American or European standards in part because Japan tends to develop a single national standard under the guidance of the Japan Industrial Standards Committee, a government office supervised by MITI. Tate emphasizes that "while major European standards organizations are also quite centralized (some more so than Japan), they are private; it's the state role that gives the system its trade barrier bite."[31] A second feature of Japan's standards process that impedes imports is the Japan Industrial Standards (JIS) system of government testing and certification, which requires JIS factory approval before goods can be labeled with the JIS seal. "Consumers who have come to rely on the JIS mark are less likely to buy products from factories that have not been granted permission to affix the JIS mark to their products." By contrast, the more pluralistic American standardization process often produces multiple, competing standards, which are not usually backed by state authority.[32]

Japan has been slow to align its standards for electrical equipment with standards approved by the International Electrotechnical Committee (IEC), and products built to conform to IEC standards may require costly adaptation to comply with Japanese standards. The Japanese government has said it will move toward IEC-based standards but plans a lengthy transition period, and for many products it plans an indefinite period in which the preexisting standards under the Japanese Electrical Appliances and Material Control Law would coexist with IEC-based standards. The European Union (EU) is concerned that the continued existence of separate standards based on Japanese national law will bias consumers toward buying domestic rather than imported electrical equipment.

The EU also complains about the Japanese requirement to obtain government certification for electrical products, rather than merely requiring a manufacturer's declaration of safety. There are 117 products that have been allowed to come in without the government certification, but the EU would like to see the remaining 165 products added to this list. Another example of regulations that appear to use safety concerns to arbitrarily discriminate against imports is those on forklifts. Japanese regulations are much more onerous for larger and faster forklifts, the category into which most European and American forklifts fall. In January 1997, Japan expanded the maximum height of "small-sized special motor vehicles" from 2.0 meters to 2.8 meters, but this covered few foreign forklifts. Negotiations are under way to determine whether Japan's limit on speed of 15 kilometers an hour should be raised to

30 kilometers an hour. Another example is elevators, for which Europe, the United States, Canada, and Russia are moving toward harmonized codes and standards. Japan argues that it needs separate standards because it suffers from earthquakes, although this seems illogical because California also experiences earthquakes but uses elevators certified under international standards. The EU also complains that Japan, under its Industrial Safety and Health Law, requires "unit testing," that is, the inspection and approval of each individual product for certain types of machinery, such as mobile cranes and electrical emergency stops for rolling mills for kneading rubber. In the EU, manufacturers may choose from various technical approaches as long as they can show they meet essential safety requirements.[33] Another problem is that Japanese utilities require expensive safety devices to prevent electric generators from feeding current into devices that have been turned off. Many European wind turbines have functionally equivalent safety features built in, but requirements for the expensive additional safety devices keep them out of the market.[34]

Unusual requirements for license plate fittings and noise tests, and a refusal to recognize foreign front crash, brake, or engine tests increase the costs of refitting and testing cars for the Japanese market. And Japan has an unusual requirement dating from 1951 that control devices be located within 500 millimeters from the steering wheel. A European truck maker puts its defroster switches outside this range and is obliged to reconfigure the control panels of vehicles to be exported to Japan. In addition, Japan has unusual regulations requiring that motorized agricultural and construction machinery be certified for extended driving on roads, even though such vehicles are not normally driven on roads except for extremely limited distances.[35] Foreign pharmaceutical companies complain about the slow and sometimes opaque approval process for foreign goods and about arbitrary regulations that, for instance, prevent certain products from being sold in gelatin capsules.[36] The EU complains about a number of other products also subject to unusual standards, including inflatable life rafts, maritime cables, food supplements and diet products, wines, starches, mineral waters, plastics that come in contact with food, pork, food additives, and berries, and about a general series of unusual phytosanitary regulations that make fruit and vegetable imports expensive.[37]

Similarly arbitrary rules block imports of auto parts. The MOT requires frequent, costly checkovers of cars at a network of certified garages that pressure car owners into making unnecessary repairs to pass government inspections (*shaken*), creating an artificial market for parts.[38] "Critical parts" for auto

repairs can only be sold by certified dealers. Onerous requirements for certification have limited it largely to shops tied to Japanese automakers. The
shops reward the MOT for its patronage by hiring a large number of MOT
retirees. The list of critical parts tends to ensure that consumers buy Toyota
parts for Toyota cars rather than cheaper alternatives, and it enables Japanese
auto firms to charge high prices for parts that cross-subsidize their sales of
autos. A 1991 Commerce Department and MITI survey found that Japanese
auto parts cost more than twice as much as U.S. parts.[39] Firms that handle
imports of American auto parts typically add a 100 to 200 percent margin to
them, discouraging consumers from buying them. The MOT has loosened
inspection requirements for specified parts, enabling the Zen Nihon Rōtasu
Dōyūkai, an association representing about 8 percent of Japan's *shaken* repair
stations, to import parts directly from Tenneco Automotive.[40] The Japanese
government agreed to changes to open up the repair, inspection, and parts
market in 1995 that brought down the cost of car inspections 13 percent by
1996.[41] In 1997, the MOT agreed to drop the requirement for inspection by
MOT land offices for do-it-yourself repairs. The U.S. government complains
that this is meaningless because few Japanese consumers do their own repairs
and that it is nonsensical to continue to require continued inspections for
repairs by certified mechanics working in garages that have not been certified if
ordinary citizens are allowed to go without inspections of their work. The
United States, the EU, and Australia are still dissatisfied with progress over
parts and are asking that more products, particularly brake parts, be dropped
from the list of critical parts.[42] Regulations still unnecessarily burden Japanese
consumers, keep imports out, and allow Japanese car companies to charge
exorbitant prices for parts.

In addition to all the cases of discriminatory standards based on design or
safety issues, in other cases cumbersome and expensive import procedures
seem to have no purpose but to block imports. For instance, imported alcoholic
beverages are taken to a tax warehouse, where a seal is affixed by hand to each
can or bottle. The cheapest beer costs 22.5 yen a can at 130 yen to the dollar,
but the cost of the seal adds about 5 to 6 yen per can, or 25 percent of the cost of
imported beer. Liquor taxes of 77.70 yen push the price of beer up to 120 yen
per can.[43] The MOT requires that each time changes are made to certain
features of an automobile (such as engine displacement), the whole car must go
through the type approval process again. This process is time consuming
enough that European manufacturers often must ship vehicles by air to Japan at
least three months before marketing to get approval. Due to the narrow defini-

tion of "vehicle type" under Japan's certification system, Japan has more vehicle types than any other country in the world, and therefore a much more cumbersome and expensive vehicle type approval system. Some measures were taken in March 1997 to deal with the problem, but the EU is unsatisfied. By contrast, according to the director of the JETRO office in Berlin, Japan finds that the EU's system of car type approval "works very well. . . . Japanese companies don't seem to have any problems with European standards for autos. . . . As in the United States, there are no technical problems or problems with physical distribution."[44] To be sure, costly and cumbersome regulations plague distributors of domestic goods as well. Japanese auto dealers complain that each time they sell a car they have to go to the police, the District Land Transport Bureau, the ward office, and specified garages for permits. The *Nikkei sangyō shinbun* notes that whereas in the United States auto sales over the Internet have begun, the scale of paperwork makes it impossible for an individual in Japan to buy a car this way, and that journalist sees no prospect of change. "Some breeze-holes have opened with regard to automobiles, but in comparison with the United States and other countries, many think this is insufficient. There is especially much left to be done in deregulating new auto sales."[45]

Japan has conducted lengthy negotiations with the United States and the EU to correct discriminatory standards. Although the examples cited here are ongoing problems, many others have been solved. However, long lag times before a solution often appear to be the result of deliberate stalling tactics. For example, Japanese tonnage-based inspection criteria for recreational boats do not conform to International Standards Organization (ISO) criteria, which are based on length. The MOT has said that it will adopt ISO standards once a complete range of ISO standards covering stability, structure, main engine, and so on, is created, but it refuses to move to international practice in the meantime.[46] Or Japanese authorities find some loophole to keep from honoring a deregulation pledge they have made. For instance, in 1996 the MOT in principle allowed the Preferential-Handling Procedure (PHP), a streamlined approval procedure for vehicles imported in limited quantities, to be used for trucks and buses. But later the MOT ruled that it would not allow vehicles subsequently customized by local body shops, as are most imported large trucks, to be approved under PHP procedures. Or trading partners find that Japan simply does not live up to its agreements. For instance, in 1990 Japan agreed that when engine type and exhaust emission system are identical for different models of commercial vehicles, emission test results are allowed to be used for the various models, but the EU has found that the MOT has not consistently honored this promise. The Japanese government has set up the Office of the Trade and Investment Ombudsman to arbitrate foreign firms' disputes over such problems as discriminatory standards, but the office has no power to enforce its decisions and foreign firms have generally not been satisfied with the results.[47]

Weak Antitrust Policy and Informal Regulation by Industry Associations

Another regulatory problem is the absence of strong antitrust policy, which is needed to create the kind of genuinely competitive markets that would bring down domestic prices and pressure Japanese firms to seek out products that are a good value, including imports. In many cases the most important rules restricting competition in Japanese markets are actually imposed by private trade associations. These private rules are often supported by discriminatory government regulation, so private and public regulations work together as a system. Opening Japanese markets in a meaningful way requires both changing government regulation, in order not to discourage imports, and using aggressive antitrust policy to do away with the discriminatory, informal rules established by trade associations. One of the strategic choices of the regulatory reform movement has been to focus on regulation by government bureaucrats and to largely ignore the market controls of private trade associations. The result has been to chip away at some public restraints on the market, which largely affect services, while leaving intact the private restraints on competition that are especially important in markets for manufactured goods. In response to U.S. government pressure during the Structural Impediments Initiative (SII) talks, the Japanese government increased penalties under the Antimonopoly Law somewhat, although not as much as the U.S. government and the Japan FTC requested. Opposition to the larger increases came from the Keidanren, the LDP, MITI, and the construction ministry and suggests a lack of interest in increased competition.[48]

Although by some measures the Japanese FTC has a budget and staff roughly comparable with that of U.S. antitrust agencies, Japan lacks the private lawsuits and award of treble damages that make American firms pay attention to antitrust law.[49] Moreover, the FTC does not enforce the Antimonopoly Law aggressively. Michael Beeman notes that this is in part because the FTC's limited power to gather evidence that will stand up to appeals in the courts restricts its ability to enforce antitrust law. He also finds that historically the LDP has responded to spates of increased enforcement with threats to water down the Antimonopoly Law, forcing the FTC to temper its enforcement efforts.[50] Although the FTC has stepped up its enforcement of the law in recent years, by and large it has had little impact on competition; prices even for internationally tradable goods are still high by world standards, and cartels continue to operate flagrantly.

Much of the "regulation" that blocks access to Japan's markets is informally carried out by private industry, often with the help of supplementary government regulation. Informal industry self-governance is strongest in the basic materials sector, which accounts for one-third of the value added in Japanese manufacturing. Such goods as steel, cement, and plastics are readily transportable and largely standardized. Although Japanese prices for such goods are high by international standards, Japan runs trade surpluses in most basic materials industries. These industries have long been considered key to Japan's economic security and have been supported by industrial policy and government-backed cartels. Official cartel policies have been discontinued because of U.S. complaints that they constituted an unfair trade barrier, but informal cartels remain strong and constitute the most powerful form of governance in the basic materials sector.

The gap between high domestic prices and low export prices reveals the cartels' success in preventing firms from undercutting one another's prices in their home markets even though they will sell cheaply abroad. The price gap is not the ephemeral result of fluctuations in exchange rates but has been long lasting. For example, domestic prices for all the major standardized ethylene-based petrochemicals averaged 60 percent over export prices for 1980 to 1992 and 64 percent over import prices.[51] From 1986 to 1995, Japanese domestic undelivered cement prices averaged 150 percent over its export prices and 72 percent over import prices.[52] The "big buyer price," used for at least half of Japan's steel, was 46 percent higher than the export price for steel plate from 1985 to 1995 and 57 percent higher than the import price from 1985 to 1991.[53] The discipline of domestic cartels can be seen not only in their prices but also in their behavior. Some analysts have emphasized individual firm preferences for long-time ties with suppliers as the reason for persistent high prices and resistance to imports in Japanese markets.[54] But in the basic materials industries individual long-term ties do not stand up on their own, relying instead on industrywide cartels for support. A good example of this is the petrochemical market, in which buyers emphasize long-term ties in order to ensure security of supply and in some cases to get suppliers to invest in producing custom-grade chemicals. Nevertheless long-term ties are never strong enough to prevent some price competition in the domestic market, and the inefficiency of domestic manufacturers makes them vulnerable to the danger that domestic competition might drive prices down to international levels. In order to prevent such competition, domestic petrochemical firms have used a price formula since 1983 that ties commodity chemical prices to the cost of materials. Petrochemical industry officials deny the existence of the price-setting formula and acknowledge that it would be illegal. However newspapers regularly report its use, and chemical buyers for the auto industry report that it is "a rule that the whole industry abides by."[55] This acknowledgment that buyers consider the cartel legitimate underscores its character as a form of informal but publicly supported regulation.

The cement industry also has a cartel that not only sets prices but threatens refusals to deal, to keep buyers from going around the cartel and buying imports. That is, the trade association threatens domestic construction companies that they will not be able to buy domestic cement if they dare to buy imports. The implementation of this industry strategy to keep imports out was supported by government nontariff barriers and appears to remain strong. Newspapers reported in 1993 that ready-mix concrete companies were hiring gangsters to scare off outsiders to the cartel that used imports and were arranging special loans from financial institutions to reimburse cartel members for price cuts designed to run import-using competitors out of business. Prices have declined somewhat in the 1990s, leading cement firms into a series of mergers that has increased concentration in the industry.

The steel cartel is not as elaborate or visible as the chemical or cement cartels, yet it is at least as strong and its existence is an open secret. In 1996 I asked a marketing executive in a large Japanese steel firm, who had been posted by his firm for several years to the United States, how competition in the Japanese steel market compared with that in the United States. He replied, "Oh, it's totally different. In the U.S. you have free competition. Here it's like we're violating the Antimonopoly Law every day. The steel companies get together and talk about what the price ought to be."[56]

Buyers buy from the cartel rather than buying cheaper imports in part because of a belief that it is their patriotic duty to support the domestic industry. For instance, shipbuilders buy Japanese steel even though it costs 40 percent more than Korean steel, and they face tough competition from Korean shipbuilders. As one shipbuilding executive put it, "People often say, 'Steel is the state.' It's true. If steel gets weak, all of industry will get weak. If we switch to imported steel, the country will stop developing."[57] That major steel buyers talk about loyalty to the national industry as a whole rather than to particular suppliers suggests that nationalism rather than long-term ties with individual suppliers keeps them from buying imports. Glen Fukushima, president of the American Chamber of Commerce in Japan, has found in discussions with American firms selling in Japan that those selling directly to consumers do not tend to find resistance to the idea of imports but that firms selling intermediate goods to industrial firms often run into a problem of *jimaeshugi,* the idea that Japan ought to be self-sufficient.[58]

Although the steel cartel benefits from the nationalist bias of its buyers against imports, it also uses coercion to enforce its monopoly in the domestic market. The *Nihon keizai shinbun* reports that "it is common knowledge that the domestic steelmakers use tacit pressure to keep out imports and support the price structure. The . . . shearing and coil center firms haven't spoken openly about using imported steel because of fear of reaction from the blast steel makers. The big trading firms haven't handled imports openly."[59] Iketani Masanari, president of Tokyo Steel, the largest of the mini-mills attempting to compete with the steel oligopoly, laughed at the suggestion that the FTC played any role in preventing the steelmakers from bullying their buyers and said that "to sell your products, you have to find some person at each company who is not afraid of retaliation [from the big steel companies.]"[60]

Iketani told me in November 1995 that nothing had changed. He added that overseas the Japanese steel firms had actually retaliated against those going around the cartel. According to Iketani, Japan's five big steel companies have handled their exports as a cartel. In China, for instance, the five companies negotiated a single price with Min Metal, the state trading company handling most of China's steel imports, and allocated sales both among themselves and among the Japanese trading companies that served as intermediaries. In 1993, the Mitsubishi Corporation, one of the trading companies, offered Tokyo Steel a contract to sell 20,000 tons of hot rolled coil to Min Metal. Though Tokyo Steel had been selling bar steel in China, its hot coil sales were seen as a threat to the cartel. The five major steel companies retaliated against the Mitsubishi Corporation by excluding it from rail sales to China. Joint sales negotiations by the five companies with Min Metal were officially stopped as of 1995, but Iketani thinks that in fact they still continue.[61] Mini-mill steel producers also charge that the integrated steelmakers have harassed them by exporting scrap and refusing to sell it in the domestic market. This is apparently part of the reason for the rise of

Japanese scrap prices in the 1990s and a reason that Tokyo Steel lost money in 1996 and 1997. The mini-mills' trade association, the Steel Mini-mill Industrial Association (Denro Kōgyōkai) has demanded that domestic integrated producers sell domestic mini-mills the scrap they are currently exporting.[62]

Japanese cartels are not omnipotent; buyers try to negotiate lower prices and are often successful. Although in the main large industrial buyers have remained loyal to their domestic suppliers, car companies have bought some foreign steel in part to pressure their domestic suppliers to lower prices. Nevertheless, the fact that major Japanese firms continue to sell cheaply overseas before they will undercut their competitors' prices in the domestic market suggests the cartels continue to exert strong discipline.

Private cartels are often supported by government regulation. MITI requires special, onerous tests for cement imports, a trade barrier that helps insulate the domestic industry from foreign competition. And the construction ministry provides regulatory barriers to keep outsiders to the steel cartel out of the construction market, which absorbs half the nation's steel. Although in principle public works projects are supposed to be open to all, the MOC indirectly fixes prices and designates suppliers. Groups affiliated with the construction ministry publish two books that list prices for construction materials and lists companies that are allowed to supply them.[63] Tokyo Steel complains that this informal rule about construction supply sources restricts government steel purchases to firms that belong to the domestic cartel, even though Tokyo Steel sells more cheaply than cartel members.

The basic materials cases show us that private regulation through informal cartels is a major force in regulating Japanese markets and keeping out imports, that the FTC tolerates blatant cartels, and that government regulation often reinforces them. They also show that private and public regulations are not the only trade barrier. Company executives say that their firms avoid buying foreign inputs because it would weaken the larger national economy. The fact that managers make this argument even for completely standardized products such as sheet steel makes one suspect that the barriers of mercantilist attitudes in high-tech sectors are at least as high. Sung Joon Roh argues that managers of Japanese corporations are able to indulge their mercantilist beliefs because widespread cross-shareholding of Japanese firms relieves them of strong pressures to produce high profits.[64] The basic materials cases show the strength of Japanese managers' adherence to the norm that Japan should produce key materials domestically whenever possible.

Industry self-regulation is also enforced through group boycotts with bu-reaucratic support in the retail sector. Kraft, Incorporated, Japan's largest pharmacy chain, ran into such problems in 1993 when it opened an outlet in Saku, Nagano Prefecture, near the area's largest hospital.[65] In retaliation the local pharmacists association expelled Kraft from the organization, which acts as a conduit for information from local health authorities and shares inventory among members, and in which membership is required to avoid burdensome equipment requirements by the Ministry of Health and Welfare.[66] The association also carried out an organized attack on the new pharmacy, distributing leaflets at hospitals that urged patients to use only pharmacies that belonged to the association. The campaign was successful in limiting business to only 10 percent of what Kraft had expected. To top it off, all three of the local pharmaceutical wholesalers refused to sell to Kraft because it is not a member of the regional association. Kraft for its part believes the wholesalers were afraid of being boycotted by the members of the association.[67]

Paradoxically, regulation by the FTC also helps industry groups organize to discourage competition through the Fair Trade Promotion Associations, set up in 107 different industries. The associations are headed by industry leaders such as the president of Matsushita, Matsushita Masaharu, Toyota's Toyoda Eiji, and Ishino Kiyoharu of Shiseido and act as liaisons between firms and the FTC. Legal affairs specialists of member firms frequent both the FTC and the Fair Trade Promotion Councils in order to discuss FTC guidelines. The Discount Cosmetic Dealers Association has complained that the tie between the FTC and the Fair Trade Promotion Councils is too close and opaque. Former LDP Lower House Diet member Kuranari Masa has said that the FTC's meetings with the Fair Trade Council "make it look like companies could avoid investigations if they join the associations."[68] Kodak complains that the Photographic Supplies Promotion Association, with FTC support, has enforced rules against discounting and promotional activities. The photographic supplies Fair Trade Promotion Council has asked members to be on the lookout for firms that are discounting cameras and other goods and report them to the FTC for discipline. Trade association members in the film industry have been quite clear that the purpose of maintaining high domestic prices is to create a sanctuary market in Japan. In 1986, when cheap, reimported Fuji film was threatening high domestic prices, Zenren, the retailers association affiliated with Fuji, criticized the retailers: "This is unacceptable. Domestic products cover the cost of selling goods cheaply abroad. Therefore, Zenren says that [reimported film] should be sold at the same price [as domestic Fuji film] so as to stabilize the market."[69]

One of the functions of the FTC Promotion Councils is to enforce FTC rules that actually limit competition by restricting the use of promotional gifts. These restrictions have been loosened in some industries, although in others, such as banking, trade associations restrict them on their own.[70] The real estate industry is currently pressuring the FTC to tighten the restrictions on promotional gifts. The FTC prohibits promotional gifts worth more than 10 percent of the value of a product worth more than 500,000 yen. In the case of housing, gifts include items as extravagant as cars. Consumer groups complain that if real estate companies can afford to give away cars with a new house, pricing must bear little relation to costs.[71] Here the prospect of tighter regulations on promotional gifts is a symptom rather than a cause of lack of competition. The deeper problem is the absence of meaningful antitrust policy.

Antitrust legal expert Harry First argues that the thrust of the FTC's stepped-up enforcement efforts since 1991 has been in enforcing laws that restrict retail price maintenance. In 1991, the FTC issued new guidelines on resale price maintenance and has pursued cases in drugs, cosmetics, and prerecorded audio products.[72] In 1997, the FTC completely banned resale price maintenance for cosmetics.[73] First argues that the decision to cut resale price maintenance favors manufacturers over the retail sector and will enable big retailers to cut distribution margins and consumer prices at the expense of inefficient small stores, which will be unable to compete. Ultimately this will force distribution companies rather than manufacturers out of business.

Although the FTC has made greater enforcement efforts in this area, its impact even on resale price maintenance has been feeble. The FTC's actions in the cosmetics industry have attracted the most attention because of the industry's extremely high prices. Yoko Sazanami, Shujiro Urata, and Hiroki Kawai estimate the rate of implied nontariff protection in cosmetics at 660 percent.[74] In October 1995, the FTC ruled that Shiseido had illegally used threats to cut off deliveries to Jusco, Daiei, and the Consumers Co-ops in retaliation for discounting. However, at the same time it continued to allow Shiseido to use face-to-face counseling requirements as an excuse for cutting off sales to smaller discounters. In 1990, Shiseido cut off deliveries to discounter Fujiki Shōten, saying it had broken its contract to only sell cosmetics through direct sales in order to provide face-to-face counseling. Fujiki Shōten argued that although it sold cosmetics over the telephone, it provided face-to-face counseling for any customers who requested it. In this regard, its sales were parallel to

Shiseido's own subsidiary, Za Ginza, and to the major department stores, which also sell by telephone. What Fujiki does do differently is deeply discount prices.[75] The FTC investigated the case but said there was insufficient evidence to decide against Shiseido. A lower court decided in favor of Fujiki, but this decision was overturned by a higher court and is now under consideration by the Supreme Court. The upshot is that Fujiki is still unable to get deliveries from Shiseido, as is Kawachiya, another discounter. In August 1997, Fujiki also asked the FTC to issue a cease-and-desist order against Kanebo, another major cosmetics producer, and against Kanebo's distribution company, for cutting off supplies to Fujiki in retaliation for discounted sales.[76] Other discount stores find that Shiseido will supply them some products but reserve other products for stores that do not discount. Shiseido's vice chairman Genma Akira says that "the retailer decides the price," but admits that "we contract with *keiretsu* stores that emphasize value [*kachi*] for our new brands."[77] According to the *Nihon keizai shinbun,* the managing director of the All Japan Cosmetics Retailers Association (Zenkoku Keshōhin Kouri Kumiai Rengōkai), which represents 17,000 *keiretsu* stores, "does not hide his warning when he says, 'the discount stores get hit because they make sales on the side' [that is, they sell to blacklisted stores such as Fujiki]."[78]

Sensui Fumio notes that although the EU also allows suppliers of certain types of products to restrict supplies to certain dealers, there must be objective criteria for excluding sellers and these must be applied without discrimination. He notes critically that the Japanese FTC has brought neither consideration to bear in reviewing cosmetics cases.[79] The *Shūkan tōyō keizai* cites an "observer knowledgeable about the FTC" as saying, "Within the FTC there are many voices that are critical of giving too much support to discount stores."[80] The larger discount stores have been cautious about discounting cosmetics. Even Daiei, frequently cited as a champion price-cutter, is only timidly discounting the high-end cosmetics that require counseling by a maximum of 10 percent in the form of stamps good for purchases only at Daiei. According to the *Nihon keizai shinbun,* "It is thought that Daiei is trying to maintain the price the manufacturer wants and thus avoid provoking a reaction."[81] Supermarkets have been discounting cosmetics that do not require counseling since 1995 but have not discounted cosmetics that do require it because of resistance from manufacturers.[82] In short, even in its showcase area of enforcement, the FTC appears ineffective and compromised.

The problem of manufacturers' pressure on distributors is also at the root of the dispute between the United States and Japan over sales of new autos in

Japan. Imported autos took only 6 percent of the Japanese auto market in 1996. This contrasts with the United States, where imports from outside North America (not counting imports from Canada and Mexico) accounted for 11.3 percent of the domestic market in 1996 and where total sales by non-U.S. firms (including their North American subsidiaries) took 27.2 percent of the market (including 22.8 percent by Japanese firms). The U.S. government has complained that the principal barrier to auto imports into Japan is the overwhelming dominance of exclusive dealerships. Of Japan's 16,200 sales outlets, only 753 handle cars produced by the "big three" American auto firms: GM, Ford, and Chrysler. The merger of Daimler-Benz and Chrysler may provide access for Chrysler cars through Daimler-Benz distributorships, although it is too early to tell. The vast majority of Japanese automobile dealers avoid taking on a second automobile brand because they fear retaliation from their current supplier. By contrast, court rulings in the United States against exclusive dealerships and strong antitrust enforcement give American automobile dealers recourse if manufacturers threaten retaliation, freeing them to sell cars from competing manufacturers. The reluctance of Japanese suppliers to take on foreign car sales significantly increases the cost of entering the Japanese market. The 1995 U.S.-Japan Automotive Agreement sought to expand the number of high-volume dealers handling foreign autos but has had little success. As of late 1997, only 142 additional dealers had agreed to handle American big three autos.[83] It is true that German automakers also insist on exclusive dealerships in Germany and that German automakers have pressured distributors not to undermine prices. The director of the Japan External Trade Organization office in Berlin, Niimura Kiyoshi, recognizes that the predominance of exclusive dealerships is a barrier to imports in both Germany and Japan. "It is not as easy to export to Europe as it is to the United States." According to Niimura, the unwillingness of distributors to take on cars from other manufacturers makes it expensive and slow to build up a network of auto distributors, in contrast to the United States, where distributors are willing to take on cars from additional manufacturers. Although Japanese companies have ultimately succeeded in the German market, "Japanese companies struggled for twenty years to build their distribution networks. You can't succeed quickly here as you can in the United States. The United States has complained to both Japan and Germany of this."[84]

The EU's 10 percent tariff on imported cars, in contrast to Japan's zero tariff and the American general tariff on cars of 2.5 percent (although a 25 percent tariff on light cars and trucks), is an important formal barrier to car imports from outside the EU. German automakers have erected further informal trade barriers by pressuring distributors in neighboring countries not to undermine high prices for cars in Germany by selling to German car buyers. In January 1998, the EU fined Volkswagen $112 million for barring its distributors in Italy from selling cars to Germans and Austrians.[85] Similar practices are apparently used by other automakers, and most car makers sell their cars some 15 to 25 percent higher in Germany than in such nearby countries as Denmark, Italy, and the Netherlands. At the same time, however, the German auto market is much more internationalized and open to imports than the Japanese market. Imports took about 40 percent of the German market in 1994 (16 percent from Japan).[86] And a third of cars produced in Germany were produced by the American manufacturers Ford and Opel (owned by GM). All in all, weak antitrust policy is a greater barrier to car imports in Japan than in Germany.

Another area in which weak antitrust policy is a concern is telecommunications. The Japanese government approved the restructuring of Nippon Telephone and Telecommunications (NTT) in December 1996, has ratified the Fourth Protocol of the General Agreement on Telecommunications Services of the World Trade Organization (GATS/WTO) on basic telecommunications services, and has liberalized telecommunications services within Japan.[87] But the EU is concerned that weak antitrust means that there will be nobody to prevent NTT, which is two-thirds owned by the Japanese government and which enjoys a virtual monopoly in local phone markets, from using its monopoly power to unfairly exclude competitors. As an example of such monopolistic practices, NTT has set connect charges at a level that makes market entry difficult, 2.4 times higher in 1997 than those charged in the United Kingdom. Although Ministry of Post and Telecommunications study groups are working on developing fair methods of pricing, these are unlikely to issue reports and rulings until 1999 or later, which gives NTT a crucial advantage in the period during which the telecommunications market is opened to restructuring.[88]

The international trade consequences of the lack of antitrust challenges to NTT are not only the exclusion of foreign telecommunications firms from the Japanese telecommunications market, but also the exclusion of equipment providers from the telecommunications equipment market. NTT has given preference to domestic suppliers, although it has expanded procurement from foreign suppliers somewhat under the 1994 NTT Procurement Agreement with the U.S. government. An example of NTT's rigid loyalty to domestic suppliers is its allowing its three domestic suppliers of cable, Sumitomo, Fujikura, and Furukawa, to maintain the same market shares they have held since 1924. Only the remaining 20 percent of the market is open to foreign suppliers. Although suppliers of fiber optic cable have had success in selling to firms in other Japanese industries, such as utility companies, long-distance carriers, and cable TV, NTT's monopoly power has enabled it to ignore the price competitiveness of foreign equipment suppliers.[89] A recent JETRO report on market access issues in the telecommunications equipment sector sharply criticizes a number of barriers to imports in Japan and favors adopting Western European and American regulations and business practices, although it expresses optimism that new policies will soon solve the problems.[90]

Lack of Business Enthusiasm for Deregulation

Both top business leadership and MITI argue that Japanese business needs regulatory reform to lower the domestic costs of production and maintain the competitiveness of domestic business. The Industrial Structure Council, which advises MITI, has called for "rapid regulatory reform" and the "correction of private practices that restrict competition."[91] Why, then, is so little changing?

Discussion of regulatory reform is earnest and meant to correct excessive bureaucratic control. However, Western observers misinterpret the deregulation movement when they see it as an attempt to establish liberal capitalism in Japan. The dominant powerholders and intellectual leaders in Japan continue to subscribe to a "developmentalist" *view* of the economy, whereas they welcome limited reforms to developmentalist *policy*. Developmentalism holds that society's primary economic goal is the development of strong and secure domestic industry.[92] The state is to set broad goals for industry and provide regulatory support for exclusive and collusive arrangements between competing firms to keep prices high, imports out, capital stable and loyal, and business well funded. By contrast, liberal economic doctrine makes consumer welfare the goal; trusts the market to achieve it; and is opposed to bureaucratic intervention, price collusion, or protectionism. Although liberalism has not achieved the mobilizing depth of belief of an ideology in Japan, it nevertheless enjoys a broad legitimacy that enables various institutions and aggrieved interests to put some limits on the inefficiencies of the developmental state and private cartels. However, the principal spokespersons for liberalism—the FTC, economists, and lawyers—do not have the power, even if they had the desire, to impose a liberal order on the economy.

The contrast between developmentalism and liberalism was behind the fruitful tension between market and state ordering that Chalmers Johnson says was key to the success of Japanese industrialization in the 1948–75 period.[93] As Japan has become more deeply enmeshed in the international trade system and as overseas expectations that it open its markets have increased, liberalism has gained great legitimacy in public discourse about the economy and developmentalist visions of the economic order have retreated into the background. The rise in the yen since 1985 and the resulting domestic-external price gap have created aggrieved parties who want particular markets loosened, and the regulatory reform movement has given a home to grievances about bureaucratic excesses. Various bureaucracies and interest groups, such as the Keidanren, MITI, and the MOF, use liberalism to argue for specific reforms, but the regulatory reform movement has not done away with discretionary bureaucratic governance of markets nor brought about aggressive antitrust policy to squelch private cartels. There is as yet no crisis to force a fundamental change in values. Developmentalism is still the common sense that guides the economy beneath the patina of liberalism.

The regulatory reform movement must be understood as a corrective and complement to Japan's system of developmentalist capitalism rather than an attempt to overthrow it. Japanese developmentalist ideology puts the building of the nation's productive capacity above efficiency or consumption gains for individuals. One of the core concepts of developmentalist ideology is the notion of "excessive competition," defined as a condition of great excess supply, prices below costs, and producers in danger of being pushed out of business.[94] Proponents of the concept argue that excess competition results from high sunk costs, which make firms reluctant to abandon production, and they say intervention may be justified to avoid the excessive monopoly rents that the remaining firms would exact after weak competitors had been pushed out.[95] Although an oxymoron to Western neoclassical economists, developmentalist ideology holds that excessive competition is injurious because it wastes productive capacity through underutilization or bankruptcy and needless scrapping of facilities and because bankruptcy causes human suffering. Many argue that economic thought in Japan is converging with that of liberal economies, but the continued strength of the concept of excessive competition suggests continued divergence between economic thought. An interesting illustration of the way Japanese business leaders think about competition is a quote by Jirō Ushio, chairman of the Japan Association of Corporate Executives (Keizai Dōyūkai), one of Japan's four main business associations.

In the Asia-Pacific region, most countries operate by what has become known as the "APEC de facto standard"—a set of fairly advanced trade rules based on market realities in the United States. Compared to this Anglo-Saxon model, the traditional market rules in Japan and Europe are closed by nature. . . . Three Japanese practices go against this Asia-Pacific model: market rigging within an industry, excessive government control, and a tendency not to throw bad eggs out of the market. Old-fashioned Japanese businesses tend to avoid competing in open markets. Some industries condone restrictive business practices and they gang up to shut out new entries. True, rigging the market is a highly efficient way to do business, no one gets hurt through government mediation, and everyone can keep the cost of sales low. The upshot is higher prices, and it is the consumer who ends up holding the bill.

This article was published in the English-language *Japan Times,* and in it Ushio presents himself as a reformer, calling for stronger FTC enforcement of the Antimonopoly Law.[96] Ushio is critical of collusion, yet he argues that "rigging the market is efficient." He deplores the higher prices that consumers must pay but notes that at the same time rigging prices reduces marketing and distribution costs for manufacturers. Although Ushio advocates reform and antitrust policy, he follows the view that too much competition is wasteful.

Quantitative measures also show that this developmentalist suspicion of excessive competition continues to run deep and that liberal ideology has not fundamentally transformed Japanese economic thinking. One would expect that if liberal economic ideas were successfully discrediting the concept of excessive competition, major newspapers covering the economy would stop using the term. The most prominent and proderegulation newspapers on the economy are the *Nihon keizai shinbun* (*Nikkei,* for short) and its three sister papers that specialize in distribution, finance, and industry. Yet a survey of articles in these newspapers from 1975 to 1997 finds that usage of the term *excessive competition* (*katō kyōsō*) has not declined significantly. It was used in an average of 120 articles per year from 1975 to 1979, 152 from 1980 to 1984, 200 from 1985 to 1989, 160 from 1990 to 1994, and 124 from 1995 to 1997. In 1997 the term appeared 150 times.[97] Furthermore, the *Nikkei* newspapers do not use the term critically, but unselfconsciously as a useful concept for describing large parts of the economy. The fifty most recent articles mentioning the term *excessive competition* up to February 20, 1998, described the phenomenon in eighteen different industries. To be sure, industries with standardized technologies—such as cement, steel, chemicals, aluminum rolling, bread baking, and shipping—are considered to suffer from excessive competition. The retail sector, covering markets from groceries and liquor to gasoline, is also so characterized, perhaps not surprisingly given the large number of small enterprises it harbors. One might be tempted to think that the term is only used for these older or low-wage industries, but this is not the case. The *Nikkei* newspapers also report that such machine sectors as autos and water meters are plagued by excessive competition, as well as a range of service industries, some with quite new technologies, such as insurance, real estate, hotels, theme parks, ski resorts, satellite transmission, and television broadcasting. Excessive competition is not simply a tired phrase used for old-line industries but is applied to industries across the spectrum.

The newspapers often use the term *excessive competition* in a quoted phrase to suggest that industry insiders think their market is so characterized. But more often the newspapers use the term simply to describe what reporters see as objective reality. For instance, the February 17, 1998, *Nihon keizai shinbun* reported that "there are eighty-nine [paper] manufacturing companies nationwide, and they are falling into classic excessive competition."[98] There is no irony in the use of the term and indeed none in any of the fifty articles. It is simply a matter-of-fact representation of the *Nikkei* newspapers' worldview and likely of Japanese business more broadly. The continued frequent use of the term suggests that there has been little fundamental change in the view that competition is sometimes excessive and by implication best reined in by state or trade association governance.

Not only has Japan's business press not moved away from certain core developmentalist economic tenets; rank-and-file business organizations also appear to maintain considerable support for time-honored patterns of industrial policy and industry collusion. Despite calls for regulatory reform by the Keidanren, the broader business community is content with the status quo. A *Nikkei shinbun* survey on market liberalization and regulatory reform found large firms ambivalent about the need to scrap informal bureaucratic supervision of business or close cooperation within industries. Although 82 percent of firms say they want regulations changed, only 35 percent want changes in administrative guidance, that is, informal bureaucratic supervision and regulation, and a mere 6 percent want to change the pattern of government-business cooperation. Although 56 percent think that there should be change in Japan's "side-by-side competition," or *yokonarabi kyōsō,* a pejorative term that means the absence of real competition, only 9 percent want to change the system of "industrial cooperation," or *sangyō kyōchō,* a positive term that also implies cooperation rather than competition. Few respondents express strong support for maintaining these features of Japan's political economy either, suggesting that firms are content to let the system muddle along as is. Overall, big business is evenly split over whether Japan "definitely needs" an "economic and business system based on market principles" or only needs one "to a certain extent."[99] The survey indicates no groundswell of business support for strong antibureaucratic, promarket reforms.

Although individual industries are naturally interested in removing the taxes and restrictions that affect them directly, a review of the journals published by Japan's auto, electronics, telecommunications, and chemical industry trade associations suggests that these industries have no broader complaint with bureaucratic guidance. The journals prominently feature articles by bureaucrats explaining future industry trends and the policies that will be taken to deal with them. They also express no urgent desire for freer markets. The *Nikkakyō geppō* (Japan Chemical Industry Association monthly), under the mistaken impression that Japan has an especially tough antitrust policy, wants it watered down to European and American levels.[100] The *Jidōsha kaigisho nyūsu* (Japan Auto Chamber of Commerce news) argues against deregulating the taxi industry, because regulatory reform would lead to excessive competition among taxi drivers.[101] Although of course the larger auto industry has an interest in keeping taxi fares high in order to give people an incentive to buy their own cars instead of using taxis, it is interesting that the industry that is the foremost representative of internationalism still uses the term *excessive competition*. Although American observers often hope that the drive to cut costs will cause Japanese industries to abandon domestic partners in favor of more efficient foreign firms, the auto industry publication urges additional subsidies to keep Japan's uncompetitive domestic shipping industry in business. It argues that Japan needs a domestic international shipping industry for the sake of security in Japan's international shipping and to give Japan bargaining power with foreign shipping firms.[102] Again, there is no broad business mandate for usurping the role of bureaucrats, introducing rigorous market competition, or running uncompetitive strategic industries out of business in the name of efficiency.

But are not global competitive pressures forcing Japan to deregulate? Economists like to think that Japanese markets cannot stay rigged, because consumers will not put up with it and because high prices make firms uncompetitive on world markets. The Keidanren and MITI also argue that high costs are driving Japanese manufacturing overseas and thus "hollowing out" Japanese industry. It is true that increasing Japanese overseas investment has closed some factories and produced some "reverse" imports from Japanese overseas plants into Japan. But MITI says that reverse imports are far outweighed by Japan's exports of parts and capital goods to its overseas factories. In 1993, exports to Japanese factories accounted for $102 billion, far more than the $28 billion in imports from these factories.[103] In my view, the cries of alarm about hollowing reflect a paranoid fear of imports of manufactured goods, more than any real threat to the economy. International trade can only plausibly be said to hollow an economy that is running a trade deficit. Although imports of manufactured goods have increased, Japan is still by far a net exporter in the vast majority of industrial categories.

It is true that Japanese goods and services are expensive compared with world prices and that theoretically this should impose high costs on firms competing in world markets. But Japanese firms do not sell most of their products in competitive world markets. They sell at high prices in a domestic sanctuary market, cover their costs there, and sell at lower prices overseas. As long as Japanese consumers pay high prices for the end product, domestic manufacturers are by and large able to make ends meet. Although proponents of regulatory reform have emphasized the drag that inefficient sectors place on the export sectors, these inefficient sectors also in turn support the export industries by paying their high prices for domestic manufactured goods. For example, Japanese construction companies charge more than twice as much as American companies for the same construction work but provide a docile and captive market for expensive domestic steel and cement.[104] Similarly, Japanese consumers may pay high rates for insurance, but the insurance companies support manufacturing by investing their capital quietly in Japanese business without pressuring manufacturers for immediate high profits. Japanese travelers pay high domestic air fares, but the airlines support the fledgling domestic aerospace industry. There is plenty of room to increase efficiency, and change will no doubt continue, but it is not an impossible situation that business is desperate to change. Fears of economic dislocation and unemployment seem to outweigh concerns about efficiency losses due to the high prices of goods.

Conclusion

Overall the impact of the regulatory reform movement has been to introduce new competition in significant, if gradual and limited, ways. It has reminded people of the discrepancy between domestic and international prices and of the imperative of introducing efficiency and rationalization. Even if it has not moved quickly, it has prepared business people for change. Although it may be slow in opening discount stores, it discourages twenty-year-olds from thinking they have a future taking over their parents' small shops.

At the same time, the persistence of developmentalist ideology ensures that debates over regulatory reform will discuss whether regulatory reform will strengthen or weaken strategic industries rather than whether it will benefit consumers. Telecommunications is an example of this. Although NTT was partially privatized with the sell-off of one-third of its stocks, it still has monopoly control over the local phone network. The Ministry of Posts and Telecommunications and NTT's competitors say NTT should be broken up because this control allows it to charge exorbitant access fees to its competitors, to unfairly restrict interconnection availability, and to acquire sensitive information about its competitors. But Keidanren opposes the breakup of NTT on grounds that it would weaken NTT's ability to invest in research and development and thus handicap its international competitiveness. David Boling notes that the contrast between the debates over breaking up telephone monopolies in the United States and in Japan reflects the difference between America's consumer orientation and Japan's industrial policy orientation. "Rather than focusing on increased consumer welfare, [Japanese] critics have focused on international competitiveness because of the power the issue has with Japanese citizens. During the debate over AT&T's corporate structure, the focus was on anticompetitive acts that harmed consumer welfare, not the ability of AT&T to compete internationally."[105]

Within the framework of the current Japanese debate over regulatory reform we are not going to see the kind of broad deregulation that would dismantle Japan's system of dense, informal governance by bureaucracies and trade associations and open Japan's markets indiscriminately to imports. Economic liberalism provides legitimacy for gradual, limited freeing of some markets, in response to market pressures and foreign governments' demands. But developmentalism will ensure that as much as possible regulatory reform will be carried out in ways understood to benefit strategic domestic manufacturing sectors. As Steven Vogel argues, when decisions are made to expose key domestic industries to greater competition to make them more efficient, the change will take place slowly and in such a way as to avoid overwhelming them.[106] Although cost pressures are pushing Japanese businesses to seek regulatory reform to lower some prices, high domestic prices also largely enable Japanese manufacturers to cover their costs. There is no broad support within business for sweeping reforms that would fundamentally change government-business relations or initiate aggressive antitrust policy. Kaneda Seiichi, a Democratic Party (Minshutō) Diet member in the Lower House who has been critical of Japan's weak FTC, says that there is almost no interest in a stronger antimonopoly policy in the Diet and that to make progress Japan is going to need more foreign pressure (*gaiatsu*).[107] For Japan to make progress with deregulation and tougher antitrust policy in ways that open up opportunities for foreign firms, the United States and other nations will need to continue to supply Japan with exactly this.

Notes

1. Kumagai Naohiko, "Nihon ni shinrai o torimodose" (Let's bring back trust in Japan), *Gekkan keidanren,* July 1996, p. 48.

2. MITI, "*Tsūshō hakusho*" (Trade and industry white paper) (Tokyo, 1995), p. 140.

3. Keizai Kikakuchō Bukka Kyoku, *Seikeihi chōsa (1996 nen) ni yoru kōbairyoku heika oyobi naigai kakakusa no gaikyō* (Purchasing power parity and domestic/international price gap based an the survey of living costs [1996]) (based on November 1996 prices) (Tokyo, May 1997).

4. Yoko Sazanami, Shujiro Urata, and Hiroki Kawai, *Measuring the Costs of Protection in Japan* (Washington, D.C.: Institute for International Economics, 1995), pp. 6–7.

5. Richard Marston, "Price Behavior in Japanese and U.S. Manufacturing," in Paul Krugman, ed., *Trade with Japan: Has the Door Opened Wider?* (University of Chicago Press, 1991), pp. 121–46.

6. Hiroshi Iyori and Akinori Uesugi, *Japanese Anti-Monopoly Law,* Antitrust Bulletin (New York: Federal Legal Publications, 1994), p. 292.

7. Interview with Glen Fukushima, published in "Minkan de dekiru jigyō wa minkan ni saseru, kore ga kihon desu" (The principle should be to leave activities that can be done in the private sector in the private sector), *Keidanren Geppō,* vol. 44 (July 1996), pp. 26–29.

8. Shōda Akira, Funada Masayuki, and Kurokawa Kazumi, "Zadankai: Kisei kanwa to hō no shiten" (Roundtable discussion: Deregulation and a legal perspective), *Jurisuto,* vol. 1044 (May 1–15, 1994), pp. 6–27, p. 9.

9. Nihon Keizai Shinbun Sha, *Kisei ni idomu* (Standing up to regulation) (Tokyo, 1996), p. 28.

10. Mark Tilton, interview with electronics executive, Tokyo, July 1994.

11. Iwasaki Hiromitsu, *Kanryō tōsei rettō nihon ga mabunai* (The bureaucrat-controlled Japanese archipelago is in danger) (Tokyo: Goma shobō, 1994), p. 11.

12. *Nikkei Weekly,* June 26, 1995.

13. Frank K. Upham, "Retail Convergence: The Structural Impediments Initiative and the Regulation of the Japanese Retail Industry," in Suzanne Berger and Ronald

Dore, eds., *National Diversity and Global Capitalism* (Cornell University Press, 1996), pp. 263–97.

14. Ibid.

15. "Itōyōkadō shachō suzuki toshifumi: Kankyō mondai, daitenhō" (Itō-Yōkadō President Suzuki Toshifumi: Environmental problems and the Large Store Law), *Nikkei ryūtsū shinbun,* January 1, 1998, p. 23.

16. Hiromitsu, *Kanryō tōsei rettō nihan ga mabunai,* pp. 14–16.

17. Ibid., p. 72.

18. Itoh Motoshige, *Nihon no bukka wa naze takai no ka, kakaku to ryūtsū no keizaigaku* (Why are Japanese prices so high? The economics of prices and distribution) (NTT shuppansha, 1995), pp. 85, 197.

19. Ibid., p. 83.

20. Tajima Yoshihirō, *Kisei kanwa, ryūtsū no kaikaku vijon* (A proposal for deregulation and distribution reform) (Tokyo: Nihon hōsō shuppan kyōkai, 1994), p. 234.

21. *Nihon keizai shinbun,* March 3, 1998, p. 5.

22. Ibid.

23. *Nihon ryūtsū shinbun,* December 27, 1997, p. 1.

24. Ibid.

25. *Nihon keizai shinbun,* March 3, 1998, p. 5.

26. Keidanren, "Ryūtsū bunya ni okeru issō no kiseikanwa wo yōbō suru" (A demand for a thorough regulatory reform of the distribution sector), cited in *Nikkei ryūtsū shinbun,* April 30, 1998, p. 4.

27. *Nihon keizai shinbun,* February 28, 1998, p. 1.

28. *Nihon keizai shinbun,* March 30, 1998, p. 42.

29. Katō Masashi, *Kisei kanwa no keizaigaku* (The economics of deregulation) (Tokyo: Tōyō keizai shinpō sha, 1994), pp. 73–74.

30. Ibid., p. 75. See also Commission of the European Communities (EC), "List of EU Deregulation Proposals for Japan" (Brussels, November 17, 1997), pp. 20–23.

31. John Jay Tate, "Making Things Better: Technical Institutions and Industrial Innovation in Japan," taik presented to the Ph.D. Kenkyukai, International House of Japan, Tokyo, November 27, 1996. Also see John Jay Tate, *Driving Production Innovation Home: Guardian State Capitalism and the Competitiveness of the Japanese Automobile Industry* (University of California at Berkeley, BRIE, 1995).

32. Tate, "Making Things Better"; *Driving Production Innovation Home,* pp. 200–03.

33. EC, "List of EU Deregulation Proposals for Japan," pp. 64, 66–69.

34. Ibid., pp. 60–63.

35. Ibid., pp. 70–78.

36. United States Trade Representative, *1996 National Trade Estimate Report on Foreign Trade Barriers* (Washington, D.C.: United States Government Printing Office, 1996), p. 179.

37. EC, "List of EU Deregulation Proposals for Japan."

38. Yoda Kaoru, *Nihon no kyoninka seido no subete* (All about Japan's licensing system) (Tokyo: Nihon jitsugyō shuppan sha, 1993), p. 24.

39. U.S. Commerce Department and Japanese Ministry of International Trade and Industry (MITI), "U.S.-Japan Price Survey 1991" (Tokyo, May 1991).

40. *Nikkei sangyō shinbun,* August 12, 1997.

41. Isowa Harumi, "Kisei kanwa keikaku kaitei de kurashi wa dō kawaru ka" (How will the changes in the Regulatory Reform Plan change our lives?), *Kokumin seikatsu,* August 1996, pp. 46–49.

42. U.S. Department of Commerce and Office of the U.S. Trade Representative, "Report to President William Jefferson Clinton of the Interagency Enforcement Team Regarding the U.S.-Japan Agreement on Autos and Auto Parts," Washington, D.C., December 4, 1997, pp. 35–38.

43. Nihon Keizai Shinbun Sha, *Kisei ni idomu* (Challenging regulation) (Tokyo, 1996), p. 17.

44. Mark Tilton, interview with Niimura Kiyoshi, director of JETRO Berlin office, June 23, 1998.

45. *Nikkei sangyō shinbun,* February 9, 1998.

46. EC, "List of EU Deregulation Proposals for Japan."

47. U.S. Trade Representative, *1996 National Trade Estimate Report on Foreign Trade Barriers* (Washington, D.C.: United States Government Printing Office, 1996), p. 178.

48. *Nihon keizai shinbun,* March 3 and 4, 1992.

49. Tony Freyer, "Japanese Antitrust in a Global Economy," paper prepared for Abe Autumn Colloquium, Tokyo, October 2, 1996.

50. Michael Beeman, "Slave, Sycophant or Cinderella? The FTC and Japan's Antimonopoly Law," presentation to Ph.D. Kenkyukai, International House of Japan, Tokyo, October 22, 1996.

51. The discussion of basic materials industry cartels here is drawn from Mark Tilton, *Restrained Trade: Cartels in Japan's Basic Materials Industries* (Cornell University Press, January 1996).

52. *Semento nenkan,* various years.

53. *World Steel Intelligence,* published by Paine-Webber, various issues. Import prices are calculated from Japan Tariff Association, *Japan Exports and Imports: Commodity by Country* (Tokyo: Japan Tariff Association, various years).

54. Ronald Dore, *Flexible Rigidities: Industrial Policy and Structural Adjustment in the Japanese Economy 1970–1980* (London: Athlone Press, 1986); Takabumi Suzuoki, "From Flying Geese to Round Robin: The Emergence of Powerful Asian Companies and the Collapse of Japan's Keiretsu," Program on U.S.-Japan Relations, Harvard University, 1996.

55. Mark Tilton, interview with chemical buyers, Tokyo, February 1992.

56. Mark Tilton, interview with marketing executive, Tokyo, September 1996.

57. Mark Tilton, interview with shipbuilding executive, Tokyo, July 1994.

58. American Chamber of Commerce in Japan President Glen Fukushima, address to the National Press Club, Washington, D.C., January 16, 1998.

59. *Nihon keizai shinbun,* May 10, 1994.

60. James Sterngold, "Elusive Price Cuts Intrigue Japan," *New York Times,* November 9, 1994, pp. C1, C11.

61. Mark Tilton, interview with Iketani Masanari, November 1995.

62. *Nikkei sangyō shinbun,* August 8, 1997, p. 9; *Nihon keizai shinbun,* October 23, 1997.

63. The books are *Kensetsu bukka,* put out by the Kensetsu Bukka Chōsa Kai, and *Sekisan shiryō,* put out by the Keizai Chōsa Kai.

64. Sung Joon Roh, "Agency Capitalism: The Logic of Managed Competition in Japan," Ph.D. dissertation, MIT, 1996.

65. *Nikkei Weekly,* July 11, 1995.

66. Nihon Keizai Shinbun Sha, *Kanryō: kishimu kyodai kenryoku* (Bureaucrats: The weakening behemoth) (Tokyo, 1994), p. 23.

67. *Nikkei Weekly,* July 11, 1995.

68. Nihon Keizai Shinbun Sha, *Kanryō,* p. 27.

69. *Zenren tsūhō,* November 1986, pp. 8–9, cited in Kodak materials.

70. Harumi, "Kisei kanwa keikaku kaitei de kurashi wa dō kawaru ka."

71. *Nihon keizai shinbun,* September 16, 1996.

72. Harry First, "Antitrust Enforcement in Japan," *Antitrust Law Journal,* vol. 64 (Fall 1995), pp. 137–82.

73. *Nikkei sangyō shinbun,* June 15, 1997, p. 13.

74. Sazanami, Urata, and Kawai, *Measuring the Costs of Protection in Japan,* pp. 6–7.

75. Toyonaga Hiroshi, "Fumon ni tsukesareru keshōhin no 'teika' hanbai" (Overlooked "discount" cosmetics sales) *Shūkan tōyō keizai,* August 1996, pp. 62–65. My thanks to Ron Bevacqua for sending me this article.

76. *Nihon keizai shinbun,* August 9, 1997, p. 8.

77. Ibid., August 13, 1997, p. 8.

78. Ibid.

79. Sensui Fumio, "Keshōhin no ryūtsū seido to dokusen kinshi hō: Sentakuteki ryūtsū seido no nichi-ō hikaku" (The cosmetics distribution system and the Antimonopoly Law: A Japanese-European comparison of the selective distribution system) *Jurisuto,* June 1, 1996, pp. 141–45.

80. Toyonaga Hiroshi, "Fumon ni tsukesareru keshōhin no 'teika' hanbai," *Shūkan tōyō keizai,* August 1996, pp. 62–65.

81. *Nihon keizai shinbun,* September 10, 1996, p. 13.

82. Ibid.

83. U.S. Department of Commerce and Office of the U.S. Trade Representative, "Report to President William Jefferson Clinton," pp. 10, 41.

84. Tilton, interview with Niimura.

85. *Economic Times,* January 30, 1998; Heinz Blüthmann, "Das erste Opfer heisst VW," *Die Zeit,* February 6, 1998; Franz W. Rother, "Blutige Nase," *Wirtschaftswoche,* February 2, 1998; "Autos in Deutschland bis 25 Prozent billiger?" *Neue Presse, Hannover,* January 31, 1998.

86. *European Market Share Reporter* (London: Gale Research International, 1995).

87. *Nikkei Weekly,* November 17, 1997.

88. EC, "List of EU Deregulation Proposals for Japan," pp. 102–03.

89. Mark Tilton, interview with representative of foreign cable manufacturer, Tokyo, December 1996. On fiber optic cable, see Ira Magaziner, *The Silent War: Inside the Global Business Battles Shaping America's Future* (Random House, 1989); Clyde V. Prestowitz, *Trading Places: How We Are Giving Our Future to Japan and How to Reclaim It* (Basic Books, 1989).

90. Japan External Trade Organization Import Promotion Department, "Tainichi akusesu jittai chōsa hōkoku sho: Denki tsūshin kiki" (Report on the state of access for imports into the Japanese market: Telecommunications equipment) (Tokyo, June 1998); summary of the same report in English: JETRO Import Promotion Department, "Points of the Survey: Telecommunications Equipment" (Tokyo, June 19, 1998).

91. "Kisei kanwa suishin shō ni henshin" (A changed ministry that is [now] promoting regulatory reform), *Nikkei bijinesu,* October 24, 1994, pp. 53–58.

92. On developmentalism, see Bai Gao, *Economic Ideology and Japanese Industrial Policy: Developmentalism from 1931 to 1965* (Cambridge: Cambridge University Press, 1997); Richard J. Samuels, *Rich Nation, Strong Army: National Security and the Technological Transformation of Japan* (Cornell University Press, 1994); and Chalmers Johnson, *Japan: Who Governs? The Rise of the Developmental State* (New York: W. W. Norton, 1995).

93. Chalmers Johnson, *MITI and the Japanese Miracle: The Growth of Industrial Policy, 1925–1975* (Stanford University Press, 1982).

94. Hiroshi Iyori and Akinori Uesugi, *The Antimonopoly Laws of Japan* (Tokyo, 1983), p. 114.

95. Itoh Motoshige, Kiyono Kazuharu, Okuno Masahiro, and Suzumura Kōtarō, "Shijō no shippai to hoseiteki sangyō seisaku" (Market failure and compensatory industrial policy), in Komiya Ryūtarō, Okuno Masahiro, and Suzumura Kōtarō, eds., *Nihon no sangyō seisaku* (Japan's industrial policy) (Tokyo University Press, 1984), pp. 225–28.

96. Jirō Ushio, "Spread the Gospel of the Market Economy," *Japan Times,* December 7, 1996, pp. 1, 4.

97. Survey done by searching through the *Nikkei Telecom* newspaper retrieval database for all articles that use the term *excessive competition* for the periods mentioned in the four *Nikkei* newspapers.

98. *Nihon keizai shinbun,* February 17, 1998, p. 13.

99. Ibid., October 19, 1996, p. 8.

100. *Nikkakyō geppō,* December 1995.

101. *Jidōsha kaigisho nyūsu,* published by Nihon Jidōsha Kaigisho (Japan auto chamber of commerce), no. 643 (September 1996), pp. 2–21.

102. Ibid., no. 642 (July 1996), pp. 2–3.

103. MITI, *Tsūshō hakusho,* p. 72.

104. Itoh, *Nihon no bukka,* p. 30.

105. David Boling, "The Debate in Japan on the Breakup of NTT: Regulatory Reform May Be Japan's Preferred Path to Increased Competition," *East Asian Executive Reports,* March 15, 1996, pp. 9, 15–20.

106. Steven Vogel, *Freer Markets, More Rules: Regulatory Reform in Advanced Industrialized Countries* (Cornell University Press, 1996).

107. Mark Tilton, interview with Kaneda Seiichi, Tokyo, February 13, 1997.

CHAPTER EIGHT

Is Japan Really Changing?

Lonny E. Carlile and Mark C. Tilton

There is an odd paradox in Japan. A long-standing deregulation movement, with Japan's top business organization, Keidanren, at its head, demands energetically that the bureaucracy step aside and let the market work. Government agencies respond to these calls with a seemingly endless parade of ambitious plans and programs that would ostensibly roll back regulations and restructure the government bureaucracy. Foreign governments hope these developments will make Japanese markets more competitive and, in the process, open them to imports. Yet prominent Japanese observers of the economy, not to mention foreign firms trying to export to Japan, continue to claim that government regulation and other nontariff barriers still block imports and that Japan has a long way to go before it can claim to have weaned itself away from government regulation and opened its markets. As the Mitsubishi Research Institute bluntly puts it, "We must recognize that the framework of Japan's economy is, by international standards, so far divorced from market economic principles that it not only creates friction with other countries, but also stands in the way of Japan's growth in the 21st century."[1] Economist Shimada Haruo, figuratively throwing in the towel, remarks that Japan needs unregulated free trade zones to serve as "airholes into the Japanese regulatory state."[2]

Under these conditions one might rightfully wonder: Is the deregulation movement just for show? Why does it seem that so little has changed, as such critics suggest, despite all the apparent time, energy, ink, and paper that has been invested in regulatory reform? What are the prospects, if any, for significant, procompetitive deregulation in Japan? It is tempting to dismiss the entire Japanese regulatory reform movement as one big cynical and disingenuous campaign aimed at duping the gullible. Nevertheless, although it is certainly true that there is a substantial public relations dimension in Japan's recent deregulatory drive, such characterizations of the situation constitute a superficial reading and are not particularly helpful in generating meaningful domestic or external policy responses.

Japanese Regulation, Revisited

In Japan, both formal and informal regulation have served as the functional equivalent of the control over enterprise gained through formal state ownership of nationalized firms and industries. As Yul Sohn shows in his chapter, the phenomenon has historical roots that date back to Japan's initial modernization in the latter half of the nineteenth century, wherein the "unequal treaties" imposed on the country induced the emergence of industrial policy mechanisms as a substitute for tariff-based import substitution. Miyajima Hideaki's description of the 1960s shareholder stabilization program, which aimed to ensure that Japan's largest firms remained in Japanese hands, can be read as an effort to sustain an environment in which national purposes could continue to be effectively delegated to private firms, as can Lonny Carlile's description of *minkatsu* in the 1980s. Both Elizabeth Norville and Kōsuke Ōyama provide concrete descriptions of how this phenomenon plays out at the sectoral level.

The protection of sectors with a large number of "economically disadvantaged" small producers is widely accepted as a proper function of the state in Japan for much the same reasons that many Western European governments find it politically and socially desirable to maintain generous social welfare policies. Such protection has been particularly conspicuous and costly in sectors, such as agriculture and small-scale retailing, with large, politically significant blocs of voters but extends well beyond such groups. Protection of domestic leather goods production, traditionally the calling of a discriminated minority group known as the *burakumin,* provides such an example. Although labor has long been excluded from representation in the ruling conservative regime, it is arguable that even the working class has been indirectly incorporated into such a "social contract," as is illustrated perhaps most vividly by the employment subsidies that have been provided to employers in designated declining industries.[3]

There are both domestic and international reasons why informal regulation pervades Japan. First, as Mark Tilton stresses in his chapter, the ideology and legal system predisposed Japan to informal policy. Developmentalist ideology, which holds that bureaucrats must be trusted as the guardians of the nation's development and security, helped generate acceptance of considerable bureaucratic discretion. The legal system, by contrast, has provided little recourse for firms or individuals to challenge informal government policy. Paradoxically, the postwar, market-oriented institutional reforms of the economy under the wing of the occupation forces have also provided incentives for informal regulation. As discussed in the Miyajima chapter, the United States attempted to shape Japan's domestic markets through occupation reforms that embedded "liberal" elements in the contemporary Japanese political economy in the form of the Antimonopoly Law and the Fair Trade Commission. Although the significance and influence of both were reduced after the occupation, and the antitrust regulatory framework they constitute is weak compared with that of other advanced industrialized countries, they nonetheless set legal limitations on the extent of both formal bureaucratic intervention and private cartel practices and for that reason have encouraged informal regulation to circumvent their proscriptions. Furthermore, Japan's nationalistic mercantilism unfolded in the context of an international system of trade and finance based on liberal principles and norms. The resultant "embedded mercantilism" required Japan to adhere formally to the letter of GATT and IMF stipulations even as it frequently undercut them in spirit with informal policies. Such embedded mercantilism was facilitated by the cold war era–U.S. policy of ignoring economic issues in order to ensure that its security concerns involving Japan were achieved.[4] The financial policy dimension of this dynamic is described by Norville in her chapter, whereas Miyajima's documentation of the promotion of stable shareholders during the 1960s in response to the external pressures for liberalization illustrates how it played out in the large corporate sector generally.

Cartels have often worked hand in hand with government regulation to promote the concentration of capital in industry hands, exclude would-be entrants, and promote the sustained financial viability of cartel members. Norville's description of the convoy system in finance provides a prime example of cartel-like arrangements being enforced and appropriated by the state. Cartels, furthermore, provide a mechanism for existing firms in an industry to undercut market forces and "regulate" the market in the absence of overt state regulation, as was borne out in several of the chapters. Tilton shows how informal government tolerance and support for cartels continues in industries such as steel and chemicals, even though official support for cartels has been discontinued. He also shows that this tolerance for cartels rests on a broadly held concern with "excessive competition." Ōyama notes that petroleum industry self-governance has been effective at maintaining prices, whereas Norville shows that the insurance industry has been able to maintain strong cooperation to keep premiums high.

Pervasive informal regulation and weak antitrust law have combined to create a context in which public and private interests supportive of existing regulatory arrangements have become fused and strongly entrenched. It is this connection, perhaps more than anything else, that accounts for the longevity, tenacity, and adaptability of the Japanese regulatory regime and makes regulatory reform so difficult politically. In industries such as steel and chemicals, cartels are allowed to flourish because they are considered important in ensuring the security of supply of basic industrial inputs (Tilton). Ministry of Finance (MOF)–managed convoy systems in the banking, insurance, and securities industries established a de facto "social contract" that guaranteed the survival of every firm in those industries as a means of assuring a nationally controlled financial sector responsive to state policy direction (Norville). Petroleum industry self-governance and state regulation were effectively combined to maintain prices while at the same time contributing to national energy security (Ōyama). Miyajima shows how Japanese financial regulation was critical to the development and maintenance of a system of corporate organization, the J-Type firm, that has been praised as a model worldwide and retains widespread support domestically today.

The findings of this volume's various chapters confirm the point, made in chapter 1, that the challenge of regulatory reform is different in Japan from that in the United States or Europe because the type of economic regulation that developed out of Japan's modernization is different. In the United States economic regulation has tended to be legalistic and formal and has involved government rate setting or controls on entry into markets in areas such as telecommunications and transportation, in which natural monopolies were thought to exist.[5] In Europe, regulation involved these markets, as well as widespread state ownership in industries such as steel and coal, whereas considerable political energy has been expended on the income redistribution and social welfare mechanisms of the welfare state.[6] Japan stands out in several ways: in its expansive application of regulation, its tendency to prefer licensing-based regulatory mechanisms over nationalization, its use of regulatory mechanisms for income maintenance and social policy purposes, its wide-spread use of informal regulation, and the great stress that it has placed on cartels as devices for ordering industry.

The Roots of Regulatory Reform

In the United States and Britain a popular explanation for why "deregulation" occurs is that in an increasingly globalized economy, market competition will inexorably force governments to sweep aside economic regulation. The Japanese experience over the past century clearly implies that increased integration of a national economy into the global economy alone does not automatically lead to the withering of state intervention. Indeed, as Yul Sohn demonstrates in his contribution to this book, before World War II Japan's integration into the international economy provided the very reason and rationale for the development of an expansive and highly interventionist form of economic regulation that gave the Japanese state the ability to control entry, investment, production, pricing, and consumption in a wide array of strategic industries. A similar illiberal, "mercantilist" logic continued to characterize the post–World War II system of economic regulation. If anything, as discussed in chapter 1, Japan's postwar democratic reforms and the changed circumstances surrounding the maintenance of Japan's international security provided additional rationales.

If it is indeed true that Japan's integration into the global economy has followed an illiberal logic, then a lack of progress in deregulating the Japanese economy should not be surprising. If anything, what needs explaining is why a Japanese regulatory reform movement calling for a greater role for market forces emerged at all. The various contributions to this volume suggest that four impulses were involved.

In the United States the seeds of the late 1970s deregulation movement were sown by a rethinking among economists of the costs and benefits of regulation and the resulting conclusion that, as a general principle, rather than benefiting society and the economy regulation tended to keep prices high and hurt consumer welfare. These ideas were then taken up by individual politicians and other "political entrepreneurs" who saw in their implementation a means to advance consumer interests and to gain, in a populist exercise, the support of the unorganized mass of American consumers. Such efforts eventually bore fruit in the major regulatory reform initiatives implemented in the financial, telecommunications, and transportation sectors. As epitomized by the elimination of the Civil Aeronautics Board in 1984, such deregulation in many instances involved the wholesale elimination of lines of regulatory authority and the outright elimination or substantial reduction of regulatory agencies themselves.[7]

As pointed out by Norville, Miyajima, and Carlile, the primary initial impetus for the post-1980 reform drive in Japan was not concerns about the invisible social costs of regulation but the concrete economics of a state fiscal crisis. With big business and the country's finance ministry at the forefront of an effort to impose fiscal discipline on a system increasingly oriented to pork barrel generosity, one would be hard-pressed to label the initial stages of Japanese regulatory reform a populist initiative. And although regulatory reform did lead to some substantial changes in the regulatory arrangements that expanded the scope of market forces in specific sectors, the intent of these modifications was only secondarily to "free" market forces. As contributors to this volume and others who have analyzed these reforms stress, the mechanisms of discretionary and strategically oriented bureaucratic oversight were maintained, if not strengthened, in the process, and aside from the privatization of government corporations, which were in any event charged with operational rather than regulatory functions, Japan's regulatory agencies have so far survived the regulatory reform process virtually unchanged organizationally.

In the case of finance, as Norville outlines in her contribution, developmental goals and security concerns dovetailed to induce the MOF to expand the role of market forces in the financial sector in a carefully calibrated way. The need to reconstitute the country's financial system so that it could effectively absorb massive state debt issues prompted Japan's financial authorities to create, virtually from scratch, a viable bond market. External capital liberalization was pursued in order to facilitate a recycling of capital that would address state security concerns and with the aim of promoting the "catch-up" of Japan's financial sector. In each instance, the mechanisms of the MOF's discretionary authority over domestic firms overseas remained intact and operative.

In telecommunications, technological innovations were creating the potential for entirely new markets for information services that simply had not existed when the regulatory regime was created. The same fiscal imperatives that induced the liberalization of the bond market provided the rationale for the subsequent decision to privatize Nippon Telephone and Telecommunications (NTT). This, in turn, provided the opportunity for a major overhaul of a system of telecommunications regulation that was showing signs of obsolescence in a period of tremendous technological change. And although interministerial turf battles make for a rather complex narrative, the fact that the primary story line in this drama consists of interministerial politics rather than political entrepreneurship based in the Diet is symbolic of the nature of the reform. So too is the fact that the Ministry of Posts and Telecommunications emerged from the scramble with its regulatory authority dramatically enhanced. As in telecommunications, privatization in the transportation sector actually strengthened Ministry of Transportation (MOT) regulatory authority and influence by eliminating the semi-independent status of the public corporations that had dominated these sectors and by reducing the scope for political intervention on these corporations' behalf via the Diet's power over their budgets.[8]

A second impetus for Japanese regulatory reform was external diplomatic pressure. In contrast to an "early deregulator" such as the United States, in which internal pressures predominated, external pressures were far more salient for "latecomers," who were faced not only with potential competition from efficient firms from deregulated markets, but also diplomatic pressure from the United States to open their markets in order that a global playing field might be created for U.S. multinationals. Such pressure typically took the form of the implicit and explicit threat that these countries had better deregulate their economies and liberalize foreign access to their domestic markets if they intended to maintain access to the critically important U.S. market.[9]

U.S. market opening initiatives had a particularly strong impact on the Japanese regulatory reform process, even though, to the chagrin of U.S. officials, the results in terms of effective liberalization almost never measured up to what was hoped for. From the outset, Japan's security dependence and its heavy reliance on the United States as an export market made it acutely sensitive to U.S. pressure.[10] U.S. pressure for Japanese regulatory reform became conspicuous in the mid-1980s. Japan's rapid rise to the status of the world's number-two economy and the fact that it became the largest single source of the U.S. trade deficit meant that U.S. benign neglect evaporated and the "Japan problem" was suddenly of great significance from the U.S. standpoint. This eventually led to the 1988 passage by Congress of "Super 301," a section of the Omnibus Trade and Competitiveness Act that mandated retaliation against countries that engaged in "unfair" trade practices. U.S. trade officials identified Japanese regulatory arrangements and domestic anticompetitive practices as trade barriers, and consequently the furtherance of deregulation-oriented regulatory reform in Japan became an important item on the U.S. agenda at bilateral trade negotiations. The Structural Impediments Initiative (SII) talks of 1989–90, with their ostensible goal of modifying the entire structure of the Japanese economy, marked a culmination of sorts, with subsequent U.S.-Japan negotiations essentially continuing on the track laid out at that time.[11]

Fear of trade sanctions induced Japanese business to lobby the government for visible deregulatory responses. Moves toward deregulation provoked resistance from politically well-entrenched groups whose interests and influences were threatened. In the process, deregulatory initiatives soon took on the quality of what one critic described bitingly as "piecemeal reforms designed to impress the uninformed."[12] Although the implied intentional malevolence suggested by this characterization may perhaps be exaggerated, it does effectively describe the external relations function served by regulatory reform proposals from the Maekawa Report to the recent Deregulation Action Plan. By consolidating various regulatory reforms that state agencies had already committed to for reasons of their own or as a consequence of trade negotiations, and then packaging them with ideas and proposals that were being studied in the abstract, the recent Deregulation Action Plan and various industry-level liberalization proposals floated by ministries and agencies over the years served bureaucratic interests by establishing a gloss of commitment and progress that could be pointed to in an effort to alleviate foreign and domestic criticism.

The third impetus for Japanese regulatory reform can be seen in the serious concerns about the long-term viability of Japan's national economy that emerged in embryo in the wake of the 1985 Plaza Accord and became a matter of sustained public concern in the early 1990s in the wake of the collapse of the "economic bubble." The appreciation of the yen during much of this period meant that the relative cost of doing business in Japan increased dramatically. Fears of a consequent "hollowing out" of the economy, combined with the need to reduce operating costs in domestic factories and offices, encouraged calls for the elimination of inefficient and high-cost regulatory practices for the sake of industrial competitiveness. Adding fuel to the fire was the emergence of telecommunications, transport, and finance as key growth sectors. In all three of these areas it was becoming increasingly obvious that despite widely trumpeted regulatory reform measures in the 1980s, firms in these sectors were hamstrung by what appeared to be anachronistic regulatory arrangements and falling behind their deregulated counterparts in the United States and elsewhere.

On top of these concerns, the standard mechanisms of macroeconomic stimulus were perceived as no longer as effective as they had been in the past.

Spurred by a recession that refused to go away, the Japanese government reversed in a grand way the principles propounded by Rinchō and passed a series of fiscal stimulus packages that raised total government debt outstanding to an estimated 254 trillion yen ($2.1 trillion) for the central government alone (521 trillion yen, or $25 trillion, if local government and various "hidden" accounts are included).[13] With the official discount rate hovering at 0.5 percent and traditional construction projects not generating the spillover effects of earlier years, regulatory reform was seen by many as about the only lever left to get the Japanese economy out of its slump. It was in this environment, as Carlile suggests, that competition-enhancing regulatory and administrative reforms came to be seen as something essential to the future viability of the Japanese economy. In the meantime, the scandal-plagued financial sector has, as outlined by Norville and Miyajima, come to be seen as a major barrier to future sustained economic viablity and for that reason a priority target of reform efforts.

Finally, a regulatory reform impetus of relatively recent vintage is developments in party politics associated with the hiatus in the long period of single-party governance by the Liberal Democratic party (LDP). The breaking down of LDP single-party rule was accompanied by the emergence of politicians and political parties both inside and outside of the ruling coalitions that have embraced an expansive regulatory reform agenda as the centerpiece of their political platforms. Indeed the perceived popularity of this kind of agenda was so great that in the October 1996 general election *every* major party campaigned on a regulatory reform platform. Unfortunately, the rise to salience of partisan politics as a major source of pressure for regulatory reform initiatives is such a recent development that it is difficult at this stage to gauge its significance with any degree of definitiveness. However, findings in the volume do bear out its significance. Ōyama, for instance, points to the establishment of the non-LDP Hosokawa government as the catalyst for a shift to a more market-oriented regulatory approach in the petroleum industry. Carlile, in his chapter, discusses the role and dynamics of party-backed regulatory reform initiatives within the context of the post-1993 coalition cabinets.

One of the striking characteristics of the sequencing of the regulatory reform impetuses in the Japanese case outlined here is its near reversal of the U.S. experience. The U.S. reforms began with procompetitive ideas and political entrepreneurship rooted in electoral and legislative politics. A political consensus on dealing with the government budgetary deficit emerged later. In

Japan, by contrast, it was budgetary concerns that initially sparked what came to be labeled the administrative reform movement and only very recently did "populist" deregulatory concerns begin to take on major political significance.

The Consequences of Regulatory Reform: Process and Outcomes

The essays of this volume concur strongly on the point that the regulatory reform measures implemented so far have had a relatively small, marginal impact with respect to increasing competition and the role of the "market" in the Japanese economy. Perhaps the most telling indicator is that, as Tilton details in his chapter, prices in Japan remain substantially higher than the norm in advanced industrialized countries. Also, a variety of import barriers and internal obstacles to market entry remain even in "deregulated" sectors. This assessment is widely shared among analysts of the Japanese regulatory reform process.

In addressing the issue of why the impact of regulatory reform has been so limited, it is useful to observe that Japanese regulatory reform has unfolded on two "planes." One plane is that associated with the centralized administrative reform movement that Carlile focuses on in his chapter. The second is that on which the ministerial- and sectoral-level decisions, or "mesolevel" decisionmaking, unfolds. In the Japanese regulatory reform processes the two planes have at best been only tenuously integrated.

The considerable press and public attention generated by developments associated with the first plane notwithstanding, it is developments on the second that have been the primary determinant of the concrete results of Japanese regulatory reform. Here, the decisionmaking process has changed relatively little from that which predominated prior to the initiation of the administrative reform movement in the early 1980s. The segmented, bureaucratically mediated mode of decisionmaking described by Ōyama for the revision of the Petroleum Import Law has characterized the vast majority of regulatory reform initiatives produced over the past decade and a half. In this mode interests are "adjusted" among parties represented on a ministry- or agency-attached *shingikai* before cabinet and legislative approval of an initiative. If an accommodation cannot be reached in the *shingikai,* appeal will be made to the organs of the LDP (or interparty organs in coalition governments) for "political" resolution. A second round of mediation occurs in negotiations between agencies and their supporters, on the one hand, and MOF officials, on the other, to obtain budgetary funding when spending is required in order to implement a reform. The regulatory reform process associated with the administrative reform movement has served off and on as a catalyst for activity at the mesolevel and occasionally has even had a major substantive impact. However, even when the latter contingency has unfolded, it has taken the form of these "higher"-level developments imposing external parameters on decisions reached on the first plane. These external impositions have left the internal workings of the routine, bureaucratic, agency-centered decisionmaking process largely undisturbed. Examples can be found in the budgetary ceilings induced by Rinchō's retrenchment effort and the establishment of a time frame–cum–output venue for reforms by the Deregulation Action Plan. The essential effect has simply been to add a deregulatory "gloss" to the business-as-usual proceedings of segmented decisionmaking.

Given that mesolevel decisionmaking is shaped primarily by producer and bureaucratic concerns and rests on a basic consensus among the represented interests in support of the existing regulatory framework's general parameters in the relevant policy arena, it is hardly surprising that the deregulatory output of this process tends to take the form of marginal modifications of existing arrangements. Thus rather than eliminate price controls altogether, when the MOT "deregulated" airline ticket pricing it established bands between MOT-dictated floors and ceilings within which airlines were allowed to set their fares. When the MOF "liberalized" the beer market and opened the way for the growth of "boutique" beers, it did so by reducing the minimal annual production capacity required to obtain a production license from 2,000 kiloliters to 60. Another favored approach to "deregulation" is to "downgrade" a licensing requirement to a less onerous type, as in a shift from a permit (*kyoka*) to a notification (*todokede*).[14] Such marginal rule relaxations can, of course, have a significant market-opening effect under the right circumstances—as when the MPT relaxed rules governing mobile telephones. But at the same time, a key feature of such reforms is that they leave the existing regulatory framework intact. It therefore should not be surprising, when looked at in this light, that the past decade and a half did not produce a major rollback of state regulatory authority comparable with the elimination of the Civil Aeronautics Board in the United States.

One reason for the persistence of the system is that the external impetuses described in the preceding section that drove the Japanese process did little to alter the modal format of Japanese economic policymaking. The coalition that

sustained the Rinchō-led movement of the early 1980s sought fiscal retrenchment rather than deregulation, and as such the issue of bureaucratic regulation
of the economy was not the core concern. If the Rinchō-led movement did have
a deregulatory impact, this impact was a latent consequence of a process aimed
at a different target. The second impetus, foreign pressure, or *gaiatsu,* stemming from U.S.-Japan trade and investment friction, also did little to undercut
the bureaucratically oriented decisionmaking system. These were after all
government-to-government negotiations in which Japanese ministry officials
were primarily responsible for the negotiations and the drafting of responses.
Naturally, bureaucratic rather than legislative processes predominated, and
they too tended to reinforce existing domestic decisionmaking practices in a
given sector.

The survival of the existing mesolevel decisionmaking frameworks in the
Japanese regulatory reform process created certain characteristic biases in
outcomes. As already noted, because the system was biased toward "insider"
interests, the process naturally tended to produce results that favored existing
players in a market. The proclivity to relax rules rather than radically redefine
the rules of competition helped ease the task of adjustment for existing firms in
an industry by allowing them to operate within a familiar environment. Consensus on a reform initiative was often premised on an implicit or explicit deal
in which disadvantages to insiders resulting from liberalization or deregulation
were compensated with "side payments," as when gasoline import liberalization was undercut by administrative reforms that kept the gasoline market
closed in a de facto sense (Ōyama). Furthermore, because Japanese economic
regulation mechanisms perform so many social regulation functions, economic
regulatory reform frequently has to be accompanied by the construction of
compensating arrangements in other policy arenas, thereby greatly expanding
and complicating the issues to be tackled in realizing a given regulatory reform
initiative. Even where regulatory reforms are engineered without an identifi-
able quid pro quo, the persistence of the regulatory regime in an industry means
that Japanese ministries and agencies have ample room to continue to play the
"managerial" role that is so characteristic of the Japanese developmental state.
The pervasiveness of licensing requirements provides bureaucratic agencies
with various alternative regulatory mechanisms to wield in preserving an interventionist role.

Pervasive private regulation provided another means to maintain the status
quo in the face of liberalizing legislation. In the context of external diplomatic
pressures that demanded visible regulatory change of some kind, a key strate-

gic choice of the regulatory reform movement has in fact been to focus on regulation by government bureaucrats and to largely ignore the market controls of private trade associations. There are numerous documented examples of licensing authority over entry into a previously state-regulated line of business being transferred to private associations.[15] Overall, the result has been to chip away at some public restraints on the market while leaving intact the private restraints on competition that are especially important in markets for manufactured goods.

It is doubly ironic, in light of the entrenched regulation discussed, that a major problematic area of the Japanese system with respect to regulatory reform issues is the *lack* of regulation in certain critical areas. Despite the fact that health and safety concerns are frequently raised as arguments against deregulation, in its emphasis on promoting developmental goals the Japanese state has often failed to develop an effective framework of social regulation in key sectors. The problem is an old one, with a prime illustration being the way that the social and health costs of pollution were explicitly subordinated to economic development needs in legislation before 1970.[16] A particularly tragic example of the kinds of problems that can crop up as a consequence of the persistence of a "developmental" style of regulation at the expense of social regulation can be seen in pharmaceuticals. As Aki Yoshikawa and Brian Woodall detail in a recent study, the pharmaceutical industry's regulatory arrangement overseen by the Ministry of Health and Welfare (MHW) is a typical one for Japanese regulatory agencies. Built upon close ties between the firms in the industry and the regulatory authorities, it is heavily oriented toward promoting and protecting the interests of Japanese pharmaceutical firms. It produces, in the words of the authors, "peculiar drugs and shoddy testing procedures" and is directly responsible for incidences of HIV transmission through untreated blood supplies and incidents involving lethal and disfiguring side effects that could have been prevented through more rigorous testing procedures.[17] Paradoxically, more effective social regulation in pharmaceuticals would probably provide expanded export opportunities for foreign pharmaceutical firms.

Even "successful" reforms have been associated with certain fundamental problems. One set of characteristic problems can occur when deregulation is only partial in character, as in Miyajima and Norville's descriptions of how the partial deregulation in the financial sector contributed to Japan's bubble by destroying the basis for the operation of the existing system of corporate governance without providing enough freedom for new market-based forms of corporate governance to take their place. Ōyama describes how for similar reasons the "success" of the recent petroleum reforms have undermined a viable energy conversion policy. It is also important to remember that in the move to deregulation many regulations are key to ensuring nonmarket goals, such as individual safety from accidents or communal and global safety from environmental degradation. There are trade-offs between short-term efficiency and goals such as environmental safety and dangers in misguided moves to efficiency.

The case studies in this book thus suggest that the developmental state model has been alive and well in the implementation of regulatory reform policies in recent years at the level of specific industries. The key to the sustainability of bureaucratic influence has been the control that the bureaucracy and allied politicians and interest groups have been able to maintain over the institutional policymaking machinery. The opaque and elusive quality of Japanese regulation, along with its often excessive orientation toward the promotion of domestic industry, implies that what is needed for substantive regulatory change may be less a matter of modifying the rules than modifying the nature of the relationship between the regulators and the regulated. The current economic policy cul-de-sac is in fact pushing regulatory reform proposals in the direction of a dramatic restructuring of the existing institutional framework of economic regulation, although it remains to be seen whether they are in fact adopted or implemented.

Japanese Regulatory Reform: The Current State of Affairs

In a 1994 book Hashimoto Ryutarō complains about what he saw as excessive "should be-ism" (*beki ron*) in the discourse of regulatory reform proponents.[18] By should be-ism he is referring to the practice of justifying reforms on the basis of abstract normative principles such as "deregulation should be promoted." In his view the problem with should be-ism is that by allowing normative concepts to drive the discussion, attention is turned away from the search for concrete solutions to practical problems. Using the metaphor of a tree, he argues that should be-ism promotes disjointed debates about "branches and leaves" without considering the larger issues at the root of the problems being confronted. In Hashimoto's mind, the root issue that needs to be addressed in the discussion of administrative and regulatory reform is that of adapting Japan's administrative structures to the harsh realities of Japan's ongoing demographic transition to an "aging society," circumstances that are

already putting tremendous pressure on Japan's fiscal and administrative resources and are fated to become exponentially more burdensome in the future.[19] Referring specifically to the should be-ism of the Gyōkakushin III, he
accuses the commission of corrupting the spirit of the movement initiated by
Rinchō back in the early 1980s, and he urges renewed attention to the latter's
stated goal of creating a "parsimonious and efficient government" capable of
addressing problems of Japan's aging society within the constraints of available resources.

Hashimoto also rejects the notion that reducing the power of the bureaucracy
through indiscriminate deregulation is the solution to Japan's ills. The point,
according to him, is not that the state bureaucracy is inherently dysfunctional,
but rather that the existing structure of ministries and agencies, which had not
changed much since it was first established fifty years earlier, is no longer able
to deal effectively with the issues of today. What needs to be done, therefore, is
to reattune them to contemporary context through a major administrative overhaul. On the subject of deregulation specifically, he notes that there are anachronistic aspects that need repair, but insists: "We must not forget that [regula-
tions] perform the practical function of protecting the lives of the people. In
addition to this, regulations are devices that perform the important function of
helping the weak and securing employment."[20] In line with this characterization, he considers the task at hand to be "regulatory review" (*kisei no minaoshi*)
rather than "deregulation" (*kisei kanwa*).[21]

The Japan Association of Corporate Executives (Keizai Dōyūki), one of
Japan's leading business associations, presented a somewhat different view of
the goals and purposes of regulatory reform in a document entitled "Shijōshugi
sengen" (Manifesto for a market-oriented economy) in January 1997. Noting
that "there are inherent trade-offs between efficiency and fairness, and between
equality of opportunity and equality of outcomes," it comments that "in the
past, Japan has attempted to achieve both at once by restraining competition, as
seen, for example, in the 'convoy escort system,' in which all members of a
domestic industry move together under government protection." This created a
"high-price, high-cost structure" that is no longer viable "amid the continuing
trends of globalization, advances in information technology, economic liberalization, and diversification of values." It goes on to argue that "no one can see
into the future without calling on the predictive abilities that the market mechanism makes available" and for that reason "as a basic principle, the operation of
the economy should be entrusted to the market to the maximum extent possible." "We are no longer in an era," it points out, "when the government can lead

by building a national consensus in order to attain a single clearly defined goal, as it did during the high-growth era of the 1950s and 60s. In the absence of such conditions, government intervention in the market to secure a preordained result restricts the free exercise of choice and initiative by market players, precludes the possibility of a diversity of outcomes, and actually increases the likelihood of failure." It asserts that "a clear distinction should be made between economic policy and policy instruments for securing fairness of outcomes by redistributing income or wealth to assist the socially disadvantaged, and these policy instruments should be clearly separated from the market."[22]

Juxtaposed and appropriately contextualized, the two statements say quite a bit about the current state of Japanese regulatory reform. Both the Hashimoto and the Keizai Dōyūkai positions are representative of larger currents of thought that have been animating recent efforts to promote deregulation and a major overhaul of the Japanese administrative system in the face of a profound sense of crisis and extreme pessimism regarding the future prospects of the Japanese economy. Hashimoto's position is reflective of the mainstream opinion of the leadership of the LDP, as well as, no doubt, more liberal elements within the Japanese bureaucracy. The connection with the former is symbolized by the adoption of the basic tenets of Hashimoto's treatise as official party policy on regulatory reform in what became popularly known as the "Hashimoto Vision."[23] The Keizai Dōyūkai position, on its part, echoes the essential stance previously outlined by Japan's leading business associations, albeit in a considerably more straightforward and systematic manner than is the norm.[24]

The two positions are rooted in profoundly different philosophical soil. Not coincidentally, the differences between them parallel the distinction between a "developmental state" and a "regulatory state" put forward by Chalmers Johnson in his classic study of Japanese industrial policy.[25] The developmental state orientation in the Hashimoto-LDP line of thought is revealed, for instance, in the way the central pillar of the LDP's administrative reform plan is the notion of attaining "an efficient and slim government." This contrasts with the centrality given to the task of fostering the market mechanism in the Dōyūkai document. In line with this difference of focus, the bulk of the LDP document is devoted to outlining ways to reform the state bureaucracy. Only two paragraphs are devoted specifically to the issue of promoting deregulation and even these are modified by the following proviso: "In addition to strengthening the oversight of the Fair Trade Commission so that the intensification of competition that accompanies deregulation will not lead to unfair practices on the part of the strong, we must implement generous assistance to employees, farmers, foresters, fishermen, the self-employed, small and medium-sized enterprise operators, and others who are expected to be severely affected, and thereby assure that the deep relations of trust that are the tradition of our society are not destroyed."[26] Although the full realization of the posited "slim government"—described by the LDP as one in which "government must be limited to only those activities deemed absolutely essential from the goals of the state"—would probably greatly reduce the overall level of government intervention in the economy, it is noteworthy that the document does not specify what should and should not constitute the parameters of state goals.[27] By contrast, the Dōyūkai document insists on the principle that "the activities of the market will be left to the free actions of individuals and corporations, while the government will avoid participating directly in market." The Dōyūkai presents, in order to attain this, a long list of actions that together amount to a systematic dismantling of Japan's regulatory system through the substitution of licensing-based mechanisms of prior restraint with minimalist regulation based on "ex post surveillance." Among the concrete items suggested are the abolition of all licensing requirements for entry into an industry; the abolition of all supply adjustment clauses relating to production, volume, and facilities; the elimination of regulatory barriers that prevent cross-sector competition; a review of Antimonopoly Law exemptions; and the elimination of private sector self-regulation through industry trade associations.[28]

Principles per se do not necessarily get in the way of practical politics, and the Hashimoto and the Dōyūkai currents of thought overlap substantially at the level of the "branches and leaves" of programmatic politics despite their profoundly different roots. The Keizai Dōyūkai along with Keidanren have declared support for a six-point program of administrative reform pushed by Hashimoto, and both sides perceive that the times demand a shift to a more liberalized and competitive economy. A seemingly endless parade of scandals have thoroughly discredited the bureaucracy and the political system more generally in the public eye, forcing even die-hard defenders of the developmental state to admit that substantial changes are needed in order to restore confidence. With the old goal of "catching up" technologically and economically with the advanced industrialized countries achieved, a new goal is needed to energize the system. Without meaningful unifying goals, it is easy for the activities of autonomous bureaucratic agencies vested with extensive regulatory authority to descend into petty and dysfunctional bureaucratism of the sort exemplified by the MOT's insistence on a wind gauge in an indoor ski slope and other examples described by Tilton in his chapter. And with the fiscal crisis demanding a substantial rollback of state programs, the developmentalist goal of reattuning the state begins to dovetail with the regulatory state-based goal of expanding markets.

In the political arena, one of the more interesting and potentially significant developments to emerge out of the recent turmoil in party politics has been the formation of parties such as Sakigake and the Democratic party that have constructed their identity around proposals to alter the terms and conditions of the exercise of state authority in a manner that would likely be conducive to the emergence of a regulatory state in Japan. With the emergence of this group, the politics of regulatory reform in Japan has taken on the attributes of a three-way struggle among (1) those who seek to turn Japan into a regulatory state, (2) politicians and bureaucrats who have embraced deregulation and regulatory reform as a means of reattuning the society and economy to the new realities without fundamentally altering the guiding role of the state, and (3) interest groups, bureaucrats, and *zoku* politicians (one could also include some public sector unionists in this group) who are fighting a rearguard action to preserve the status quo. At the moment the center of gravity seems to be located closest to the struggle between the latter two groups and as such would appear to be leaning toward a modified version of the current Japanese developmental state. However, the situation is extremely fluid, and minor shifts in political currents external to the processes directly associated with administrative and regulatory reform could potentially shift the balance in the regulatory reform arena in an unpredictable direction.

In terms of sociopolitical context, the commonly cited characterization of the archetypal attitude individual sectors in Japan have toward deregulation— what in the United States is referred to as the "not in my backyard" syndrome (*sōron sansei, kakuron hantai*)—grows directly out of the economic situation Japan currently faces. On the one hand, deregulation of the economy became widely accepted as economically beneficial in that it would help to reduce the costs of doing business and benefit the Japanese consumer. By the same token, to the extent that the survival of domestic firms is often dependent on protection, industries and their bureaucratic and political allies are inclined to adamantly oppose any deregulation that introduces further competition in their own industries. These circumstances create a high-pressure gridlock in which demands for change and resistance to them tend to escalate even as they cancel each other out.

In surveying the contemporary landscape of Japanese regulatory reform, it would appear that progress in meaningful deregulation is most likely in sectors such as telecommunications, finance, and international transport, where technological change has made the old regulatory structures obsolete, interconnectivity with the international system is a key requirement for establishing a viable Japanese presence in the market, and lowered costs are essential to preserving the competitiveness of other domestic industries. In such circumstances, market opening becomes industrial policy. The temptation will be to structure the new regulatory regime in such a way that Japanese national champions are given an advantage, but here foreign governments are in a position to insist that Japanese liberalization be implemented and a more level playing field be established as conditions for Japanese access to their domestic markets. It is also useful to encourage joint ventures, alliances, and mergers between foreign and Japanese firms as a way of discouraging the mercantilist impulse, with the effect of such measures the strongest where cross-national alliances are formed with multiple Japanese players.

In other areas the industrial policy impetus is more prone to conflict with the mercantilist and employment protection impulse of the Japanese state, and the assurance of a more open and competitive environment will require that several conditions be met. First, existing protectionist barriers need to be dismantled without being replaced by informal or formal functionally equivalent arrangements. Second, there need to be assurances that the policies to cushion the impact of deregulatory change that will inevitably be adopted as a condition for the acceptance of deregulation do not turn into permanent arrangements. Third, and this also represents an important way to attain the second goal, rules must be put in place that prevent discriminatory and anticompetitive practices. Strengthened competition policy and rules that mandate open decisionmaking processes are important here. So, too, as paradoxical as it might sound on the surface, are *strengthened* social regulation and social welfare in order to ensure that economic regulation does not need to be turned to for social policy reasons.

Although foreign governments and other external actors are in a position to influence the course of Japanese regulatory reform to some extent, the engineering of a fundamental restructuring of the Japanese system will inevitably rest on whether the domestic political system can produce the political will and leadership that is the prerequisite for a major reorientation of the regulatory regime. As for the likelihood of this contingency unfolding, the opinions of the

contributors to this volume range from guarded skepticism to qualified optimism. On the one hand, there are signs of the development of political forces
willing to champion such a course. On the other, mercantilist practices and the
values that sustain them appear to remain deeply rooted, and the Japanese
electorate may not ultimately allow such forces to control the government.
Indeed the ultimate outcome of regulatory reform in Japan may well be determined less by how parties and politicians stand on issues of regulatory reform
than by the latent consequences of political realignments stemming from ad
hoc responses to fiscal and financial crises, as well as on security issues, on
which political parties have much stronger and emotionally held differences.

For governments outside of Japan seeking to encourage liberalization, it
would be useful to encourage, where possible, those elements in the Japanese
political spectrum that are trying to push the system in a deregulatory direction
and are serious about a major overhaul of the basic administrative institutions
and practices of the Japaense state bureaucracy. "Positive" appeals reflecting
arguments being made inside Japan, such as the contribution of deregulation to
domestic growth, the competitiveness of Japanese industry, and the enrichment
of the lives of the average salaried, white-collar employee (*sarariiman*) are to
be encouraged. In addition, deregulation can be promoted as a way for Japan to
live up to its international responsibilities. Given the historic moment of Japan
desiring and needing change, such "pressure" can be effective if handled with
skill and grace. The challenge is to encourage the Japanese to shift away from
insular cronyism to a more open-minded and principled "should be-ism."

Notes

1. Mitsubishi Sōgō Kenkyū Jo (Mitsubishi Research Institute), *Nihon kaikaku* (Re-
forming Japan) (Tokyo: Daiyamondo sha, 1996), p. 44.

2. Shimada Haruo, *Japan Crisis* (Tokyo: Kōdansha, 1995), p. 65.

3. Kent Calder, *Crisis and Compensation: Public Policy and Political Stability in
Japan, 1949–1986* (Princeton University Press, 1988); T. J. Pempel, "Japan and Swe-
den: Polarities in Responsible Capitalism," in Dankwart A. Rostow and Kenneth Paul
Erikson, eds., *Comparative Political Dynamics* (HarperCollins, 1991), pp. 408–38;
Frank K. Upham, *Law and Social Change in Postwar Japan* (Harvard University Press,
1987), pp. 78–123; Sheldon Garon and Mike Mochizuki, "Negotiating Social Con-
tracts," in Andrew Gordon, ed., *Postwar Japan as History* (University of California
Press, 1993), pp. 145–66.

4. The concept of embedded mercantilism is from T. J. Pempel, "Regime Shift: Japanese Politics in a Changing World Economy," *Journal of Japanese Studies,* vol. 23, no. 2 (1997), pp. 333–61. See also Donald C. Hellman, "Japanese Politics and Foreign Policy: Elitist Democracy within an American Greenhouse," in Takashi Inoguchi and Daniel I. Okimoto, eds., *The Political Economy of Japan,* vol. 2: *The Changing International Context* (Stanford University Press, 1988), pp. 345–78.

5. Steven K. Vogel, *Freer Markets, More Rules: Regulatory Reform in Advanced Industrial Countries* (Cornell University Press, 1996), pp. 217–69.

6. Raymond Vernon, ed., *Big Business and the State: Changing Relations in Western Europe* (Harvard University Press, 1974); Mark Kesselman and Joel Krieger, "European Politics in Transition," in Mark Kesselman and Joel Krieger, eds., *European Politics in Transition* (Lexington, Mass., and Toronto: D. C. Heath, 1987), pp. 1–24.

7. Thomas K. McCraw, ed., *Regulation in Perspective: Historical Essays* (Harvard University Press, 1981); Roger E. Meiners and Bruce Yandle, eds., *Regulation and the Reagan Era: Politics, Bureaucracy, and the Public Interest* (New York: Holmes and Meier, 1989); Martha Derthick and Paul J. Quirk, *The Politics of Deregulation* (Brookings Institution, 1985).

8. Vogel, *Freer Markets, More Rules,* pp. 137–66, 196–213; Kent E. Calder, "Assault on the Bankers' Kingdom: Politics, Markets and the Liberalization of Japanese Industrial Finance," in Michael Loriaux and others, eds., *Capital Ungoverned: Liberalizing Finance in Interventionist States* (Cornell University Press, 1997), pp. 17–56.

9. Members of the European Union experienced the further "external" pressure from the EU to pursue regulatory reform as a prelude to deepened regional integration. Stephane Ducable, "Application of the European Community Competition Rules in the Telecommunications Sector," January 10, 1997; Deregulierungskommission, *Marktöffnung und Wettbewerb* (Market opening and competition) (Stuttgart: C. E. Poeschel Verlag, 1991).

10. Leonard J. Schoppa, *Bargaining with Japan: What American Pressure Can and Cannot Do* (Columbia University Press, 1997), pp. 96–103.

11. Ibid.; Kozo Yamamura, ed., *Japan's Economic Structure: Should It Change?* (Seattle: Society for Japanese Studies, 1990).

12. Katsuhiko Eguchi, "Changing Japan: Administrative Reform, Deregulation, and the New Generation of Politicians," speech given before a forum of the Japan Information Access Project, March 27, 1997, as reproduced at World Wide Web URL http://www.nmjc.org/jiap/dereg/papers/eguchi.html.

13. Ibid.

14. *Kisei kanwa suishin no genkyō* (1996), pp. 2–3, 11. See Sugimura Tomio, *Koredake wa shitteokitai kisei kanwa: Ukabu gyōkai, shizumu gyōkai* (I just want to know this about regulatory reform: which industries will go up and which will go down?) (Tokyo: Jitsugyō no nihonsha, 1994) for detailed explanation and anlaysis of deregulation and its concrete impact in a broad range of industries and sectors.

15. For numerous examples, see Nihon Keizai Shinbun Sha, *Kisei ni idomu* (Challenging regulation) (Tokyo, 1996).

16. Norie Huddle and Michael Reich, with Nahum Stiskin, *Island of Dreams: Environmental Crisis in Japan* (New York and Tokyo: Autumn Press, 1975).

17. Aki Yoshikawa and Brian Woodall, "Prescription for Japan's Ailing Drug Industry: Regulation and Deregulation," in *Japanese Deregulation: What You Should Know, Proceedings* (Washington, D.C.: Japan Information Access Project, 1997), pp. 91–101, quote p. 95. See also Masao Miyamoto, "Mental Castration, the HIV Scandal, and the Japanese Bureaucracy," Japan Policy Research Institute Working Paper 23 (Cardiff, Calif., August 1996).

18. Hashimoto Ryūtarō, *Seiken dakkai ron* (Tokyo: Kōdansha, 1994), p. 178.

19. John C. Campbell, *How Policies Change: The Japanese Government and the Aging Society* (Princeton University Press, 1992).

20. Hashimoto, *Seiken dakkai ron*, p. 202.

21. Ibid., pp. 187–93, 202, 219–20.

22. Keizai Dōyūkai, "Manifesto for a Market-Oriented Economy: Action Program for Japan toward the 21st Century," (January 1997) at World Wide Web URL http://www.doyukai.or.jp/database/teigen/970109_2E.html, accessed April 1997. The original Japanese text was available at World Wide Web URL http://www.doyukai.or.jp/database/teigen/970109_2.htm as of April 1997 and was entitled "Shijōshugi sengen: 21 seiki e no akushon puroguramu."

23. Liberal Democratic Party Administrative Reform Promotion Headquarters (LDP), "Hashimoto gyōkaku no kihon hōkō ni tsuite," June 18, 1996. Translated as "Prime Minister Ryutaro Hashimoto and the Liberal Democratic Party's Fundamental Approach toward Administrative Reform." Downloaded World Wide Web documents, September 9, 1996, URLs http://www.sphere.ad.jp/ldp/saisin/saisin-12B.html (Japanese) and http://www.sphere.ad.jp/ldp/english/e-topics/reform-1.html (English).

24. See, for instance, Keidanren, *Miryoku aru nihon: Sōzō e no sekinin–keidanren bijon 2020,* October 1996, World Wide Web URL http://www.keidanren.or.jp/japanese/policy/vision/index.html, accessed April 1997.

25. Chalmers Johnson, *MITI and the Japanese Miracle: The Growth of Industrial Policy, 1925–1975* (Stanford University Press, 1982), pp. 18–23.

26. LDP, "Hashimoto gyōkaku no kihon hōkō ni tsuite."

27. Ibid.

28. Keizai Dōyūkai, "Manifesto for a Market-Oriented Economy."

Contributors

Lonny E. Carlile
University of Hawaii at Manoa

Hideaki Miyajima
Waseda University

Elizabeth Norville
University of Puget Sound

Kōsuke Ōyama
University of Tsukuba

Yul Sohn
Seoul National University

Mark C. Tilton
Purdue University

Index

Administrative guidance (*gyosei shido*), 9
Administrative Management Agency, and administrative reform, 81
Administrative practice, Japanese, 6–9
Administrative reform (*gyōsei kaikaku*), Japanese: *1990s* revival, 91–103; *1996* shift in focus, 98–99; action plan for, 95–96; bureaucracy and, 88; coalition backing, 80–82; concerns giving rise to, 77; cumulative aspect of, 104; definition, 76–77; deregulation in, 89–91; fiscal crisis and, 77–78; format, 103–04; Gyōkakushin-led, 83–85; Hiraiwa Commission and, 94–95; Hosokawa administration and, 93–94, 95; *minkatsu* projects, 85–88; political parties as agents of, 96–98, 109n52; politics of, 91–93; resistance to, 82; Rinchō-led, 77–83
Administrative Reform Council (ARCounc; Gyōsei Kaikaku Kaigi), 101–03

Administrative reform outlines (*gyōkaku taikō*), 88
Agency of Natural Resources and Energy (ANRE), and oil industry reform, 153–54, 157
Akinori Uesugi, 164
Anglo-American tradition: competition in, 5; convergence of J-Type firm toward, 59, 61; economic regulation according to, 4, 200–01; interpretation of deregulation in, 3; regulatory reform in, 77, 201
ANRE. *See* Agency of Natural Resources and Energy
Antimonopoly Law (*1947*), 9, 36, 39, 174; *1949* amendment of, 37; U.S. and, 199; violations of, 176
Antitrust policy, Japanese, weak nature of, 174–84
Aoki Masahiko, 62
ARCounc. *See* Administrative Reform Council
Autarky, Japanese, 25–26

221